To Mary –
One of the highlights of ou[r]
has been meeting you and the
Welbourne. Serendipity, again!
The journey's the thing!

Following the Plume

Adventures in Exploring Mosby's Confederacy

Compiled and written by *Brian Buntain*

Photographs

All photos are property of the family of trekkers with the Historic Mosby's Rangers, with the exception of the cover photo and the photo on page 102 which have been used with permission from Eddie Pole, photographer, the back cover photo used with permission from Karin Anderson, and the photos of Ayrshire courtesy of Claiborne Stokes. All others are from the public domain.

Cover Design: Mary Anne Lauby, Grey Dog Services

ISBN: 978-0-9978963-0-5

Table of Contents

James E. Taylor sketch from James J. Williamson's Mosby's Rangers

Foreword

Brian Buntain, one of the founding members of the living history organization, *Historic Mosby Rangers,* has written a retrospective that is different from any other narrative concerning the Confederate Guerilla Chieftain Colonel John Singleton Mosby and his daring ranger exploits.

Brian portrays Captain Robert Stringfellow Walker, as a heroic member of Colonel Mosby's Partisan Rangers. It was his portrayal of Captain Walker that brought a yearning and a strong desire for him to travel to Northern Virginia to learn firsthand about Mosby and the men who rode with him. His mission was to explore and walk the hallowed ground where Mosby's Rangers rode over a hundred and fifty years ago during the four most tragic years in American history. These yearly rituals were packed full of excitement and adventure. Some of the trips brought closure to countless questions and other visits brought more puzzles to solve. Each trip was more exciting than the last.

Brian has done a tremendous service to all Mosby historians and enthusiasts by conveying his successes, failures, and sometimes amusing predicaments in his attempts to find the hidden camps, safe houses, roads, burial plots, and ambush sites documenting the life and times of Mosby and his Rangers from January 1863 to April 1865.

Without question, this composition is the most entertaining book of its kind. Brian has been able to vividly tell these wonderfully written short essays on his various visits searching and finding the countless skirmishes, scouts, patrols, raids, and reconnaissance forays of this most famous Confederate guerilla unit.

I was fortunate to join Brian on many of his scouts and learned a great deal of invaluable information from him regarding various previously unknown locations and sites concerning the Gray Ghost and his men. Only Tom Evans, the revered co-author of *Mosby's Confederacy* has supplied me with more information than Brian.

In conducting research for this labor of love, Brian has collaborated with many wonderful and amazing experts and individuals who assisted him immeasurably in finding, gaining access to, and/or confirming countless sites and escapades.

I hope and trust you will read this narrative and use it as a valuable reference tool for present and future researchers who are driven to learn more about the history of John S. Mosby, his men, and the hallowed ground that made them famous.

Donald C. Hakenson Alexandria, Virginia

Introduction

The most daunting challenge to describing this adventure is where to start. Does it begin when, as a young lad, I couldn't wait for Saturday morning and the next episode of *The Gray Ghost*? Or perhaps in my teens when I pored over my grandad's *National Geographic* articles about the centennial anniversary of the War Between the States? I cannot recall a time when I was not drawn to the topic.

As an adult my interest amplified when I took two graduate courses that were field studies of Civil War battlefields. One summer it was the Eastern Theater, and the following summer we examined the Western Theater campaigns. The legend, which became a running gag during those classes, was that by rubbing the nose of Col. Patrick O'Rorke's bas relief memorial on Little Round Top at Gettysburg, I had "condemned" myself to a life-long pursuit of Civil War studies. So far, I don't mind!

The contemporary focus on John Singleton Mosby and the 43rd Battalion Virginia Cavalry came as three comrades sat around my dining room table one afternoon beneath the Stars and Bars. We had been members of an Indian Wars cavalry reenactment unit, Company L, 7th US (Custer's at Little Big Horn). At the time, it was the only mounted cavalry unit in our area, and we were not entirely satisfied with the experience. Each of us had reasons, but personally, I sided with the Indians. As we sat quietly considering what unit we would form for our own, the three of us looked from one to another, and without hesitation, in unison, said, "Mosby's Rangers!" Why Mosby? Each of us had his own twist, but in general, we respected Mosby's leadership qualities, creative tactics and the incredible accomplishments of his Partisan Rangers during The War Between the States

So began the modern chapter of this adventure. That was 1988, and for the first few years we recruited members, participated in Civil War reenactments (yes, here in the Pacific Northwest!), and read the few books we could find on the 43rd Battalion Partisan Rangers. The first was V.C. Jones' *Ranger Mosby*, followed by J.J. Williamson's *Mosby's Rangers*. The events were fun; we even started doing school and civil war roundtable presentations. Eventually, the horses and shooting were not completely satisfying. We realized that we needed to do more; to actually honor the men who had served with Mosby. Around 1992 we determined that each of our members would research and portray an actual Ranger.

This is where we first noticed *synchronicity* would become a prominent theme in our adventure. As each of our men decided on a Ranger, it became clear that it might be a case of the Ranger choosing the man! I thumbed through the 1895 roster of former Rangers in the Williamson book. As an educator, I was searching for a Ranger who had become a teacher after the War. I found Robert Stringfellow Walker, identified as a high school principal at Woodberry Forest School. Close enough for me! Eventually, I was to meet and become friends with Ranger Walker's grandson (not great-grand), and to learn that Woodberry Forest is not only still in existence, it is one of the county's premier prep schools. (More on this later….) "*Living history*" became another theme of our experience.

In 1994, we incorporated as a non-profit education and historic preservation organization, "Historic Mosby's Rangers" (HMR). We still participated in reenactments regularly. We drilled monthly at our own "Camp Spindle" near Tumwater, Washington. We sponsored authentic tactical events and various living history programs. It was always our goal to accurately portray life of the Rangers and the civilians they lived with and protected.

By this time, I had expanded my Mosby library and began to have many more questions. There were accounts of skirmishes or fights written by Rangers who were participants, but their views were conflicting or the lay of the land was confusing. We needed more information. We needed "eyes-on" to truly understand the story of Mosby's Rangers. One of the books added at that time was *Mosby's Confederacy* by Tom Evans and Jim Moyer. Their "Guidebook" provided the spur for the horse. In June 1995 six members of our organization made our first research trek to Virginia, to Mosby's Confederacy. From the moment our feet hit the ground, we learned that another theme of our adventure was *serendipity*. Nearly every day provided another epiphany, an unexpected revelation, another door opened, a more accurate perspective.

Now 20 years, 14 treks, and many Mosby friends later, it is time to tell our story, our journey in: ***Following the Plume: Adventures in Exploring Mosby's Confederacy.***

Brian Buntain,

Joyce, Washington

December, 2015

Acknowledgements

Across 20 years of treks in Mosby's Confederacy, we have met incredible people, learned some fascinating history, and encountered amazing experiences. For each trek, we developed an itinerary based on points of interest which evolved from our continual research. The more insight we gained the greater the attraction to new discoveries. This book is a tribute to the trekker family and to the legion of Virginians who made our journey so memorable.

First, I offer a huge thank you to all our trekkers. I will not try to name you all. Often making sacrifices in time, energy, and money to join the trek, your enthusiasm for the quest was contagious. Individually, your research and questions inspired further adventures. Your willingness to go with the flow and to go the extra mile added to the pleasure and successes of our journey. Above all, the camaraderie we shared throughout our travels brought a new highlight to each day.

Second, to the Mosby Crew in Northern Virginia I cannot find words enough to express my gratitude for all you gave to facilitate our treks. A note of special appreciation goes to those who have gone to the great bivouac on the other side of the river: Virgil Carrington "Pat" Jones who instigated the modern interest in Mosby; Jim Moyer who so generously shared his knowledge and time; John Gott who never failed to have the answer and always provided much more information than I thought was possible; and Bob Daly who cheerfully opened his collection of Mosby artifacts for our examination.

To the contemporary Mosby historians I can say that there was never a finer group of people; ever ready to assist us in the pursuit of our objectives. Tom Evans is one of the original Mosby Crew. A gentleman and scholar, he co-authored with Jim Moyer *The Guidebook* that has been the beacon since our first trek. Tom has been a constant source of encouragement and is a veritable fount of obscure Mosby-related information. We never would have dared to begin the journey without *The Guidebook*! For enlightening and entertaining Mosby lore, there are no better raconteurs than Eric Buckland and Don Hakenson. Gentlemen, you are an inspiration! A new trekking "rule" is: "If you have an opportunity to join one of Don and Eric's Mosby tours, take it!" Don Hakenson has trekked with us more often than any of the Mosby Crew. It has been a splendid journey, and Don has made it even more awesome!

No matter which museum or historical society we visited, our reception was always professional and courteous. Our appreciation is especially extended to the helpful staffers of the Clarke County Historical Society, the Fauquier Historical Society, the Jefferson County (WV) Historical Museum, the Warren Rifles Museum, the Old Gaol Museum, Sky Meadows State Park, Brentmoor, and the Stuart-Mosby Historical Society. From its beginning, we have supported the goals of the Mosby Heritage Area Association education mission. Thank you Childs Burden, Judy Reynolds, Rich Gillespie and the rest of the MHAA crew for all you do to preserve the rich heritage of Mosby's Confederacy.

It is close to impossible to recognize everybody that has helped make our journey memorable. At the risk of omission, I want to thank the following people for their support, assistance, sometimes patience, and most of all friendship: Nat and Sherry Morison, Jolly de Give, Frank and Bernice Walker, Win Meiselman, George Wiltshire, Doc and Annie Mitchell, Jim Glymph, and Al and Sheryl Kellert. You all are a big reason we keep returning to Mosby's Confederacy.

Todd Kern has helped us with our Mosby Rides, providing horses and proper, "period-correct" tack. We hope you have learned something from us, because we certainly are more knowledgeable due to your instruction and friendship.

The infinite patience and support of Mary Anne Lauby and Jim Yount at Gray Dog Services has been a gift beyond description. Thank you for the peace of mind you provided!

Almost last, but definitely not least, my esteem and gratitude go out to my sisters, Rosie Roberts and Dixie Brown, my cousin, Carol Jeffords, and friend and advisor, Laurie Tanguay. Rosie is my Gray Ghost "reader" and Dixie has been a constant cheering squad. Also, I cannot thank enough Carol Jeffords. Carol has joined several treks, and made the mistake of volunteering to be my editor. She is simply amazing! Furthermore, I want to thank Rosie and Carol for the remedial lessons on punctuation. Apparently, I was playing hooky from grammar class during commas, colons, and semicolons! Even though Laurie's fee for advice is only five cents, I am certain my tab now rivals the federal deficit. Laurie's friendship is priceless! Thank you!

The biggest thank you of all goes to my Darlin' Lynn. Despite only a cursory interest in the War Between the States, Lynn has been an abiding pillar in my quest of Mosby lore. Without your support, Darlin', this book would not have become a reality. Thank you!

Dedication

To John C. Buntain, my Dad, from whom I learned to dig deeper, go the extra mile, and give it all you've got.

Chapter One: *Mounting Up*

Prepare to Mount

Before beginning this journey, there are a few items that will need clarification. First, the body of published Mosby resources is enormous. It is not my purpose here to replicate the excellent work done by the many fine Mosby historians. To them I owe tremendous homage and appreciation. My effort here is not an academic treatise; it is merely an accounting of many fondly remembered people and experiences encountered on my journey through Mosby's Confederacy.

Second, although I have studied and visited almost all of the events and sites connected to the Mosby lore, not all will be included in this work. Some of the major episodes – the Stoughton Raid, the Point-of-Rocks Raid, the Mt. Zion Church Fight, the Harmony/Hamilton Fight – are well worth a story, but may best be told another time.

Third, I will be guilty of the shameful use of acronyms, first-only names, cavalry terms, and local place names. Please accept my apologies ahead of time! To assist the reader in understanding the lingo, I offer the following definitions and explanations:

HMR – Historic Mosby's Rangers is the name of the non-profit corporation organized for educational and historic preservation purposes. It was founded to honor the men who served in the 43rd Battalion Virginia Cavalry also known as Mosby's Partisan Rangers. HMR is headquartered in Washington State.

MHAA – Mosby Heritage Area Association was formed as a non-profit educational and preservation organization in northern Virginia. MHAA offers many educational and heritage programs each year, and is active in historic preservation projects in the region where Mosby operated during the War Between the States.

SMHS – Stuart-Mosby Historical Society was organized to preserve the memory and heritage of Gen. J.E.B. Stuart and Col. John S. Mosby. SMHS provides educational and heritage programs and operates the SMHSMuseum in Centreville, VA.

The Guidebook – *Mosby's Confederacy: A Guide to the Roads and Sites of Colonel John Singleton Mosby*, by Thomas J. Evans and James M. Moyer, White Mane Publishing Co., 1991.

For any further confusion, I apologize. It is my fervent wish that the reader is able to forge through the chaos of our adventures and finds enjoyment in the following pages.

No Pedestal, but…

Another challenge in telling this adventure is how to describe the man, John Singleton Mosby, in his own time referred to as "The Gray Ghost." It would be all too easy to fall into extravagant superlatives, leaving the impression that Mosby was an immortal with super-human powers; stand him on a pedestal. From everything I read about the man, he was good, even great as a leader of troops and an innovator in small unit, close quarter combat tactics. It is my belief that Mosby demonstrated a level of integrity that few others over time have possessed.

Col. John Singleton Mosby

Prior to The War, Mosby was practicing law in a far western neck of Virginia. He spoke out against secession with rational argument, but when Virginia left the Union, Mosby joined a local militia to defend his home from the impending invasion. For the duration of his command, Mosby refused to accept any share of spoils. Even in his post-war career, Mosby continued to fight for what was right. Was the man vain? Yes, but his well-earned self-confidence did not hinder in the achievement of his mission. I am convinced that very few commanders could have achieved the successes while operating, almost with impunity, entirely within enemy occupied territory.

Mosby understood his mission implicitly. His command, the 43rd Battalion Virginia Cavalry, was formed to disrupt Yankee supply and communication lines, gather reconnaissance, induce the Union command to pull troops from the front line, and, in general, to demoralize the Federal war effort.

Starting in January 1863 with nine men loaned by Gen. Jeb Stuart from his 1st Virginia Cavalry, Mosby blazed a path through The War, into military history. At first the raids were on Yankee picket posts; then gradually grew more aggressive. In March, slightly two months into his partisan career, Mosby's reputation soared with the capture of Gen. Stoughton in Yankee headquarters, without firing a shot or losing a man, and 25 miles into Union occupied Fairfax City.[1]

An attribute that made Mosby popular with his men was his careful planning. Rangers knew prior to going into a fight or raid that Mosby had been in the saddle continuously, scouting, gathering information that he developed into a favorable battle plan. They had confidence that there would be two or more avenues of escape should things turn sour, as they were wont to do. The Rangers knew that Mosby would not lead them into anything that he could not get them out of safely. These are indicators of a good leader!

Slight of build, Mosby did not have the imposing appearance of a famous, great warrior. Several first-hand accounts expressed surprise that Mosby was not a mountain of a man, fierce in expression and aggressive in manner. He did not look the warrior visage that his legend had built. To the contrary, there was no shiny saber, no flashy uniform, no Robin Hood or Richard the Lion-Heart! Mosby was calm, soft-spoken, and except on visits to Richmond, plainly attired. He did not give a demonstration of physical strength; there was no swagger. What was the secret of his absolute authority over his men? According to Ranger John Munson, it was Mosby's deep blue eyes that flashed and sparked as he spoke. I am not certain that was the only qualifier, but Mosby definitely held sway over the Rangers. He demanded absolute obedience to his orders and had little tolerance for misconduct. Mosby's expectations for his men were simple: obey orders and fight. A Ranger needed a horse and pistols. If a man did not measure up, he was dismissed for inefficiency or sent back to the regular army.[2]

While some Rangers carried carbines, all used pistols. Rare is the report of a Ranger using a saber in battle. Mosby claimed, "My men were as little impressed by a body of cavalry charging them with sabers as though they had been armed with cornstalks." It was the use of pistols that proved to be ideal for the Ranger style of warfare. It was one of Mosby's innovations. Most Rangers went into a fight with two pistols; many went with four. We have been fortunate to find many examples of Ranger pistols in museums and in private collections. The most common models were Colt Army .44 and Colt Navy .36 calibers. We have seen Remington .44 models that belonged to Rangers Bob Walker and John Lunsford. Of course, other models were in use, too. [3]

Aside from the lure of spoils, the attraction of Mosby's command was that it was not the regular army. Ranger life spared the men the dull routine of camps and hours of drill. They did not live in tents or dine on fatback and hardtack, the standard army rations. Most of Mosby's men were in their teens or early twenties and could not refuse the romantic adventures of Ranger life. Once, when Mosby was asked why he preferred to have the youngsters as soldiers, he replied, "Why they are the best soldiers I have. They haven't sense enough to know danger when they see it, and will fight anything I tell them to."[4]

Mosby brought selected men on a mission, whatever number was needed, but usually less than fifty. Occasionally, as with the Point of Rocks Fight and in the Berryville Wagon Raid, more than 300 Rangers formed the force. The Rangers often "skedaddled" at the end of the action, each man on his own hook. They would return to their homes or safe houses, until they were called to rendezvous for the next mission.

As Mosby's successes mounted, so did the appeal of the battalion, which eventually grew to eight companies and regimental strength. The numbers vary according to the source, but approximately 800-900 men had enrolled in the command by the end of The War. It is estimated that maybe as many as 2000 men, including soldiers on leave or recuperating from wounds, had "ridden" with Mosby during the life of the battalion.[5]

Mosby's strategy was to "use and consume the northern cavalry in hard work." It was a strategy that was hugely successful. By the surrender, the ubiquitous Rangers were striking the enemy in multiple spots nearly every day across the breadth of northern Virginia. The Gray Ghost was everywhere! Depending on the source, the battalion managed to keep about 40,000 Union troops occupied and away from fighting Gen. Lee's army at the front lines. In addition, the Rangers destroyed or sent to Lee's army hundreds of thousands of dollars' worth of war materiel.[6]

Most difficult to quantify is the effect of Mosby on the morale of the Union troops. From the private soldier to the general officer posted in Mosby's Confederacy, the fear of another attack by the "Gray Ghost" was persistent and palpable. In my mind I see young, gray-clad warriors rising from the dark mists, closing silently, until…!

For his contributions and innovations in non-conventional combat tactics, Colonel John Singleton Mosby is the only Confederate officer to be inducted into the United States Army Ranger Hall of Fame. No pedestal for Mosby, but I do admire his achievements.[7]

COLONEL JOHN S. MOSBY
Photographed in Richmond in March, 1865

---

[1] Virgil C. Jones, *Ranger Mosby*, pp.89-99; James J. Williamson, *Mosby's Rangers: A Record of the Operations of the Forty-Third Battalion, Virginia Cavalry, from its Organization to the Surrender*, pp.33-47; Hugh Keen and Horace Mewborn, *43rd Battalion Virginia Cavalry, Mosby's Command: The Virginia Regimental Histories Series*, pp.32-38; Major John Scott, *Partisan Life with Col. John S. Mosby*, pp.43-53

[2] John Munson, *Reminiscences of a Mosby Guerrilla*, pp.14-22; Jeffry D. Wert, *Mosby's Rangers*, p.75-78

[3] John S. Mosby, *Memoirs of Colonel John S. Mosby*, pp. 30, 151-152, 284-285; Williamson, *Mosby's Rangers*, p. 21; Munson, *Reminiscences*, pp.22-25

[4] John H. Alexander, *Mosby's Men*, p. 24; Munson, *Reminiscences*,p.8-9

[5] Wert, *Mosby's Rangers*, pp.73-74

[6] James A. Ramage, *Gray Ghost: The Life of Col. John Singleton Mosby*, Lexington, Kentucky: The University of Kentucky Press, 1999. Pp344-347

[7] U.S.ArmyRangerHallofFame, http://www.ranger.org/resources/Documents/RHOF%20Documents/RHOF_Master_List.pdf, p.7;

[8] Eric Buckland, *Mosby Men II*, p. vii

Chapter Two: *Riding a Raid*

A Day in the Life

People often snicker when I respond to their query about my "Virginia vacation." "Riiiiight! You *worked* hard. Long hours. Little rest. Uh-huh!"

Well, just for kicks and giggles, I selected an itinerary from an old trek and randomly (really!) picked a day to use to illustrate a typical day in the life of a "trekker."

Monday, October 11, 2004

0500 – Wake up. Shake the cobwebs from the brain. Finish making notes from yesterday's itinerary in the Valley tracking Mosby's Hollow-Jordan Springs-John Alexander account, Myerstown Fight, and Loudoun Heights visit. Then check today's itinerary for connections, routes, sites.

0630 – Morning ablutions, then dress for breakfast and the weather.

0700 – Meet in library with Burke, Steve and Constance to review yesterday, to browse the Welbourne library, to begin spooling for the day.

Welbourne library with the portrait of Col. Richard Dulany

0730 – Breakfast in the dining room, southern style hot biscuits, sausages, scrambled eggs, fried tomatoes, juice, coffee (or tea)! Thank you kitchen crew, Mary and Ann! Toward the end of the meal, Sherry comes in to visit with us and the other guests. A most excellent start for a full-tilt journey!

0815 – Excusing ourselves from the pleasant conversation, we retire to our rooms to wash up and gather materials for the day's adventures.

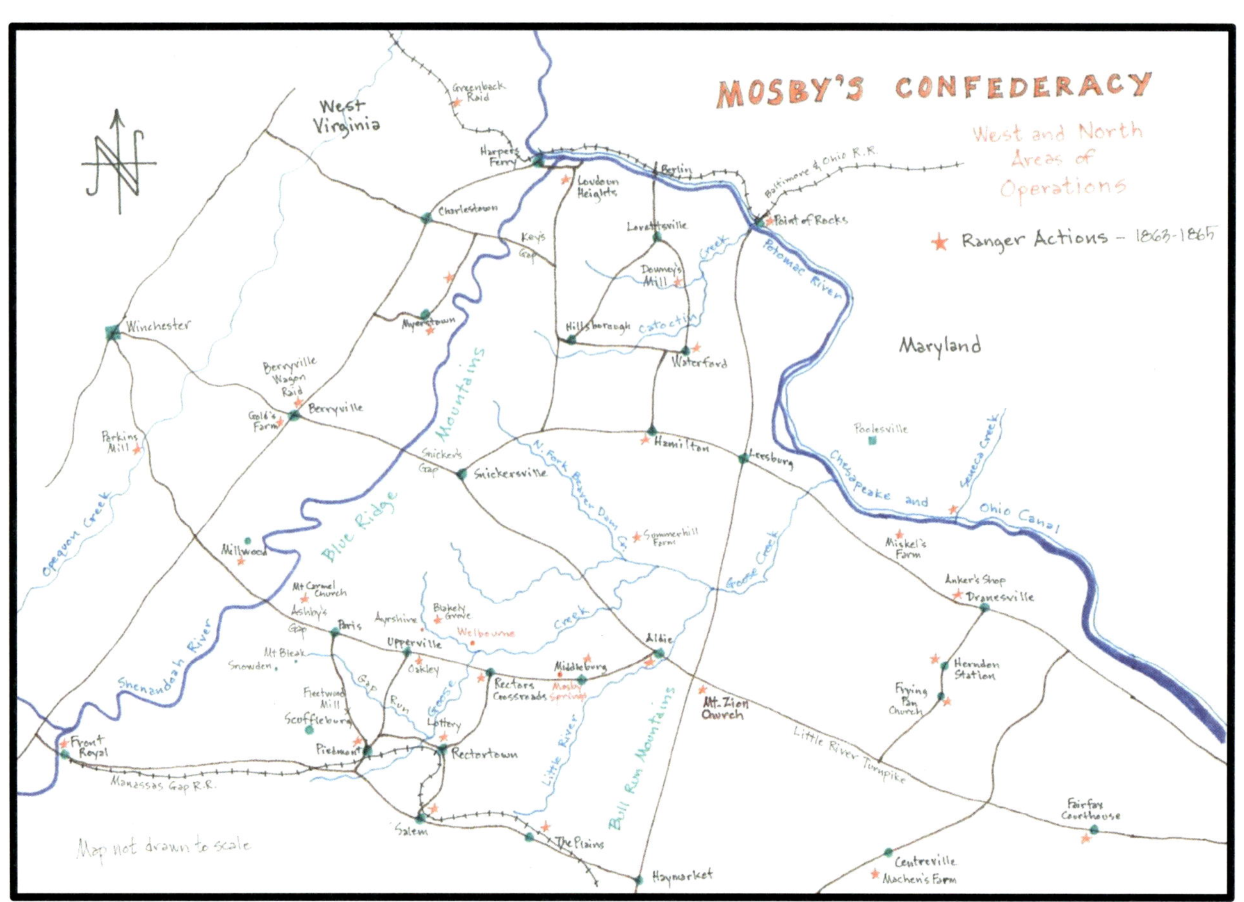
MOSBY'S CONFEDERACY
West and North Areas of Operations
Ranger Actions – 1863-1865
West Virginia
Maryland
Greenback Raid
Harpers Ferry
Loudoun Heights
Berlin
Baltimore & Ohio R.R.
Point of Rocks
Charlestown
Keys Gap
Lovettsville
Downey's Mill
Potomac River
Catoctin Creek
Myerstown
Hillsborough
Waterford
Winchester
Berryville Wagon Raid
Gold's Farm
Berryville
Blue Ridge Mountains
Hamilton
Leesburg
Poolesville
Parkins Mill
Snickers Gap
Snickersville
N. Fork Beaver Dam Cr.
Chesapeake and Ohio Canal
Seneca Creek
Opequon Creek
Millwood
Summerhill Farm
Miskel's Farm
Goose Creek
Mt Carmel Church
Ashby's Gap
Anker's Shop
Dranesville
Blakely Grove
Ayrshire
Welbourne
Paris
Upperville
Aldie
Mt Bleak
Snowden
Oakley
Middleburg
Mosby Springs
Herndon Station
Rectors Crossroads
Shenandoah River
Fleetwood Mill
Scuffleburg
Gap Run
Lottery
Frying Pan Church
Mt. Zion Church
Little River Turnpike
Front Royal
Piedmont
Rectortown
Little River
Bull Run Mountains
Manassas Gap R.R.
Salem
The Plains
Fairfax Courthouse
Map not drawn to scale
Haymarket
Centreville
Machen's Farm

0830 – Load into the vehicle – quick equipment check: spectacles, water bottles, maps and snacks – then drive out from Welbourne to our first stop in Manassas.

1000 – Meet Don Hakenson and Frank Hall at the Stone House in the Manassas Battlefield Park. Make introductions. Prank on Steve; well done, but best left untold.

1015 – Drive to Widow Machen's Farm. Museum Visitor Center, then jog across Walney Road to the site of the barn ruins. Don interprets the July 23, 1864 event.

Trekkers examine the ruins of Widow Machen's barn

1045 – Drive to Oakton Baptist Church Cemetery. Honors are paid to Rangers Ab Wrenn, Phillip D.C. Lee and Ben D. Utterback.

1115 – Drive to Mosby's Rock near Frying Pan Church. Don interprets.

Mosby's Rock - Don regales the trekkers with the legend

1145 – Drive to Laura Ratcliffe's grave. Push through the hedges, then honors to Laura.

Constance Boudreau at Laura Ratcliffe's grave

1200 – Drive to Herndon Station. Don interprets the March 17, 1863 raid. Special interest is given to the Hanna House portion of the raid.

1230 – Conduct our own raid on a nearby deli for lunch.

1330 – Drive to a location that my map indicates might be Rowser's Ford. After parking at the end of a back road and hiking through a tangle of underbrush, we approach the Potomac River. Don takes a plunge while trying to cross a slippery log. We manage to reach the bank of the river. Wide and shallow, and just above Seneca Falls, it is a likely spot for the ford. We see the Seneca locks on the old Chesapeake & Ohio (C&O) Canal across the river. This location matches the description.

Trekkers discussing the Dranesville/Anker's Shop Fight at the marker for the Anker family graveyard

1600 – Drive to Dranesville. Check out two possible sites for Anker's Shop – a Starbucks and at a stone marker on the Northern Virginia Community College grounds. The marker sits on a knoll adjacent to and north of the Leesburg Pike (Rt.7). Don, shivering, interprets.

1700 – Drive to Miskel's Farm off of Broad Run Drive. Don interprets the April 1, 1863 fight. Keep the heater on, trying to warm a soggy Don.

Trekkers at Miskel's Farm; after the Stoughton Raid, this fight put Mosby on the Union's front page news

Our Fount Beattie, Burke Nebeker, at Lt. Fountain Beattie's grave

1800 – Drive to Falls Church; first to St. James Cemetery to honor Fount Beattie, Burke's Ranger; then to the "Hanging Tree" where Don tells the legend; finally, to the Old Falls Church Cemetery to visit the grave of the Rev. John Read (Yankee spy).

1930 – Drive to Springfield for dinner at Mike's American Grill. Don's wife, Carol, joins us for an exceptional meal with the finest companions. Don is a real trouper, still shivering from his dip in the muck and mire at Rowser's Ford, but he's in great form throughout the meal.

2100 – Farewells to Don & Carol, then we head back home to Welbourne.

2230 – Arrive at Welbourne, weary but glowing. Sit in the parlor to unwind and review the day's journey.

2300 – Good nights all around. We retire to our rooms. I attempt to make notes on the day but eventually, nodding off ends that effort.

2400 – I wash up, and fall into bed. Another splendid day in Mosby's Confederacy!

This truly was a typical trekking day. Treks have ranged in duration from seven to fourteen days. Are we tired at the end of a trek? Absolutely! Why do we keep coming back? It could be because of the camaraderie, the discoveries, and the resolution of mysteries. But, really, the journey's the thing!

On the Road with Tom and Don

A lot of research hours have been shaved by conversations with Jim Moyer, Tom Evans, Don Hakenson, and Eric Buckland, among the gang of published "Mosbyites." Full of anecdotes and good humor, if they could not provide the answer, they could point me in a direction that might lead to my goal. For their willingness to share their expertise and wealth of knowledge, I am forever in their debt. They have contributed so much to my journey!

Better even than the conversations are the days when the "Mosby Crew" leads me around to visit sites, obscure as well as famous. The eastern portion of Mosby's Confederacy, mostly Fairfax County, has been smothered by rampant development. For an old country boy, it is not easy to negotiate the chaos of the east-coast urban/suburban civilization. Tom Evans and Don Hakenson have witnessed the surge in modernization and have been able to keep pace. It's home field for them. They are still able to pick out a Mosby site from a mini-mart or a condo or a business park. Hallelujah!

While there are many days from which to choose, the 2008 trek provides a good example. A typical day on the road with Tom and Don started at Merrybrook Farm, near Herndon. It was fairly early morning as Andy and I had just left Dulles Airport and the red-eye out of Seattle. Win Meiselman welcomed us in her usual charming manner to Laura Ratcliffe's post-war home. After a brief but lively chat, we departed. First stop was to see the new marker for Mosby's Rock. A short drive further southward on the Centreville Road brought us to a new site for me. Don and Tom wanted us to see Laura Ratcliffe's wartime home. I had never been to the site and would not have found it without Mosby Crew guidance. The silo is the landmark to spot at least until it is torn down for "progress." There are a couple other overgrown structures, too. Tom presented me with a button he had found on the site.

The tag mis-spelled "Ratcliffe"

From Laura's farm we drove south again across Rt. 50 and followed Walney Road to the site of Widow Machen's farm. This is another little known, but favorite Mosby site. Located in today's Lawrence Park, the interesting story for us takes place June 24, 1864. The Rangers had been scouting in the Centreville area, looking for opportunities. At the widow Machen's, the Rangers attacked a detachment of New York cavalry. The New Yorkers had stopped to rest and water their mounts and themselves. Some of the Yankees had climbed cherry trees in the widow's orchard and were availing themselves of the tasty fruit. Needless to say, the Union troopers were caught off guard. While the Rangers did not lose a man, the Federals lost 37 men and 38 horses.

The most interesting part of the tale is this. One of the Yankees, lying in a ditch under a persimmon tree, and using a Spenser repeating carbine, repulsed two assaults by the intrepid Ranger Bushrod Underwood! On the third assault the Yankee was overcome by an irate Bushrod and about 20 fellow Rangers. Bushrod was about to put a bullet into the Yankee's head, when Capt. William Chapman ordered him to back off. The Yankee's name? Thomas P. "Boston" Corbett! Boston Corbett is later given credit for killing President Lincoln's assassin, John Wilkes Booth. Obviously, Corbett was sent south as a prisoner, and was exchanged in time to become famous later. Not part of our quest here, but a worthwhile project would be to look into the life of Boston Corbett because it is most interesting. Don and I have looked for a persimmon tree as the possible site; with no success![1]

Next we drove back north to Carterville Church, then north again to Brown's Chapel Cemetery near Reston. There we did honors to Ranger M. D. Harrell, Company C before taking a short jaunt down the Leesburg Turnpike to Colvin's Run Mill. The 1810 mill has been restored and is the centerpiece of a county park. Another short sprint brought us to St. Andrews Chapel Cemetery, where we did honors to Rangers Dallas Bonnell, John Follin, and Dorsey Warfield.

Tom Evans honors Ranger Dorsey Warfield

Andy Harris honors Ranger John Follin

Somehow we ended up at Freedom Hill Fort. I don't know how! It was a warren of turns and stops and chaos. The earthworks are still quite visible. Late in The War the picket post here was converted into an artillery redoubt to protect the capital. Mosby's activities had caused so much concern that the trees were cut back along both sides of the pike, for several hundred feet distant! Aside from the reason for building the fort, there are two interesting Mosby connections. First, Capt. Henry Flint led his 1st Vermont Cavalry from here to what became known in Mosby lore as the Miskel's Farm Fight. That rout of the Yankees established the reputation of the Rangers for posterity. Second, nearly at the time of Lee's surrender at Appomattox, Rangers under Capt. Alfred Glasscock soundly defeated a Yankee patrol just south of here.

The author, Andy Harris, and Tom Evans inside the remains of Freedom Hill Fort

We had lunch somewhere around Vienna. I don't know how. It was a mystery! My notes say we had "Scottish" food then we stopped at Lydecker's Store after lunch. Lydecker's Store is now Freeman's Store and Museum. Opened early in 1861, the store was a polling place for Virginia's Ordinance of Secession. While Virginia and Fairfax County voted overwhelmingly in favor of secession, the Lydecker's store was one of the few precincts to reject secession. The store was briefly used as a Union hospital, also. I tried shopping in the store, but did not find any "cool" period items. They did carry Moon Pie Sandwiches, though.

Don Hakenson and Tom Evans reenacting the secession vote at Lydecker's Store

Now we were onward to Oakton and the Flint Hill Cemetery. There we honored Rangers John P. Chinn, Lewis B. Hunt, and Thomas H. Walker.

Not far from the Flint Hill Cemetery, driving north on Hunter Mill Road, we stopped to investigate Mosby's Oak Tree. In 1862, before Mosby began his partisan career, he attempted to capture a Quaker and Union sympathizer, Alexander Haight. Haight managed to escape his Confederate interrogators at this oak tree.[2]

Mosby's Oak – over 400 years old, 100 feet tall

Following Hunter Mill Road to the north, Tom and Don brought us to the "Hidden Valley Horse Camp." Parking next to a tennis court, we walked down into a draw where a stream struggled to run. There are bushes and small trees in the valley cluttering up the view. I attempted to blaze my way into the thicket to see if I could find the stone-ringed fire pits. Years ago after a lot of research and interviews with a Ranger son, Tom had located this site. In 1864, Mosby established a camp here to collect captured horses until they could be transferred south. Tom's exploration of the site revealed a wealth of evidence: tent stakes made from RR spikes, horseshoes, horse tack, blacksmithing tools, and soldier artifacts, in addition to the fire rings. An exciting discovery![3]

The Hidden Valley Horse Camp is hidden in there somewhere!

Tom has presented us with several artifacts recovered from the Hidden Valley Horse Camp. Tom Evans is a generous gentleman!

Relics from Mosby's Hidden Valley horse camp; broken snaffle bit,

and, a railroad spike tent stake

After Hidden Valley, we made our way to Hunter's Station. The station was located on the Alexandria, Loudoun & Hampshire Railroad. By 1862, however, the Confederates had destroyed the tracks. During the greater part of The War, the roadbed served as a convenient thoroughfare for both sides, connecting Vienna, Dranesville and Leesburg.

Several wartime events occurred around the station. Two stand out in my mind. In April 1864, a young writer accompanied a Union cavalry detachment on a search for Mosby. They rode along the old rail bed through this area. The writer later wrote a poem about the experience, *The Scout Towards Aldie.* In my opinion, it is a less than memorable poem, but one line does resonate for me. "...As glides in the seas the shark, Rides Mosby through green dark...." The poem rambles on and on; I have never bothered to count the stanzas. The primary point seems to convey a timorous attitude in the Yankees. Mosby is portrayed as a dark, ghost-like force that gobbles up careless Union soldiers. Of Mosby beware! It certainly reflects the effect of Mosby on Union morale. Oh! The young writer? Herman Melville! He eventually gains fame for his novel, *Moby Dick*.[4]

The second significant event to note was the Rangers' execution of a Union spy not far from Hunter's Station. The Rev. John D. Read was a Union sympathizer and spy. He was pastor of the Falls Church Baptist Church and was also a schoolteacher. On October 18, 1864 Rangers under the command of Capt. Montjoy were in the area to capture horses. During that evening, the Rangers entered the Union camp and were making away with Federal horses when a horn alerted the slumbering Yankees. The Rangers escaped with their captures and quickly identified Read as the horn-blower sounding the alarm. Montjoy sent Rangers to capture Read. They took him to a location near the Hunter's Station, and for his spying activities summarily executed him.

When Tom Evans was researching this story, an elderly woman told him about a song sung by the young local girls as they skipped rope: "Isn't any school; Isn't any teacher; Isn't any church; Mosby shot the preacher." It is interesting to note that the children's song mentions Mosby because he was not there for the execution. This further underscores Mosby's fearful reputation.[5]

The next site was Dead Man's Hill, named by the local residents because at the top of the hill was a graveyard for the black servants that died. When it snowed, the local children would go sledding down the hill. Their mothers would be thinking it was too dangerous, something like "Dead Man's Curve" in the old '60s song.

A short drive brought us to Hospital Hill. In 1861, there was a Confederate hospital located here, and downhill is Hospital Spring that provided water for the hospital and for troops camped nearby.

By this hour in the day, we could see the sun was making its departure for lands in the west. Reluctantly, we turned our vehicle homeward. It had been another memorable day in Mosby's Confederacy, visiting sites that Andy and I had not before visited, and likely never would have been able to locate on our own.

While each of the Mosby Crew is knowledgeable about everything connected to the Mosby lore, each also has a specific area of expertise. For example, Tom Evans is the expert in Ranger activities in the Hunter Mill/Vienna/Falls Church region of Fairfax County. Don Hakenson is the go-to-man for Alexandria and its outlying communities. For the histories of individual Rangers and their final resting places, Eric Buckland is your man. Other "Mosbyites" fill the gaps with special interests. There always seems to be new material popping up and always room for more research.

Without diminishing my esteem for any of the Mosby Crew, I will add a little more attention to trekking with Don Hakenson. Simply because we have shared more time on the road, there are more "Don adventures." When we get together, Don will say, "Have you been to see…?" Most often, I have not been to that particular site. That sets in motion another day of trekking. Don's passion for history and his enthusiastic presentations are contagious, and exponentially add delight to the journey.

On the 2015 trek, Don and I met for breakfast in Oakton. Catching up was fun, as always, and we planned out the day's itinerary. Don drove. That was better since we were going to be traveling through the chaos of modern Fairfax County. Our immediate destination: Alexandria.

Mosby Ranger marker in Bethel Cemetery, Alexandria

I had been to Alexandria once in 1985 and again in 1995. Our first stop was the Bethel Cemetery where there is a memorial to ten Rangers who are buried there. However, George H. Ayre really is not resting in the Bethel Cemetery as the memorial states. Ranger Ayre actually was buried in Tennessee. We did not try to locate the individual graves, but did honors at the memorial.

Where we went after that was a sampling of sites that Don has presented in his book, *This Forgotten Land*. I highly recommend this book! You won't find these stories anywhere else. Some of the sites were connected to Mosby, some to the War Between the States, and some to colonial history. Rather than recount each site I will merely list our stops that day and refer the reader to *This Forgotten Land*: Fairview the John Fairfax house (Don's testimony helped save this house from demolition!); Burgundy Farm and the railroad trestle destroyed by the

Rangers in 1864; the William S. Reid house; Rose Hill, one of my favorite Mosby sites where Col. Daniel F. Dulany was captured by Mosby and French Dulany, the Colonel's son; Potter's Hill and the "spy with the glass eye"; Hayfield; Round Hill, home of Triplett brothers who were Rangers; and Mt. Air, with Chichester, Landstreet, and Mosby stories. Peruse Don's book for some fascinating history![6]

"Fairview" the Fairfax House; Mosby was here twice during The War

"Mt. Air" ruins; here Gen. Lee sipped buttermilk under a poplar tree

The author with Tom Evans and Mosby's Colt revolver at the Stuart-Mosby Historical Museum

Our next stop was at the Stuart-Mosby Historical Museum in Centreville, where we were joined by Tom Evans. After a pleasant visit with Tom, who had to get to an appointment, Don and I headed to Waxpool and the Brambleton Golf Course to visit the grave of Ranger Richard "Dick" Moran. I have often wondered where Ranger Moran was buried. Where is Waxpool, and how would I ever know to look for a cemetery on a golf course?

The author honoring Ranger Dick Moran

Born in 1814, Moran was one of the oldest to serve with Mosby, and was definitely one of the early Ranger stalwarts. Ranger Moran was a key factor in the Rangers' decisive victory at Miskel's Farm. As he galloped cross-country to warn the Rangers of the imminent Yankee attack at the farm, Moran's booming foghorn voice sounded the alarm. Even though the attack surprised the Rangers, they were able to rally and deliver a crushing defeat to the attackers.[7]

At the golf course, we got permission from the club pro to go out to the family cemetery. Don had taken a tour group here the year before. They were loaned golf carts to take the entire 40-member group to the site. We were loaned a golf cart, too, for transport to the sixth hole near the cemetery. The cemetery is overgrown, and Moran's grave is now unmarked, lost among the tangle. There is a historical marker, however. We honored Ranger Moran with an appropriate toast, and savored the moment.

From the golf course, we drove north to Taylorstown. During The War, Downey's still house was located there. Burke and I had located the site in 2013, and Don wanted to see what we had found. The still house was an intriguing story that had merited further attention. Because James Downey was a Union sympathizer, he spent most of The War in Maryland. His wife continued operating their business ventures (farm, store, mill, distillery) in James's absence. Col. Mosby believed that the distilling business was harmful to the local population. The grain that went into production of alcoholic beverages was needed to feed families and livestock. Whenever a new still was discovered, Mosby would order it destroyed.

On March 28, 1865 Rangers J. Wright James, William "Major" Hibbs, and John Bolling were in northern Loudoun "pressing corn" for the battalion. James was the battalion quartermaster and Hibbs was famous in the battalion for his uncanny sense for locating forage, especially "Yankee forage." The three Rangers stopped at Downey's where they most likely would find corn. The record is not clear on whether or not they also dumped out product (or in some other manner eradicated the spirits). As the Rangers were leaving, they were captured by a Federal patrol.[8]

Possible Downey mill site along Catoctin Creek

There is no direct route to Taylorstown. The isolated location would have been perfect for a still house. We meandered over little-traveled roads until we finally reached the village. Catoctin Creek runs through the center of town, which was quite a thriving center of commerce at one time. Crossing the bridge over the creek, we turned immediately onto Downey Mill Road (Rt. 663). A short distance brought us near the creek bank. There are extensive stone ruins adjacent to the creek and it appears to flood frequently. Larger than one would expect for a distillery, perhaps it was site of the mill. Further along the road turns sharply away from the creek. Two large farmhouses, barns and outbuildings are found in here. Fields stretch out away from the farm structures. An old map locates the still house back by the creek near where the road turns away. Don and I are convinced we found Downey's establishments.

By this time in the day, the sun was beginning to abandon Mosby's Confederacy. I needed to get back to Welbourne for the gathering there. Don had an exceptionally long drive to his home in Franconia, plus I needed to pick up my vehicle in Oakton, so we nosed our way southward to call it a day. Another splendid day on the road!

For these days and for all the days Tom Evans and Don Hakenson shared with us, we are eternally grateful! The generosity and camaraderie of the whole Mosby Crew is above and beyond!

---

[1] Keen-Mewborn, *Regimental*, pp.133-134; Scott, *Partisan*, pp.232-233; Williamson, *Mosby's Rangers*, pp.464-466

[2] Hakenson, Donald C. and Mauro, Charles V., *A Tour Guide and History of Col. John S. Mosby's Combat Operations in Fairfax County, Virginia*. Franconia, Virginia: HMS Productions, 2013. pp.8-10

[3] Ibid, pp.94-95

[4] Melville, Herman, *Battle-Pieces and Aspects of the War*, 1866; Reprinted as Battle Pieces: Civil War Poems of Herman Melville. Edison, New Jersey: Castle Books, 2000

[5] Hakenson and Mauro, *Fairfax*, pp.122-127

[6] Hakenson, Don, *This Forgotten Land: A Tour of Civil War Sites and Other Historical Landmarks South of Alexandria, Virginia*. Alexandria, Virginia: Privately printed, 2002 (ISBN: 0-914927-38-8)

[7] Williamson, James J., *Mosby's Rangers*, pp.51-56; Jones, *Ranger Mosby*, pp110-111; Scott, pp. 62-69;KeenandMewborn,*Regimental*,pp.44-48

[8] Scheel, Eugene M., *Loudoun Discovered: Communities, Corners and Crossroads*; vol.5, pp.75-82. Leesburg, Virginia: The Friends of the Thomas Balch Library, 2002. Keen and Mewborn, *Regimental*,p.255

Chapter Three: *Headquarters*

It has been said that home is where your heart is. I have also heard that home is where you lay your head at night. For me home is Mosby's Confederacy. Especially comforting to me is that part of northern Virginia lying between The Plains and Paris and Middleburg and Marshall. Beginning with the first trek, this section of Mosby's Confederacy has been a magnet. It seems only natural that Welbourne is situated within the region that feels most like home, and serendipitous that it is a bed and breakfast. Traditionally, Rectortown was considered to be the capital of Mosby's Confederacy with his unofficial headquarters at nearby Heartland. Located between Middleburg and Upperville, Welbourne is the headquarters for our treks. It definitely holds my heart and I think of it fondly wherever I lay my head at night.

I think of Mosby Springs Farm as headquarters, too. George Wiltshire's farm has a Mosby story of its own. George is a genuine character, full of life and a good friend. According to George's grandfather, Ranger Lt. James Wiltshire, the springs on the farm were actually utilized by the Rangers during The War. For these reasons, Mosby Springs Farm qualifies as a trek headquarters, a place for centering the Ranger energy.

Another type of headquarters is the inspiration I find in the life of Ranger Captain Robert Stringfellow Walker. Frank Stringfellow Walker is the personification of the integrity, intelligence, and courage passed down from his grandfather, Captain Bob Walker. It is headquarters in the sense that my thoughts and actions relative to the trek are guided by the example of the Walker family.

Robert Stringfellow Walker

The phone rang….

This was in the "old" days before cell phones or even caller ID; however, we did have a portable phone that worked fine so long as the handset was not too far removed from the base. It was a pleasant summer morning so I was sitting on the deck reading a book on Mosby. I answered the phone to a voice that could only be described as succulent and melodious, an accent that I could imagine hearing from the quintessential Virginian, Thomas Jefferson.

"Hello, my name is Frank Stringfellow Walker. I understand you are interested in my grandfather, Robert Stringfellow Walker? So, I decided to call to introduce myself."

To say I was shocked and momentarily at a loss for words would be a gross understatement! Earlier in the month the Stuart Mosby Historical Society (SMHS) had published my article introducing our organization, Historic Mosby's Rangers (HMR). After explaining our mission and describing our practice of portraying individual men of Mosby's command, the article detailed our plans for a research trek to Virginia. Although I had invited SMHS members to contact us while we were in Mosby's Confederacy, actually being contacted was still unexpected.

The author with Frank Walker at "the Residence," home of Robert Walker, Woodberry Forest School

Robert Stringfellow Walker is "my Ranger" to honor. As I was an educator, I selected this particular Ranger based on his listing in the appendix to J.J. Williamson's *Mosby's Rangers*. In 1895, Robert S. Walker is identified as "principal Woodberry Forest High School, Orange, VA." Close enough for me. It was a while before it occurred to me to research Woodberry Forest, and when I did, I admit to being surprised that the school still existed. Further research revealed that not only was "Captain Bob" the principal he was the founder of the school. He proved to be one of the visionaries following The War, understanding that education would be a key for the recovery and rebuilding of the South. With six Walker sons to educate, the school naturally evolved from tutors for the family, then to neighboring children, and eventually the formal establishment of the school.

As a Ranger, Bob Walker served with distinction. He was involved in multiple battalion actions and was wounded several times. By the end of hostilities, Walker was promoted to Captain in command of Company B. The more I learned about the man, the more I believed he deserved to be honored.

When I finally recovered my tongue, I managed to express my pleasure that Frank Walker had taken the time to contact me. Now that I was aware that there was a family connected to Captain Bob, I needed to ask for permission to portray him. When I explained my request, Frank chuckled and remarked, "Well, the family *is* puzzled why you have chosen Captain Bob, and we are rather wondering who *you* are."

After listening to my response, Frank graciously granted permission. Believe me, I consider it an honor! From that first phone call, Frank and I have been in frequent communication, written and phone, then email when it became convenient. We have not managed to connect on every trek, but whenever we do get together, it is like no time has passed.

Frank Stringfellow Walker is an energetic, multi-talented man, a farmer, running Rosni farm which had been in the Walker family for many generations, as well as an attorney, published historian, tour guide, civic leader, and devoted husband and father. Bernice is the long-time love of Frank's life and is just as active, talented and gracious. Bernice and Frank may have had struggles but no one would ever know. They are so perfectly matched in humor, respect, and support. I thank Captain Bob for bringing us together! My life is much richer for it.[1]

Frank's support of our treks has been generous and constant. Always ready to show us "new" sites in Madison, Orange and Culpeper Counties, Frank is ever willing to share family stories, too. Whenever possible, I try to return the kindnesses. On the 2003 trek, Frank and Bernice joined us for a day of visiting sites connected to Robert Walker.

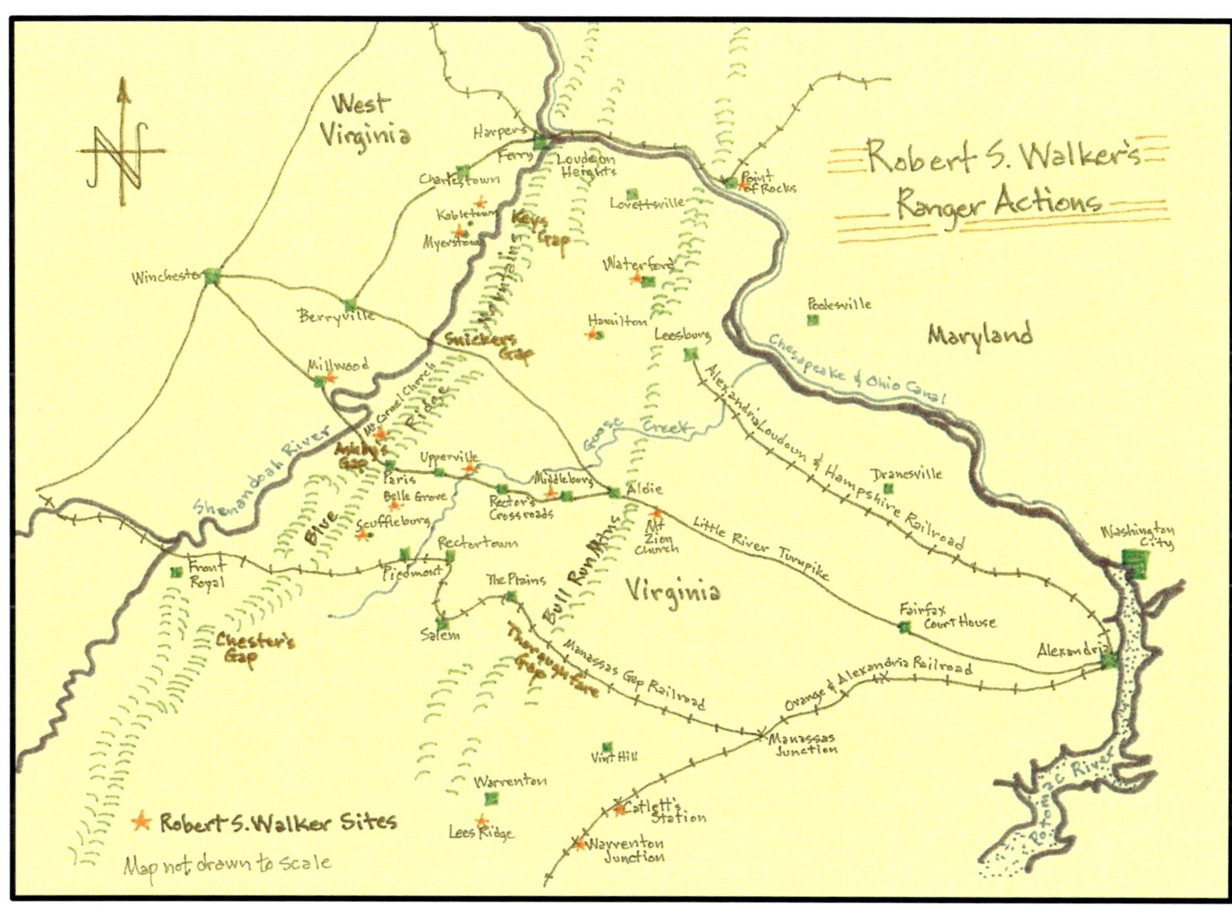

Frank and Bernice met us at Welbourne on Friday morning. I was eager to have them meet Nat Morison. Both Frank and Nat are University of Virginia alumni, both lawyers, both from long-standing, prominent Virginia families, and both share an agricultural heritage. I have never asked either man his impression of the other, but their initial meeting was a positive exchange of pleasantries. We had a long itinerary ahead of us, so we departed soon thereafter.

Rather than recount the exact order of sites visited that day, since we went by location and proximity, I will instead present sites in the sequence they occurred for Ranger Robert Walker. He was a young man but demonstrated bravery and leadership qualities from the beginning of his service with Mosby's Partisans. His service record shows Captain Bob was usually in the thick of the action. The following events are those where Robert Walker's participation can be documented.

Warrenton Junction – May 3, 1863: R.S. Walker WIA and Captured

In response to Gen. Stuart's suggestion to attack the Union rear, the Rangers charged the station depot on the Orange and Alexandria Railroad at Warrenton Junction. The Union troops were unprepared for an attack. At first they mistook the advancing Rangers as one of their own columns returning from a scout. When they realized their error, the Yankees took shelter in a house and outbuildings located within the triangle of tracks at the junction. During the ensuing hot fight, Robert Walker's horse was shot through the head. Walker rolled away from his dead mount, jumped up, grabbed a Federal horse and rejoined the fight.

The turning point in the contest came when Sam Chapman, Robert Walker and other Rangers stormed the house under scathing fire. They managed to wound or capture about 100 Union soldiers from the interior rooms of the house.

The author interpreting the Warrenton Junction Fight

The Rangers set about rounding up prisoners and plunder, but were late in noticing Yankee reinforcements arriving. The entire affair reversed fortunes. The Rangers beat a hasty retreat, their first, and suffered casualties. Among them Robert Walker was wounded during the melee, and captured.[2]

Scuffleburg – October 1, 1863: Company B Organized

Mosby's early successes enabled him to organize a second company. Company B was formed in Scuffleburg. Apparently Robert Walker had been exchanged and returned to duty by then because he is listed on the roster.

Lees Ridge (Billy Smith Raid) – October 3, 1863:

Mosby's custom was to send a new company out immediately to earn their spurs. Company B was commanded by Captain William Rowley Smith, so their first action was termed the "Billy Smith Raid." At 4:00 am Capt. Smith led the attack on a Federal camp located in a ravine on Lee's Ridge, about a mile south of Warrenton. Even though the Rangers were outnumbered by the Yankees about 1:6 the Federals were completely surprised. The Yankee officers did manage to rally their men, but the Rangers escaped with six prisoners and 27 horses.[3]

<u>Kabletown Road</u> (Near John Chew's House) – March 10, 1864:

After completing a successful raid on a Federal picket post located on the Bloomery Turnpike near Charlestown, the Rangers sent their prisoners under a small guard back to Loudoun County. The remaining Rangers broke into small groups and made their way across the Shenandoah by various paths. In command of the Ranger detachment, Captain Dolly Richards detailed six Rangers, led by Robert Walker to form a rear guard.

The Yankees had organized a pursuit of 25 troopers and quickly approached the six Rangers riding on the Kabletown Road. Upon hearing the Union troopers coming up behind them, the Rangers wheeled and charged the surprised enemy. Six against 25! In the sudden assault, the Federals suffered several casualties and the Rangers came away with eight more prisoners. They also liberated Ranger Willie Martin who had been captured earlier.[4]

<u>Waterford</u> – May 17, 1864:

Early on the northern section of Loudoun County was settled by German immigrants and Quakers. A significant number of the families held allegiance to the Union. One unit of Federal cavalry, the Loudoun Rangers, was formed from that population loyal to the north. The Loudoun Yankees were a frequent opponent of Mosby's men.

A party of the Loudoun Rangers had been raiding near Hillsboro, and had captured four of Mosby's men. Captain Dolly Richards gathered about thirty Rangers to pursue the Yankees. The Yankees had ridden to Waterford the previous night. Richards concealed his men near the village, and with two Rangers rode forward hoping to lure the Yankees into an ambuscade. The ruse worked, again! A dozen Loudoun Yankees chased the three Rangers south from town. At a signal from Richards, the hidden Rangers charged and only one of the Yankees safely escaped. Mosby's men continued their assault through the village and routed the rest of the Loudoun Yankees who fled in all directions. Some even scurried all the way to the Potomac River![5]

Around this same time and in the general Waterford area, Robert Walker escaped capture. In a skirmish with a Union patrol, Walker's horse was shot down. As the Yankees swept in, Ranger Walker climbed an apple tree, thus narrowly avoiding detection.[6]

<u>Point of Rocks</u> – July 4, 1864:

In support of Gen. Early's campaign on Washington City in July 1864, Mosby formed a force of about 250 Rangers. The objective was to disrupt Federal communications and supply lines in Maryland. The target was the Point of Rocks, a critical juncture for Union rail and telegraph lines, and a center of trade along the Chesapeake and Ohio Canal.

The Rangers arrived at a spot across the Potomac from the town. With artillery support from their new 12-pound Napoleon, accurate sharpshooting from their carbineers, and heroics by several of the men, the Rangers captured the town and one canal boat. The Yankees abandoned their defenses, retreating out of harm's way to the north. The Rangers availed themselves of the opportunity to requisition supplies and goods from the Federal supply depot and from the village stores. The Union camp was burned, telegraph lines connecting Harpers Ferry and Washington City were cut, and a Federal train was persuaded to reverse direction, back toward Harpers Ferry.

Aside from inflicting a demoralizing effect, the Rangers had captured or destroyed a sizable amount of Union supplies. More importantly, the raid had prevented the Federals from sending reinforcements from Harpers Ferry to oppose Gen. Early's attack on Washington City.[7]

Mt. Zion Church – July 6, 1864: WIA

During the days following the Point of Rocks raid, Mosby's scouts reported that the Federals had sent out a large force to capture the Rangers. At first light on the 6th, Mosby moved his men from the Potomac toward Leesburg to intercept the Yankees. With a number of the Rangers released to return to their homes to deliver the merchandise liberated at the Point of Rocks, Mosby's effective force now numbered about 175 men. Trying to catch the Yankees became a bit of cat-and-mouse as the Rangers followed rumors. Finally, Mosby determined to position his force between the Federals and their camps in Fairfax. The Yankees, numbering about 150 troopers under the command of Maj. William Forbes, were found in a field near the Mt. Zion Church, east of Aldie. The Rangers remarked later how perfectly Forbes had formed up his men to receive the anticipated charge. The Federals were confident that Mosby was about to be defeated and captured – finally.[8]

Mosby deployed his Rangers, artillery from the turnpike, carbineers along a fence line, and mounted troopers to charge from two directions. After an initial exchange of carbine fire, Mosby noted that the Yankee horses were unaccustomed to gunfire. It was exactly the opening for which he was looking. When the cannon lobbed a round into Forbes's formation, the Yankee lines broke. Mosby's men charged like demons unleashed, completely routing the Union soldiers. There was a significant amount of hand-to-hand combat. Most of the Ranger wounds were inflicted by Yankee sabers. Six Rangers were wounded, with one killed in the action. The Rangers captured 55 men and more than 100 horses. In the Mt. Zion Church Cemetery, 12 Yankee markers memorialize the sacrifice of the Union soldiers who fell on that day.

CAPT. ROBERT S. WALKER, CO. B.
From a War-time Photograph.

Myerstown battlefield

Myerstown – November 18, 1864:

Blazer's Scouts was a Federal unit formed specifically to eradicate Mosby. Blazer's men had caused difficulty for the Rangers in the Shenandoah Valley on several occasions. Finally, Mosby sent Companies A and B across the Shenandoah to settle accounts with Blazer. Under the command of Capt. Dolly Richards, 150 Rangers rode into the Valley searching for Blazer's Scouts. Richards concealed half his force and then lured the Scouts into an ambush. It was a perfectly executed tactic that annihilated the enemy. With the exception of two of his men who straggled into Federal headquarters the next day, Blazer's entire command was either killed or captured.[9]

Millwood (on the road to Berry's Ferry) – December 17, 1864:

About a mile and a half south of Millwood, about 50 Rangers led by Lt. John Russell were caught on the west side of the pike by a detachment of Union cavalry. The Yankees were between the Rangers and their avenue of withdrawal to the Shenandoah. Perceiving their situation accurately, Russell told the Rangers that they could not make it to the river without damage, so they "must whip the enemy." Charging with a yell, the Rangers proved to be an insurmountable force. A few of the Yankees stood their ground, but to no avail. A cut and bruised Bob Walker prevailed in hand-to-hand fighting, his carbine against a Yankee saber. Walker succeeded in disarming and capturing his foe.[10]

Trekkers considering the possible location of the "Millwood Fight"

Fauquier County (skirmishes) – December 26, 1864:

After Mosby was seriously wounded at Lakeland on December 21, the Rangers were on constant alert to protect their commander. As the Federal troops scoured the countryside around Middleburg, Rectortown and Salem, searching for the wounded or dead Mosby, they were constantly under fire from the Rangers. Contrary to Federal reports of his demise (rumors purposely spread by Mosby's men?), Mosby proved to be too elusive. After all, Mosby was the Gray Ghost![11]

Belle Grove (Tee Edmonds social) – December 29, 1864:

This was not a skirmish or a raid, but an evening spent at Belle Grove socializing and dancing. Writing in her journal the following day, Tee Edmonds polishes the wax on her feelings about Robert Walker, *"Tis not often I meet a gentleman whom I admire as extravagantly as him – am almost in love with him. Wish I had the opportunity of knowing him better. Who could not help but admire him…noble in carriage and oh! such a splendid size!"*[12]

'Nough said!

Frank and Bernice Walker with Steve and Constance Boudreau at Belle Grove

Mt. Carmel Church – February 19, 1865:

During the previous night, the Federals were combing the Upperville and Paris neighborhoods searching the homes for Rangers. At Green Garden, the Richards family farm, Major Dolly Richards, Captain Robert Walker and Private John Hipkins, escaped being captured by dropping through a trapdoor in the home. The three Rangers immediately set out to round up other Rangers to pursue the Yankees.

The hastily formed Rangers caught up with the retreating Yankees at Mt. Carmel Church west of the summit of Ashby Gap. The Ranger assault struck like lightning and thunder! The "road" from the church down to the Shenandoah at Shepherd's Ford is narrow and rocky, not much more than a path meandering through the thick undergrowth and forest. This played to the advantage of the Rangers' use of revolvers. The carbines and sabers of the Yankees were effectively neutralized in the close-quarters struggle.

The Federals put up a gallant effort but succumbed to the hard-charging, rapid-firing Rangers. When the last echoes of the fight cleared, 63 Union soldiers and 90 horses had been captured and the road was a bloody scene with a large number wounded or killed. All the Rangers who had been scooped up by the Federal raid the previous night were liberated.[13]

The author with Frank and Bernice Walker at Green Garden, site of Capt. Bob's narrow escape

Hamilton (Harmony) - March 21, 1865:

A large force of Union troops, 1000 cavalry and infantry combined, had set out from Harpers Ferry in search of Mosby. The Federals were marching eastward through upper Loudoun County. Mosby's scouts kept him posted on the Yankees' progress. At the village of Hamilton (also known as Harmony to the locals), Mosby decided to set a trap. The winding and undulating road out of Hamilton leading south to the village of Lincoln made a perfect spot for an ambuscade. A detachment of Union cavalry took the bait and chased the lure into the trap. The Federal loss was significant and the Yankees withdrew toward the Valley. [14]

Millwood (Armistice Negotiations) – April 18, 1865:

After Gen. Lee's surrender on April 9, the Federals hoped that Mosby would surrender his command. Arrangements were made for a meeting between Col. Mosby and Union Gen. George Chapman on April 18. Mosby attended the meeting at Carter Hall accompanied by about 60 of his officers and men, including Captain Robert Walker. At the meeting, Mosby declined to surrender, and asked for an extension of the armistice so he could gather communications from Richmond. An extension was granted for two days.

The author and Burke Nebeker at the Clarke Hotel in Millwood

The armistice was set to lapse at noon on the 20th. Realizing he was going to arrive late, Mosby sent Captains Robert Walker and Tom Richards ahead to Millwood. At the Clarke Hotel, the meeting was disrupted by a warning of a trap. Mosby and his men quickly declined any further discussion and galloped back to Fauquier County.

Rather than surrender his command, Col. Mosby decided to disband his regiment. In Salem, on April 21, 1865, Mosby assembled his men for the last time. In disbanding the Rangers, he made it possible for each man to decide on his own about parole.[15]

A Tribute

The most meaningful compliments come from peers or colleagues. In Robert Walker's case, the highest praise came from his commander, Col. John S. Mosby. Granted, Mosby's letter to James Seddon, Confederate Secretary of War, would present Walker's qualities in the most positive light. However, to balance that, Mosby was known for being tight-lipped with praise except when richly deserved. The letter reproduced here is dated February 10, 1865.

Sir:

I respectfully recommend that Pvt. Robert Walker be promoted for valor and skill to be Captain of his company (B, 43 Va. Battalion) to fill the vacancy caused by the promotion of Captain A. E. Richards to a majority. During a connection with my command for nearly two years, he has never failed, in the numerous engagements in which he has met the enemy, to distinguish himself by deeds of conspicuous daring and valor, whilst his intelligence and high moral character give full assurance of the skill requisite to command. As the law requires specific instances of the exhibition of these qualities, I will enumerate the following, although these must not be regarded as mere examples of his skill and courage and not as embracing every occasion on which he has been distinguished. On the 3rd of May 1864 his horse was killed while leading a charge at Warrenton Junction. Undeterred by this accident, he immediately mounted a horse which he captured and was among the first to enter a house occupied by the enemy, which we stormed and was one of the last to leave when heavy reinforcements compelled us to retire. On the 10th of March 1864 he was one of a party of six men composing the rear guard of an expedition returning from a successful incursion near Charlestown.

The enemy pursued in strong force for the purpose of rescuing their prisoners, but were repulsed with severe loss (including the Major commanding killed) by the rear guard, who promptly turned upon them. On the 17th of December 1864 he received several severe sabre strokes in a cavalry fight near Millwood, and on the 6th of July last was seriously wounded while in the front of a charge on the enemy's cavalry near Aldie. If brilliant courage, unblemished honor, and devotion to duty constitute titles to advancement, then no one can prefer superior claims to the position for which he is now recommended.

Very Respectfully,

Your Obedient Servant,

Jno. S. Mosby

Colonel[16]

Would that more of us could live up to the standards presented on Walker's behalf! The promotion was endorsed by Sec. Seddon and Gen. Lee. Mosby was very particular about his associations. That he and Robert Walker remained friends throughout the rest of their lives speaks volumes of the character of Robert Stringfellow Walker. Perhaps the random selection of Capt. Bob for my ranger was no fluke after all? It seems to me that this is another element supporting the serendipity and synchronicity themes of our journey.

Welbourne

With their decades of researching and field study, and an amazing depth of knowledge, trekking with Jim Moyer, Tom Evans, Don Hakenson, and Eric Buckland has always provided an adventure and an education. It has never failed to be a most pleasurable and rewarding experience. On the early treks, Jim Moyer was our mentor and guide. Jim seemed to enjoy randomly showing us Mosby sites. Normally a quiet, soft-spoken guy, Jim would keep a nearly non-stop narrative going as we drove. It seemed you could not go fifty feet without it being another significant historical site. When we interrupt with questions, Jim had the answers. As was often the case with Jim, he would ask if we had been to or seen a site. If not, he would direct us there and interpret.

Prior to the 2000 trek, we always arranged for our lodging to be located in or near whatever town we were in at the end of the day. This required an inordinate amount of planning and complicated logistics. It also meant packing and unpacking almost daily, which was a challenge for those trekkers who did not grasp the concept of "traveling light."

One day during the 1997 trek we motored across the verdant landscape near Middleburg. Jim Moyer had already guided us to several Mosby sites – Heartland, Rosenvix, Brookside, Rectors Crossroads – and we were heading back toward Middleburg. Jim inquired if we had ever been to Welbourne. We answered no, and wondered what it was.

Welbourne is a farm. At one time it was among the largest and most productive in Loudoun County. Built around 1770 it has been the family seat of the prominent Dulany family since 1833. It is not my intention here to give a detailed history of the Dulanys. An excellent source for that is *The Dulanys of Welbourne: A Family in Mosby's Confederacy*, edited by Margaret Ann Vogtsberger.

Germane to our interests is Richard Henry Dulany, the proprietor of Welbourne at the time of The War. Although he was a unionist with business and political ties to the north, Dulany joined the Confederate cause early on, even financing a company of cavalry, the Dulany Troop. Dulany's leadership qualities brought him promotions throughout The War. He was promoted to the rank of Colonel and at one point he commanded the famed "Laurel Brigade." Because of Col. Dulany's prominence both economically and militarily, Welbourne witnessed a variety of interesting events and visitors during the war years.

At the time Jim mentioned Welbourne, we were not aware of its historical significance. Later we discovered that Mosby men boarded at the house, including Ranger John Peyton de Butts, who was the Colonel's nephew. Welbourne holds many stories within its hallowed walls; however, Jim brought it to our attention as a possible remedy for our itinerant ways. The current owners, Nat and Sherry Morison, were managing Welbourne as a bed and breakfast.

Jim directed us to the B&B farm. We stopped the vehicle. Snapping photos from the lane, we expressed wonderment at the grandness of the house and its park-like setting. We questioned Jim about the truth that it was a B&B. Oh, yes! We needed to stay there! We drove on to more adventures that day in 1997, but the vision of Welbourne was imbedded!

Welbourne Hall

When planning a trek, one of the first steps is to arrange lodging. The first time I contacted Welbourne, I had to dig through old notes to locate the phone number.

I dialed and waited several rings before Nat answered, "Welbourne...."

I introduced myself and indicated my desire to make a reservation. There was a pause. I heard an exhale, then, "Are you sure you want to stay here? Do you know what Welbourne is?"

"Yes, yes!"

"Do you realize Welbourne is rustic? It is not like the Marriott. If you haven't stayed with us before, you may not like it."

"Yes, we want to stay at Welbourne!"

"Welbourne is a historic home. Furnishings are original, floors creak, there might be peeling paint."

"Perfect! That is exactly what we are looking for!"

It was Nat's mother who opened the home for bed and breakfast guests. Nat is the seventh generation of the Dulany family to own the farm. Nat and Sherry's son, Joshua, is now the eighth generation. That is something of a rarity in Virginia in these modern times.

Our first lodging at Welbourne was magnificent. It is definitely not the Marriott! Stepping through the front door into the foyer is a journey into the past. To the right is the library. Above the mantel are oil portraits of Dulany ancestors. On another wall is a life-sized oil portrait of a uniformed Col. Dulany, who oversees the reading of the visitors. Except for the old telephone and electric lights, one would have no way of knowing it is the 21st century.

Across the foyer from the library is the parlor. On a chilly night the parlor is where guests gather to chat and share stories, sitting around a cheery fire. Again, electric lights are about the only clue that we are not in the nineteenth century. Well, there is a well-stocked bar in the corner, too - all modern labels! The library and the parlor are the primary public spaces in the house. With the varied backgrounds of the guests, conversations are always stimulating. In warmer weather, the guests gather on the front porch or, in case of rain, on the back porch, which is covered. No matter where, the confabs are engaging and lively.

As with Dulanys before him, Nat has ties to the north. His father had a business headquartered in New York, so as a youth, Nat spent summers at Welbourne. Make no mistake. Nat is proud of his Virginia heritage, and at the same time is a New York Mets fan. Sherry is from Vermont or New Hampshire – I only remember that she is from one of those small New England states. You will have to ask them how they met. Together, Nat and Sherry are wonderful, entertaining hosts.

Trekkers enjoy an evening with Nat and Sherry Morison at Welbourne

I should mention that the guest rooms are comfortable, not modern, and each one is unique, yet appointed in tasteful historic furnishings. Yes, electric lights, too! The bathrooms have indoor plumbing, with hot and cold running water and flush toilets being modern concessions. If floors sag a bit, it only adds to the ambiance. Think about it. Welbourne is over 200 years old! It has experienced a lot of living in its lifetime. At that age, I believe I might sag a little, too!

Welbourne is also a working farm. With just under 600 acres remaining of the original land holdings, Nat is able to maintain a retirement farm for old horses. With room to roam the retirees are able to live out their final days as horses should, free-ranging.

Nat and Sherry grooming a retiree at Welbourne

Just walking in the front door makes me feel like I am home! Wait! I would be remiss if I failed to mention the famous Welbourne breakfasts. Served in the dining room, which is in the original 1770s section of the house, breakfast is a major element of the Welbourne experience. Breakfast varies from day to day, but could include cornbread, eggs, ham, and spiced apples, along with coffee or tea. Breakfast is seasoned with spirited conversation among the guests, and when Sherry and Nat join the table toward the end of the meal. Needless to say that after our first stay, Welbourne became our home away from home, and our headquarters from whence we could launch our daily expeditions. Welbourne *and* Nat and Sherry Morison have become good friends and a cornerstone in our journey. Now, on to some of our Welbourne adventures.

Our first stay was exciting; everything was new. The Morisons were gracious hosts, but they did not know us nor did they understand our mission. When I tried to explain to Nat how we were Mosby scholars, it was difficult for him to accept that these folks from Washington State (Yankees, from way up north and the far west) could be sincerely sympathetic to the southern struggle.

To prove our interest and because we were headed out for our annual Mosby Ride that day, we decided to attend breakfast in uniform (without advance warning for Nat). Breakfast was splendid as always, warm conversation to complement the perfect repast. When Nat walked into the dining room, we stood to attention as we would for a general officer. Nat's reaction was priceless. In a matter of moments a succession of expressions flashed across his face. First, what is going on here? Then, you have got to be kidding! Then, at least you are in the "right" uniform. Finally, maybe you Washington guys are all right. "Please, sit!"

I am not certain, but I do believe that we had then convinced Nat of our honorable intentions. He did express relief that we wore the proper uniform unlike some uncouth fellas who had shown up in Union blue.

HMR rangers taking their ease at Welbourne L to R: Burke Nebeker (Fount Beattie), Brian Buntain (Bob Walker), Steve Boudreau (James "Big Yankee" Ames)

We are grateful to Nat and Sherry for welcoming us into the Welbourne fold. We have been fortunate to meet many interesting people there over the years. Being centrally located in Mosby's Confederacy, having Welbourne as our trek headquarters has helped increase our exploration time. Also, using his connections, on several occasions Nat has helped to gain us access to sites normally beyond our means. Through Nat we have been able to get up close and personal to significant Mosby sites: Oakley, Green Garden, and Ayrshire.

There are several versions of this story told at Welbourne, but the bottom line is that Ranger John Peyton de Butts escaped capture here one night. Yankee patrols were sweeping through the area looking to scoop up careless Rangers. As the Yankees rode up in the darkness and surrounded the house, the occupants warned the Ranger. De Butts was hurried off to the children's bedroom. When the Union soldiers searched the house, they did not find him or any other Ranger. Looking into but not searching the bedroom, the Yankees only saw the children jumping and playing on their bed and did not discover de Butts lying under the blankets. It was a close call for Ranger de Butts, but provided giggles and excitement for the children.

Like many safe houses in Mosby's Confederacy, Welbourne was equipped with a concealed trapdoor. This one was in the back hall and dropped into the basement. Another story relates a quick exit by another southern soldier who made his escape through the trapdoor. Leaping onto his horse that was stabled in the basement, he slipped away while the Yankees searched the house.

A huge shock greeted us as we drove up to the Welbourne house on the 2001 trek. There were long poles cantilevered against the exterior front walls. Not a good sign for an aging structure! Passing through the front door, an even greater vision stunned us. The walls of the foyer and the parlor were a dismal, moldy gray of peeling paint. Oh, no! Welbourne was finally surrendering to the ravages of time. When I called to make our reservations, Nat failed to warn me about this grim state of crumbling.

What Nat had failed to warn me about was that Welbourne was starring in a movie! The set designers had "made up" Welbourne to fit its role. Sherry had a good laugh at our shocked response but assured us all would be returned to normal after production was finished. Whew! It is surprising to me that I had developed such a strong attachment to the place.

We carried on with our trek itinerary while at the same time witnessing some of the filming in and around the house. The film, *Crazy Like a Fox*, starred Mary McDonnell (*Dances with Wolves*) and Roger Rees (*Frida*), in a story about the struggle of rural people to protect their land and heritage from rampaging development. The viewer may find a slight resemblance to Sherry and Nat, but they are very clear – the movie is not about them!

We were able to attend the premier showing in Leesburg. It is an independent film that has been featured in many film festivals around the country. The film was released on DVD in 2006 and it is worth the effort of locating it for the Welbourne scenery alone.

Fortunately, Welbourne is now placed under the protection of a historic land preservation trust so we rest easier knowing the developers will not be able to destroy this amazing place.

The author with cousin Carol Jeffords in the Welbourne parlor with the "peeling paint" effect for the movie set

Welbourne Hall at sunrise

Mosby Springs Farm

At the genial Welbourne breakfast table one Sunday morning the conversation turned to the topic of our treks. As much as possible, we briefly explained the major aspects and history of our mission to the other guests. Among those genteel guests was Brenda, who spoke of her friend who was a grandson of a Mosby Ranger. Of course the mention of a Mosby descendant pings our radar. Brenda offered to arrange for us to meet George Wiltshire, grandson (not great-grandson!) of Ranger James Girard Wiltshire. Offer enthusiastically accepted!

After breakfast our trek took us to Cool Springs Church Cemetery near Delaplane. We were there to assist in a marker re-dedication ceremony for Ranger Henry Clay Pearson. Ranger Pearson, who died in 1933, was one of the last surviving former Rangers. Following the ceremony, we invoked "Rule 2 – Go with the flow" and jettisoned the day's itinerary because Brenda called to let us know she had set an appointment to meet George Wiltshire. Already late for the appointed hour, we had to make haste to Middleburg and Mosby Springs Farm.

At the marker re-dedication for Ranger Henry Clay Pearson – Cool Springs Church, Delaplane

James "Jim" Wiltshire had served in the 12th Virginia Cavalry before joining Mosby's Partisan Rangers in July 1864. From that time on, Jim was involved in most of the 43rd's major engagements. His family home must have been located near Charlestown, WV, as Jim provided informed scouting for the Ranger attacks on the B & O railroad, especially the "Greenback Raid." Mosby's confidence and trust in Jim was clear because he detailed Wiltshire with Charlie Grogan and Charley Dear to spirit the greenbacks to safety in Loudoun County. In studying a wartime map by S. Howell Brown, I discovered properties under Wiltshire ownership just a mile or so from the attack site. Mosby's practice was to reward Rangers for their courage on the field of battle.

We know Jim Wiltshire fought gallantly. Before the end of The War he was promoted to 2nd Lieutenant of Company H. It is also believed that it was Jim, at Arundel's Tavern, who fired the final shot by a Ranger in The War.

Mosby Springs Farm sits adjacent to and north of the Ashby Gap Turnpike (Rt. 50) west of Middleburg. [Rt. 50 is also known as the John S. Mosby Highway!] A sign next to the entrance proclaims its identity. The Mosby name is ubiquitous in this neck of the woods. Mosby apartments, Mosby plumbing, Mosby Inn, Mosby Pub and more are scattered around the area. I had driven by many times and wondered if it really had a connection to the Rangers.

George greeted us like long-lost family. He is a friendly chap with a twinkle in his eye, always ready for the humor. George gave us a tour and explained his grandfather, Jim, had shown him where there was a spring hidden back on the farmland. The spring had served as a rendezvous point for the Rangers. That was one of the reasons Jim purchased the farm.

We also learned that after the Greenback Raid, Jim needed a safe place to store his share, $2100. Jim brought a servant to a hollow tree (George did not know that location) and placed the money inside. Jim's instructions were that if he did not survive The War, the servant was to bring the money to his family. George said that not only was the money still there at the end of The War, Jim used it to purchase the farm, and to put himself through medical school. Amazing the stories that are tucked away in family lore!

George loaded us into his well-worn Jeep Wagoneer. He drove us rapidly through his woods, barely escaping contact with forest entanglements and all the while chatting with us more than watching for obstacles. I do not know how he managed to avoid a collision, but I began to understand why his jeep had that broken-in look. We dismounted at the springs that became Mosby Springs. With George's orientation, we could easily envision the Rangers coming off the old Sand-and-Clay Road into the safety of the springs, watering their mounts, and watching for opportunities to attack Yankee patrols out on the Ashby Gap Turnpike.

Burke Nebeker, George Wiltshire and the author at the Mosby Springs

We piled back into the jeep and barged out to Rt. 50 where George drove us around the immediate vicinity giving us more of the local lore he recollected from his boyhood. Returning to Mosby Springs Farm, George warmly sent us on to Western View, the famed Hathaway House of Mosby legend.

Visiting George has become a mainstay of our treks. He is always generous and supportive of our mission. A couple of treks later I arranged with George for us to do our Mosby Ride over his and neighboring farms. On the appointed morning, we showed up at the farm in uniform of course. George's daughter was visiting and it was she who answered the door. She gasped, asked us to wait, and ran upstairs to wake her napping father. George was laughing later as he told us that she ran into his room, shook him awake, saying, "Dad! Dad! There are Confederate ghosts at the door!" He had forgotten to advise her of our plans.

Todd Kern arrived with horses and period-correct tack. Once mounted, we moved out with George on point. I was surprised and pleased to see that there was less development than I anticipated so close to Middleburg. George is a lifelong horseman. It showed as we rode through park-like vistas in gorgeous sunny weather. It would be difficult to find a more pleasant riding companion than George. It was late afternoon when we returned to the barn and Todd's trailer. Not only had it been a splendid ride, we had confirmed the location of Benton's Ford on Goose Creek.

HMR rangers fording Chinn's Branch near Mosby Springs

In the aftermath of the great battle at Gettysburg, the Federal army marched south through the Middleburg area. Mosby's men were active, capturing prisoners, horses, and supplies. On July 20, 1863 Rangers Bush

Underwood, Sam Underwood and David Hixson captured a Union colonel, a major, a sergeant, and a private as they rode out of Goose Greek at Benton's Ford. The Yankees surrendered without a fight.[17]

As was the case with Mosby, our headquarters are spread out in the heart of Mosby's Confederacy.

HMR rangers searching for Yankees near Benton's Ford

---

[1] Frank Stringfellow Walker, Jr., *Remembering: A History of Orange County, Virginia*. Orange, Virginia: Orange County Historical Society, 2004. Frank Stringfellow Walker, Jr., *Echoes of Orange*. Orange, Virginia: Orange County Historical Society, 2013

[2] Williamson, *Mosby's Rangers*, pp.56-57; Jones, *Ranger Mosby*, pp.117-122; Scott, *Partisan*, pp.84-86

[3] Scott, *Partisan*, pp.152-153; Keen and Mewborn, *Regimental*, pp84-85

[4] Keen and Mewborn, *Regimental*, p.115; Scott, *Partisan*, p.205; Adele Mitchell, ed., *The Letters of John S. Mosby*, pp. 37-38

[5] Keen and Mewborn, *Regimental*, p.127; Williamson, *Mosby's Rangers*, pp.167-168

[6] Crawford, *Mosby and His Men*, p.115

[7] Williamson, *Mosby's Rangers*, pp.185-186; Scott, *Partisan*, pp.239-243; Keen and Mewborn, *Regimental*, pp.137-142

[8] Keen and Mewborn, *Regimental*, pp.142-145; Williamson, *Mosby's Rangers*, pp.187-188; Jones, *Ranger Mosby*, pp.186-187; Scott, *Partisan*, pp.247-249

[9] Williamson, *Mosby's Rangers*, pp.302-309; Scott, *Partisan*, pp.366-371; Alexander, *Mosby's Men*, pp.119-128; Munson, *Reminiscences*, pp.117-125

[10] Scott, *Partisan*, pp.381-383; Keen and Mewborn, *Regimental*, pp.233-234; Williamson, *Mosby's Rangers*, pp.325-326

[11] Keen and Mewborn, *Regimental*, p.379; Williamson, *Mosby's Rangers*, p.337

[12] Edmonds, *Journals*, p.211

[13] Williamson, *Mosby's Rangers*, pp.342-351; Scott, *Partisan*, pp.446-451; Keen and Mewborn, *Regimental*, pp.244-248

[14] Ibid., pp.355-359; Scott, *Partisan*, pp.456-459; Keen and Mewborn, Regimental, pp.252-253

[15] J.H. Kidd, *Personal Recollections of a Cavalryman with Custer's Michigan Cavalry Brigade in the Civil War*, Ionia, Michigan: The Sentinel Press, 1908; Reprinted, Grand Rapids, Michigan: The Black Letter Press, 1969; Stuart E. Brown, Jr. and Ann Barton Brown, *Carter Hall and The Civil War*, Berryville, Virginia: Virginia Book Company, 2003

[16] Adele Mitchell, ed., *The Letters of John S. Mosby*, pp.37-38

[17] Scott, *Partisan*, p.109; Williamson, *Mosby's Rangers*, p.81; Keen and Mewborn, *Regimental*, p.73

Chapter Four: *My Favorite Corner*

Crooked Run begins its path on the eastern shoulder of the Blue Ridge Mountains a short distance south of the village of Paris. The creek meanders its course through verdant pasture land and thickets of bushes and woods before joining Goose Creek near Delaplane (Piedmont). For about half its journey, Crooked Run flows over pristine historical properties. Many of the homes and farms are 200 years old or more and most have been carefully maintained. Being transported back in time is a natural reaction when trekking in this history-filled land.

The other half of Crooked Run lazily gurgles beside the Winchester Turnpike (Rt.17) from Leeds Manor Road to Delaplane. Even though the modern highway is busy, it mostly follows the old roadbed which is visible in several places. Modern intrusions aside, this corner of Mosby's Confederacy is the least developed. Along the Blue Ridge from Paris at Ashby Gap south to Delaplane, then over to Upperville and down to Rectortown, the ghosts of Mosby's Rangers still roam. It is my favorite corner of Mosby's Confederacy!

Scuffleburg (Mechanicsville)

Welcome to Scuffleburg!

Before The War, Scuffleburg was known as Mechanicsville because of the industries operating there – a blacksmith, a cabinetmaker, and a wheelwright. The tiny hamlet was located on a remote shoulder of the Blue Ridge, not far south of Paris and Ashby Gap. I do not recall how I came across the story, but it explains that the Yankees referred to the hamlet as the "second Gibraltar" and avoided going there as much as possible. According to Ranger lore, the Yankees would hurriedly "scuffle in and scuffle out." Hence, the new name.

Scuffleburg became important to the Rangers due to its isolated location. It provided a haven where the Rangers could gather in relative safety. Mosby formed Company B here on October 1, 1863, and the Rangers utilized several homes in the surrounding area as "safe houses." Also, the Yankees conducted several nighttime raids through the region. So exploring Scuffleburg became an important objective in our early treks. Because of its pristine condition and an early exciting experience exploring there, Scuffleburg also became a favorite site to visit annually. One of our earliest visits presented the serendipity that became a trademark to our Mosby experience.

It was an overcast but pleasant fall day when we drove the mile-long graveled road from the Pleasant Vale Church into Scuffleburg. In spite of our eagerness to get there, it was a slow drive through the tree-lined lane. The washboard surface and the potholes prevented any faster approach. Through the shrubs and trees crowding this original roadbed, we could see farm fields and pasture lands rolling over hill and dale. In our mind's eye we could see Mosby's men riding. Watching. It was an appropriate entry to a Scuffleburg that seemed to be stuck in the 1860s. We were in a time machine!

Finally, arriving and pulling over to one side of the narrow, almost path-like road, the six of us piled out of the vehicle. Even though there were only a couple of houses with their associated outbuildings, there was so much to see! All the houses could have been "period," but one definitely was built antebellum. In front of its door there was a plaque explaining this had been the home of William Martin, a cabinetmaker, who was the last surviving member of the jury that sat in the trial for John Brown at Harpers Ferry in 1859. Martin had moved here from West Virginia before The War commenced.

The 1800s home of William Martin, Scuffleburg

As we hurried around, snapping photos, excitedly discussing what we were discovering, one could not help but think of ants scurrying over a watermelon rind at a summer's picnic.

Suddenly, coming from beyond our view an anachronistic sound shattered our intensity. It clearly was the engine of a tractor, and it seemed to be headed toward us. A panic seized us. Were we trespassing or doing anything illegal? What seemed like an hour, but in reality was only a minute, passed before a tractor, a shiny green and yellow John Deere, appeared from a lane that came in from the north. The driver was an older chap. He wore a tweed driver's cap, a matching tweed sport coat, a button-down light blue shirt, and khaki trousers tucked into his barn boots. The epitome of the English country squire! The gentleman steered into the path where we were standing, as we tremulously awaited our fate. He stopped the tractor, shut off the engine, and pondered the sight before him with a puzzled expression.

At this point, I applied a lesson learned from Jim Moyer, who had demonstrated this practice several times during previous treks. I approached the gentleman sitting on the tractor, holding up *The Guidebook*. I introduced myself: "Hi! My name is Brian Buntain. We are historians from Washington State researching Mosby's Rangers. We hope we are not intruding." With a twinkle in his eye, he introduced himself as Harry, and asked me to tell him more about our mission. Harry was knowledgeable about Mosby and the activities of the Rangers in the Scuffleburg area. He suggested that we explore up on the hill above the point where we then stood. There we would find the ruins of an original house and the blacksmith's shop. Before resuming his interrupted mission, Harry said, "And when you come back out, be sure to stop at our place. I know my wife, Susan, will want to meet you."

Scuffleburg ruins – once a house perhaps?

We went on to explore the ruins, and found the remnants of the old road that originally intersected the Winchester Turnpike (today's Rt. 17) at Fleetwood Mills. The visit was magical. The presence of the Rangers was palpable; however, we had an itinerary with many more sites for the day, and knew we needed to saddle up.

Now, we weren't certain that Harry really meant we should stop. As we approached their house, we were surprised to see Harry and Susan standing on their front porch smiling and waving us in. They welcomed us into their home almost like we were long-lost family. While we were exploring the ruins at Scuffleburg, Susan had prepared a table of refreshments. After chatting and getting to know each other, Susan brought out maps and charts. Susan shared all that she knew of The War with regards to their neighborhood. How long we were engaged in exchanging information has escaped my memory, but it was a lively and productive session. No way did we mind missing some of that day's scheduled sites!

A visit with Harry and Susan became a requisite for future treks. The energy was always high, the conversation stimulating, and the camaraderie was genuine. On a subsequent trek Harry and Susan arranged for us to track a Mosby skirmish by horse, to better understand and interpret the evolution of the fight. The horses and period-correct tack were provided by our friend, Todd Kern. To get a "Ranger's perspective" of the fight, we rode in uniform over the neighbors' fields, following wartime maps and written accounts. So far as we knew, no one had ever attempted that. That evening, Harry and Susan hosted a soiree' where they invited their neighbors to hear our presentation and learn about our mission and its progress. Again, it was a pleasant affair. Many of the neighbors' homes had been safe houses or homes where Rangers boarded. The closing comment at the end of the evening: "And these guys have to come from Washington State to teach us about our neighborhood!"

The story does not end here, however. Eventually, Harry and Susan moved away from Mosby's Confederacy, but through Harry and Susan we were able to meet other friends who have helped expand our knowledge of Mosby's Rangers. Among these are historian Norman L. Baker, and David and Jolly de Give, current owners of Belle Grove, an antebellum home prominent in Mosby history.

Scuffleburg ruins – possibly the site of a blacksmith's shop – where Rangers likely frequented

Belle Grove

Checking the index of any of the contemporary books on Mosby's Rangers will reveal references to Amanda Virginia "Tee" Edmonds. Tee was a spirited lass, the daughter of Edmonds-Settle families, which had been established in the Crooked Run Valley since 1780. Like many young women of the day, Tee kept journals, entering commentary as often as her busy life permitted. From her observations, we have a view of what life was like, 1857-1867, in the Piedmont region of northern Virginia. Her journal was passed down through her family and was eventually published as *Journals of Amanda Virginia Edmonds: Lass of the Mosby Confederacy.*

Tee's journals are not the only primary source available to the modern researcher of Mosby lore. There are several published references that have proved valuable: *In the Shadow of the Enemy* (Ida Powell Dulany, Upperville); *Dark Days in Our Beloved Country* (Catherine Hopkins Broun, Middleburg); and *My Heart is so Rebellious* (the Caldwell family, Warrenton). Each provides added perspectives to the effects of war in the Mosby Confederacy. What makes Tee's account so useful is that her home, Belle Grove, is located on a ridge overlooking the Winchester Turnpike with farmland extending to the Blue Ridge, providing a pivotal position to view and often become a participant in events of The War.

Belle Grove was home and safe house for several Rangers, including Tee's brothers, "Bud," Ben Syd, and Clem, as well as Matthew Magner and brothers Richard and George Triplett, as well as others. Tee was also related to the Blackwells, Fletchers, Fergusons, and Carters, local families with Ranger sons. Not only was Tee able to follow the troop movements, both blue and gray, up and down the turnpike, she was able to stay current on Ranger actions. With such a lively household, Belle Grove became a center of perpetual entertainment for the lass of the Mosby Confederacy.

Tee was fervently supportive of the southern cause and did not mince her thoughts regarding the Yankee invaders. After reading the journal, several points about wartime life jump out for further note.

First, the civilian population initially was largely supportive of The War, then less so as the depredations and hardships piled up. There was not a perceptive diminishing of resolve for the southern cause, gaining independence, simply an overwhelming desire for the Yankees to go home and The War to end.

Second, the civilians were necessarily creative in obtaining the essentials: food, clothing and tools. Mosby's men filled a role in this regard, sharing with their families and safe house hosts items captured from the Yankee sutlers and supply trains. Sometimes Rangers smuggled contraband items through the Federal lines for their neighbors and families, as well as generously sharing "greenbacks" liberated from Union soldiers throughout the area.

Third, the people of the Piedmont were starved for news about the progress of The War to hear word of the safety of their sons, fathers and brothers who were serving in the military, as well as to hopefully hear of great southern victories. While there existed an unofficial network for gaining news about The War, the grassroots gossip often misinformed rather than enlightened families. People were eager to obtain current newspapers, which unfortunately became increasingly scarce as The War dragged on over weeks, months and years. In the absence of local papers, even Yankee publications were sought-after items. At least one could see what untruths and exaggerations the enemy's propaganda was spreading. Mosby's men helped in this regard, too, by bringing first-hand accounts of skirmishes, and by delivering letters and local and contraband newspapers to the families.

Because of the frequent references to Tee's journals in our Mosby readings, such as Jeffry Wert's *Mosby's Rangers*, we knew we needed to find a copy. It was not a widely available book through our Washington State bookstores. On our first trek we succeeded in locating one copy (the only one in stock) at the visitor center in the Manassas Battlefield Park. Progress!

As we drove in search of Belle Grove, one of our crew looked up key subjects in the journal's index, hoping to uncover tidbits relating to our Rangers. I was driving the minivan while another trekker, serving as the navigator, consulted *The Guidebook*. At the guidebook-indicated mileage, we observed a grand mansion on the hillside to the west of Rt.17. Lacking any signage to the effect, we presumed this must be Belle Grove! It was a stately, red brick manse with expansive lawns and an appropriately meandering driveway quaintly bridging Crooked Run. We hopped out of the minivan, snapped photos rapidly, and savored the moment. In our minds-eye was the vision of Tee watching the turnpike for any imminent danger from the despised Yankees.

As we continued to drive northward on Rt.17, a voice from the back of the van began quoting from the journal,

> *"Oh! I had the pleasure of becoming acquainted with Mr. Bob W [Robert S. Walker], the nicest fellow in the crowd. 'Tis not often I meet a gentleman whom I admire as extravagantly as him – am almost in love with him. Wish I had the opportunity of knowing him better. Who could help but admire him, when he is so like Theodore, noble in carriage and oh! such a splendid size. And a greater recommendation than all – he does not indulge in any kind of spirit. I must stop eulogizing his goodness – he may disappoint me on further acquaintance."*

When the reader reached the part: "… and oh! such a splendid size" the guffaws and ribbing roared for an interminable time. My Ranger is Robert Stringfellow Walker, the Bob W. of Tee's adoration. Suddenly, over my protests within our coterie, and until taps' final note floats across the valley, I became "Splendid Size Bob!"

Ever since discovering the above reference, I have wondered what Tee meant by "such a splendid size?" After sharing the passage with Frank Stringfellow Walker, Bob's grandson (not great or great-great!), he laughed his splendid philosopher's chortle, and posed his own question, "Yes, indeed! What was her connotation? The implications are amusing."

You might imagine our chagrin, then excitement, once we drove about a half mile further on Rt.17 and pulled off to the east of the road across from a sign that read: "Belle Grove, 1780." This was our earliest example of the wisdom of "Rule 3 – go further!" The *real* Belle Grove is much older than our first, faux Belle Grove (we never did determine its true identity!). While the real Belle Grove is not as fancy, it has much more soul! The house majestically sits further back from the highway on a rise and is surrounded by ancient trees. The usual photo drill followed and then we piled back into the rental vehicle to ride on to the next site on the day's itinerary.

It became a goal to get up close and tour Belle Grove. On our third tour, Jim Moyer took us up to the house. Jim was brave; we were in awe. It did not occur to us that maybe he actually knew the owners and maybe he had been there before. We knocked on the front door, which we later learned was one of the finer front doors in Virginia. Nobody was home, so we snapped some close-up photos and departed, determined to return some day for a more in-depth investigation.

Jim Moyer on the Belle Grove front porch

From the Belle Grove house, one has a clear view to the highway. It is easy to picture Tee watching the troops filing up and down the road. It is also easy to understand how the family could detect Yankees when they came to search the house for Rangers, contraband, and plunder. As was the case with many of the safe houses in Mosby's Confederacy, there was a trapdoor that could be used by gray-clad soldiers to escape capture. Other times the Belle Grove Rangers would skip out the back when Yankees approached, and would scoot up to a "shebang" hidden in the Blue Ridge woodlands.

Looking east from the Belle Grove front yard; Rt. 17 runs along the middle-distance tree line

"Someday" came several treks later. I had not quite made progress for a planned visit when by accident (really?) we met the Belle Grove owners, David and Jolly de Give, through Scuffleburg's Susan and Harry. Serendipity! Synchronicity!

Jolly guided us through the house, sharing insights and anecdotes about Belle Grove and the Edmonds family, especially Tee. Jolly is an elegant and gracious person; it felt like we were with Jackie Kennedy touring the White House! We saw the trapdoor. It dropped into a kind of cellar space beneath today's kitchen, the war-era dining room. This hidey-hole has an opening to a latticed front porch that could be concealed by a rick of firewood. A visit with the de Gives became a highlight of subsequent treks! Belle Grove's owners have been conscientious about the physical maintenance of the home and protecting its historical integrity. We thank them every visit!

There is a story that one day someone heard a creaking sound coming from the attic. Upon investigation, a rocking chair was found next to a window. On the attic flooring next to the chair were several apple cores. The story goes that Tee would sit by the window watching for Yankee invaders while eating her favorite fruit, an apple. The apple cores were recent, and there had been baskets of harvested apples on the back porch not long before. The implication was that the spirit of Tee was still on the lookout for Yankees! We had always believed that the story had been given to us by Jolly. However, during my September 2015 visit with her, Jolly said that was her first time hearing the rocker-apple-core story. It's an entertaining story, but where did we get it?

The 2013 trek purposely coincided with the 150th anniversary celebration of the formation of the 43rd Battalion Virginia Cavalry, Mosby's Rangers. In conjunction with the celebration, the Mosby Heritage Area Association was sponsoring several events, including a public tour of Mosby safe houses. I volunteered for service and was assigned Belle Grove as a living history interpreter. I was posted as Robert S. Walker, Captain, Co. B, Mosby's Rangers. On civilian duty was Eric Buckland, resplendent in a new period-correct suit. We greeted visitors outside while Jolly and another volunteer conducted the interpretation inside. It was a beautiful sunny day but not too warm. There was a steady flow of visitors who appreciated the heritage of Belle Grove. It felt good to be able to give back to those who had assisted us over the years of trekking.

A goal now has become to do a "Mosby Ride" over the Belle Grove land to Mt. Bleak, home of Tee's Uncle and Aunt Settle, as well as maybe some neighboring fields, too.

A short distance from the house is the Edmonds family cemetery. Resting beside Tee are her husband, John Armistead Chappelear, her brother, Ranger Clement, and other members of this historic Edmonds family.

Reading Tee's journals are the best way to understand Belle Grove's story. For those desiring more information, look for a newly revised edition to come out in 2016 with Lee Lawrence as editor.

Looking toward the Belle Grove house from the Edmonds family cemetery

Mt. Bleak (Sky Meadows State Park)

The itinerary for the 2001 trek seemed busier than usual. We started within minutes after arriving at Dulles International Airport with a splendid southern breakfast hosted by Win Meiselman in Laura Ratcliffe's post-War home, Merrybrook. Merrybrook is outside Herndon about a seven-minute drive from the car rental agency. After a warm visit with Win, we went on to a very full day's itinerary. We did not slow down again until we were on the homeward bound plane nine days later.

Mt. Bleak house in Sky Meadows State Park; the log structure to the right was a summer kitchen

Mt. Bleak was the farm of Abner and Mary Settle, uncle and aunt of Tee Edmonds. Their sons, Abner and Isaac Settle, were Rangers. The farm and house are set on the shoulder of the Blue Ridge. The views toward Paris and Ashby Gap are spectacular! Belle Grove is visible from the south-facing back porch of Mt. Bleak house. After The War, Mt. Bleak became the home of former Ranger George M. Slater, and remained George's home for 55 years. He had been one of the first nine men detailed by Gen. Jeb Stuart in early 1863 to join Mosby's independent command to operate behind Federal lines in northern Virginia. Mosby's son John Jr. had stayed for a while with George at Mt. Bleak to recuperate from medical issues.

One of the highlights in a trek full of highlights, was the annual Mosby Ride. We met Todd Kern again at the Lost Mountain Trails Stables. Riding this year were Todd, Sgt. Ames, A.G. Babcock, Billings Steele, Robert Walker, Mrs. Wilson, and Col. Mosby (portrayed by Jeff Smith). Beginning with a pleasant ride up Lost Mountain, we eventually crossed the Winchester Turnpike (Rt. 17). The fields we crossed were part of the Sky Meadows State Park. The goal was to arrive at the Mt. Bleak house around noon to help with a living history presentation. We were Rangers returning to our safe house, Mt. Bleak, from a raid.

We were rangers returning from a raid to our safe house, Mt. Bleak

We strutted and swaggered around the house and grounds, posed for photos, talked with visitors about The War and life as a Ranger. A surprise was that "Col. Mosby" seemed only vaguely familiar with the history of his command and their operations. His thoughts must have been focused on the next raid. Around 2:00, though, we needed to take our leave. The horses remained with Todd at Mt. Bleak while we drove down to Rt. 17 and headed south toward Piedmont, today's Delaplane.

HMR rangers presenting a "living history" program at Mt. Bleak – Sky Meadows State Park

This was the inaugural trek for Steve, our Sgt. Ames. Unbeknownst to him, there was a dedication today of a Virginia State Historic Marker to honor James F. "Big Yankee" Ames. James F. Ames began The War as a Union trooper in the 5th New York Cavalry, a frequent foe and target of the Rangers. He abandoned the northern cause when Lincoln's Emancipation Proclamation became law, and walked 25 miles to join Mosby. After an initial trial period, Ames not only proved himself, he ultimately was promoted to 2nd Lieutenant of Company F, becoming one of Mosby's most trusted men.

In our tradition, Steve believes he might have been chosen by Ames. Steve's ancestors were Yankees, and both Steve and Ames had ties to the state of Maine and sailing. We had worked on Steve for several years before he finally agreed to join our outfit and the gray uniform stopped giving him a rash. Steve was promoted to our sergeant position and became one of our best rangers. Steve eventually moved to Virginia and is currently living in the Valley.

When we arrived at the ceremony and walked over to the marker, the people already assembled wondered if A.G. wasn't portraying "Big Yankee." A.G. had played defensive lineman at the University of Florida; he definitely was big. But Steve is tall, about 6'1", so he qualifies in the size department. Steve got a starring role during the dedication. Pretty good for a newbie experience!

Steve Boudreau as "Big Yankee" Ames at the dedication of the historical marker

The historic marker stands on the east side of Rt. 17; however, the location of the actual spot where Lt. Ames was killed is over the hill behind the marker on the Delaplane Grade.

It was long believed that the site of Ames' killing was at Kitty Shacklett's home, Yew Hill. Along with the Ashby and Shacklett families, the early years of Yew Hill itself have an interesting history. In 1769 a young George Washington stayed here for several days while he was surveying in the area. On June 17, 1863, Gen. Jeb Stuart met with Mosby regarding recon on Federal troop movements prior to the Battles of Aldie, Middleburg and Upperville. Mosby also presented Gen. Stuart with a fine sorrel mare that recently had been "liberated."[1]

Yew Hill - home of Kitty Shacklett

The Shackletts were loyal to the south. Kitty's brother, Hezekiah, had been repeatedly hanged and let down from a tree limb by the Yankees hoping to convince him to change his loyalties. He remained a good Confederate. From her upstairs window, Kitty would signal Mosby about Union troop movements in the area. The Shackletts did what they could for the cause.[2]

It was not until much later, when a letter surfaced, that we learned Kitty's was not the scene of Ames' killing. The letter had been written by a Union soldier and described the actual site to be on the Kerfoot Road (now the Delaplane Grade Road), just north of Piedmont (now Delaplane). Four Rangers were scouting in the neighborhood. They knew Yankees were near, so they split up to gather additional Rangers. Ames ranged up the Kerfoot Road where he encountered a Federal patrol. Ames apparently ducked into Cook Shacklett's lane at Ashland, but was shot by a hidden Yankee scout. The other Rangers were close enough to hear the gunfire and rode to the Ashland gate. There was Ames on the ground with the Yankee over him rifling his pockets. Ranger Ludwell Lake, Jr fired his revolver and killed the Yankee.

Steve Boudreau examining Ames' telescope

In cleaning out the Yankee's pockets, Lake recovered Ames' telescope, buttons from his uniform and some other personal items. Legend says that Ames was buried near the Ashland gate under a poplar tree. So far as we know Ames' remains were never transferred, but sometime after The War, Ranger Alexander G. Babcock arranged for a headstone to be placed in the Hollywood cemetery in Richmond.[3]

Poplar tree and springhouse at Ashland's gate, possibly Lt. James "Big Yankee" Ames' resting place

Ayrshire and Snowden

The first notice of Ayrshire in the various Mosby accounts comes as a mention of coffee. For several reasons Mosby eschewed liquor. One, the distilling of alcoholic spirits robbed much-needed grain from the tables of Confederate families and the mangers of the livestock. Two, his Rangers boarded with local families who would not welcome the drunken behavior most likely to result from young men imbibing. Three, Mosby needed his men to be ready to mount up and charge into the fight, sometimes with only a moment's notice. A drunken Ranger would be useless in the fight and most like become a casualty.

However, the elixir of Mosby's choice was coffee. He was known to carry beans with him on a scout. Due to the Federal blockade of southern ports, coffee was not readily available in Mosby's Confederacy. It was said that the Colonel knew every kitchen within his realm that could be relied on to provide a steaming cup of goodness upon request. Ayrshire was one of the fortunate households frequented by Mosby.

Ayrshire was also the family home of one of Mosby's young Rangers, George Hyde Ayre. James J. Williamson and several other Rangers boarded with the family as well. Located a short distance north of Upperville, Ayrshire was peaceful through most of The War, at least after the Battle of Upperville in June 1863. Occasionally there was a midnight Yankee raid through the neighborhood seeking to gobble up Rangers sleeping in their safe houses.

The original house at Ayrshire Farm - Courtesy Claiborne Stokes

In correspondence with an Ayre historian, and a one-time resident of the farm, I learned an interesting anecdote. Apparently George, Sr. owned a lot of land in the area and had a lease with option to buy on the Llangollen Farm. Ayre family legend tells how Ranger George in April 1864 was on his way to the courthouse with some $20,000 in gold for his father, George, Sr., for the purpose of purchasing Llangollen. The bullion had been stitched into the young Ranger's saddle. Unfortunately, George, Jr. ran into a patrol of the 2nd Massachusetts Cavalry and was captured about a mile north of his home. He sat out the remainder of The War as a prisoner, and was paroled at Fort Warren in June 1865. No official mention of the gold or saddle has surfaced.

The Battle of Upperville raged over Ayrshire's fields on June 21, 1863. This was not a Mosby action. The fight actually started several days prior at Aldie with the Union cavalry attempting to discover Robert E. Lee's intentions with the Army of Northern Virginia over in the Shenandoah Valley. Using delaying tactics, the Confederate cavalry was screening Lee's march northward, which ultimately resulted in the massive battle at Gettysburg. The Federal brigades had been slowly advancing, pushing west attempting to gain Ashby's Gap and a view into the Valley. The Confederates had to hold Trappe Road fronting Ayrshire to delay the Yankees. It was fiercely contested ground involving four to five thousand combatants, especially around the farm's sunken road. The Confederates exacted a dear price for every bit of ground conceded, but the Yankees did not get a peek at Lee in the Valley.[4]

Like most families in war-torn areas, the Ayre family suffered hardships. Their oldest son, Tom, died in Pickett's Charge at Gettysburg. Their second son was a prisoner of war. Federal troops confiscated 26 wagons of corn and provender at one point. Ayre suffered raiding parties that took whatever they fancied. In the fall of 1863, George, Sr. went to Lynchburg to dispose of a large amount of tobacco that he had stored. On his return journey, George was arrested and the $80,000 in proceeds was confiscated. He spent nine months in Old Capitol Prison suspected of being a spy before being allowed to return home.

Soon after his release from Old Capitol Prison in 1864, George, Sr. moved his wife, Mary Ann, and four daughters away from Ayrshire to a safer location, Snowden. Sheltered on the shoulder of the Blue Ridge near Mt. Bleak, Snowden was clearly more isolated from intrusions of the Union troops roaming the area. The move was an effort to protect his family from the frequent ravages of the invaders.

Unfortunately, the Ayre family hardships were not over. George, Sr. continued to work Ayrshire Farm and an abundant crop resulted that year. On November 28, 1864, Union forces, some 5,000 strong, invaded northern Virginia with the purpose of destroying crops and provender, barns and outbuildings, and running off or killing livestock. This became known as the "Great Burning Raid." Very few barns survive from the 1860s or earlier in Loudoun County. Ayrshire's losses that night were 8,000 bushels of wheat, 130 tons of hay, 70 acres of corn in the shock, a new barn with all the machinery and farming implements, and 80 fine sheep driven off.[5]

Following The War, they were never compensated for their losses at the hands of the Union Army, and consequently, sold or lost most of their land to debts. The Ayre family never regained their former stature.

Over the course of our trekking journey we have benefitted from the generosity and expertise of many people. So often the source of assistance has been a surprise – serendipity! One such surprise came in the form of our "Angel of Welbourne," Constance Boudreau. She was Miss Constance when we first met her, then Mrs. Boudreau after marrying Steve, our ranger Big Yankee Ames!

Aerial view of Ayrshire, the original house and several outbuildings – courtesy Claiborne Stokes

Constance revealed her researching talents early in her connection with our treks. She is an amazing, thorough investigator, and has been an enthusiastic contributor to our mission. Constance's skills really shone when she worked at the Sky Meadows State Park. Sky Meadows is set on the historic Settle farm, Mt. Bleak, an important Mosby site, and with family connections to Belle Grove.

During her tenure at Sky Meadows, Constance was able to access their extensive historic archives. Among other treasures, she discovered the Snowden-Ayrshire story for us. We were surprised again when Steve led us on a hike from the Mt. Bleak house to see the ruins of Snowden. The house sat along the old mountain road that meandered southward from Paris and Ashby Gap. It definitely was secluded, especially now with the new growth of trees. We had Constance's notes to interpret the site. Since our visit, the park people have improved the trail with a plethora of nature markers. The historic marker briefly explains the Ayre story, but I am more curious about the story behind the story!

Snowden foundation wall and chimney ruins

Don Hakenson and HMR rangers, Andy Harris and Burke Nebeker at the Snowden trail marker

Crooked Run Fight

After several treks, it was decided that in order to truly understand and interpret the activities of Mosby's battalion not only was it necessary to have feet on the ground, we needed to ride the ground. So much insight can be gained from walking the ground, much more than simply reading the accounts. Likewise, we determined that by riding over the terrain we would actually get the "Ranger view." With that in mind, I proceeded to make arrangements for our annual Mosby Rides.

For our second ride, we were able to arrange horses through a local wrangler, Doc Mitchell. With a name like that, we expected a tall, rugged looking fellow, handlebar mustache and all, something out of the Wild West. We were not disappointed! Doc looked like he had just walked out of an old Tombstone photo. He is quite the affable fellow, energetic, very knowledgeable about a wide variety of subjects, and an occasional standup comic.

At the appointed hour, Doc and horses met us at the Lost Mountain Trails riding barn, which is part of Sky Meadows State Park, near Paris, VA. The trails are set on fields and hills leading up to Lost Mountain. We rode in uniform. It was easy to visualize the Rangers scouting, watching the enemy, riding to the fight. From a vantage point atop the mountain, we were able to observe traffic on Rt.17, the old Winchester Turnpike, and across the Crooked Run Valley to Paris and Ashby Gap through the Blue Ridge. The Rangers had to have done the same from this spot, observing enemy troop movements, preparing to attack a Yankee column or wagon train. We were in the glow!

HMR rangers ride with Mrs. Wilson; Lost Mountain in the background

It was not a long ride – at least not long enough for us, but it was glorious! After returning to the parking lot, we un-tacked the horses. In casual conversation with Doc, a cavalry reenactor friend of ours from Oregon who had joined us for the ride mentioned that her husband was going to pick her up. Lynn's beard and kit were the best adaptations I have ever seen. Her voice was kind of gravelly, too. If you did not know ahead of time that this trooper was not a he, you would never be the wiser. When she stated that her husband was on his way there, it did not sink in for several moments. Suddenly, as the words registered, Doc let out a whoop! His shocked response was worth the price of admission! Doc brought this anecdote up frequently over passing years.

After the first ride in 1997 had hooked us, a Mosby Ride became a requisite entry for each trek itinerary thereafter. The area around the old Winchester Turnpike, from the Blue Ridge across the Crooked Run Valley toward Upperville became a favorite destination. Several significant Mosby events occurred there, as well as many Rangers' family homes and safe houses were found in the area. Once away from the modern traffic on the highway, it does not require much effort to step back into time. Much of the terrain is like it was a hundred and fifty years ago.

An essential element for each trek was a visit with Harry and Susan at Scuffleburg (at least until they moved away). On one trek, Susan had arranged with neighbors, Jolly and David de Give, to host a soiree at their home, Belle Grove; Tee Edmonds' home! Jolly and David were wonderful, gracious hosts. A highlight of the evening was meeting a neighbor, Norman L. Baker, who had just published a history of the Crooked Run Valley. We tried to obtain the book, but they were all spoken for; however, we managed to get a copy of Norman's account of the fight at Crooked Run.[6]

A few days after the Greenback Raid, Mosby sent William Chapman and Sam Chapman with their respective companies, C and E, to the Crooked Run Valley where the Federal soldiers continued to cause problems. On October 17, 1864, the Chapman brothers were positioned on an elevation above the Scuffleburg road. From there they were able to observe Yankees plundering homes along the Turnpike. While the Union troopers were looting Mt. Independence, the home and barns of the Widow Fletcher, the Rangers rode from their elevation, down a ravine, unseen by the looters. The Chapmans posted their men to be between the Federals and their camps at Piedmont, to the south. At a point where the turnpike meets a junction with the road to Pleasant Vale Church, the Rangers gave the plunderers a warm greeting. It was nearing dusk as William's squad charged the front and Sam's men hit the flank of the Union cavalry. Nearby was the landmark known as the "Indian Grave." The Federals were bottled up; the Rangers had the bulge on them. The fighting was intense. The Rangers were furious that the Yankees had abused innocent civilians. If not for the darkness, the Federals might have been completely wiped out. It was a lopsided affair that brought a formal complaint from the colonel commanding the Union cavalry in the area. Apparently, plundering civilians was not a Federal concern.[7]

We had ridden in the Scuffleburg neighborhood several times, but for our 2003 trek we had a mission. We wanted to locate the road, the elevation and ravine that the Rangers used in the Crooked Run Fight. We were determined to view the fight from the Rangers' perspective – from the back of a horse. Susan and Harry once again obtained permission from the neighbors for us to ride across their lands. Todd Kern met us at the Pleasant Vale Church with mounts and period-correct tack. With a wave from Susan, we moved out.

HMR rangers pause at Manley Iden's house near Scuffleburg

Once in Scuffleburg proper, we rode around looking for the remnants of the old Scuffleburg road. At the time of The War, it wound up the hill to an arm of Bushy Mountain, then dropped down again to meet the Winchester Turnpike at Summerset Mill. We soon found the old road. It was overgrown, of course, but not as much as I expected after 150 years. Along much of the roadbed the stone walls still did their job holding the encroaching soil at bay. At one point, we needed to dismount in order to make a path through a tangle of old barbed-wire fencing. Steve picked up a rotting fence post only to be surprised by a rattlesnake. Fortunately, it was hibernating and we got away without mishap. Eventually, the summit was reached. Though there must be more trees now, through a light haze we were able to view the valley north to Paris and to clearly observe traffic on Rt.17. This is the vantage point that the Chapmans had on the 17th of October! This was a moment to be savored!

The view is similar to that of William and Sam Chapman, from Mt Edy looking north toward Paris

Now the game was on! We searched for and found a ravine leading down toward Mt. Independence. In our minds we could see the Yankees loading hay, chickens, sheep, hogs, and household goods onto their wagons. We hurried down toward Deep Branch, a tributary of Crooked Run. It was important to us to ride out of view from the turnpike as had the Rangers; however, we were not able to complete the track to the turnpike to the site of the ambush. The intervening terrain has changed since the fight. The return to Pleasant Vale was, well, pleasant! We felt we had gained an intimate understanding of the fight. And it made sense now that we had an orientation from the Rangers' perspective.

It would not be until our 2015 trek that the actual site of the fight was refined to our satisfaction. Using the modern highway as our guide, we had interpreted the fight, but it was not quite right. It was not until Steve observed the old turnpike roadbed following the flow of Crooked Run, curving in and out, along both sides of Rt.17, that we found the solution.

Retracing the route down Deep Branch taken by the Rangers before clashing with the Federal plunderers

The accounts of the fight have William Chapman's Rangers hitting the Yankees at the entrance to Henry Dixon's farm, Courtney (today's Sky Hill). Previously we had set that entrance at the point where it joins Rt.17, at the junction with the Pleasant Vale Road. As we followed the original turnpike roadbed, the actual entrance to Dixon's farm is about 100 yards through a ravine to the east of the highway. Here we could see a much better location to form an ambush, and across the highway was a better spot for Sam Chapman's company to attack the Yankees' flank. This interpretation satisfied our persistent questions.

We stopped at Norman Baker's home to consult with him. Then we brought Don Hakenson and Eric Buckland to the ambush site to check out our new perception. All parties were satisfied that using the old roadbed improved the interpretation. It now seems like a simple thing to consider the terrain as it was, not as it is. Sometimes "simple" provides a good solution!

A side note on Henry T. Dixon: He was the only man in Fauquier County to vote for Lincoln in the 1860 election, and was an unabashed Unionist throughout The War. Shortly after The War, Dixon was killed in a street duel in Alexandria.[8]

---

[1] Jones, *Ranger Mosby*, p.137; Keen and Mewborn, *Regimental*, p.68

[2] Evans and Moyer, *Guidebook*, pp.67-68

[3] Williamson, *Mosby's Rangers*, p.255; Keen and Mewborn, *Regimental*, p.291

[4] O'Neill, Robert F., Jr., *The Cavalry Battles of Aldie, Middleburg and Upperville, June 10-27, 1863.* Lynchburg, Virginia: H. E. Howard, Inc., 1993

[5] Claiborne Stokes, *A History of Ayrshire Farm*, Manuscript, August 2000

[6] Norman Baker, *Valley of the Crooked Run: The History of a Frontier Road.* Delaplane, Virginia: Summerset Printing, 2002 (First Edition)

[7] Ibid, pp.157-158

[8] B. Curtis Chappelear, *Maps and Notes Pertaining to the Upper Section of Fauquier County, Virginia*; Warrenton, Virginia: The Warrenton Antiquarian Society, 1954

Chapter Five: *Only on a Trek*

Only so much can be learned from books, maps and other print materials. So much more can be learned through field studies, interviews and hands-on experiences. With the study of Mosby and his Rangers, there is an abundance of print resources currently available. An integral part of our adventures has been to examine the ever expanding body of work on Mosby. Nearly every year there seems to be a new Mosby book published. That suits me just fine! The journey never ends!

Our treks are proof of learning outside the book. We have been fortunate to absorb incredible experiences, meet fascinating people, and to hold and study historical objects. On our treks, we have been able to go to sites the average reader only visualizes. The treks have opened doors to advanced learning, but the best reward has been the new friendships formed.

To read about Mosby is enlightening. To walk Mosby's ground is inspiring. To study Mosby from the back of a horse while in uniform is divine! Only on a trek! The following episodes are a few examples of experiences that could be gained only on a trek.

Confederates in the Deli

During monthly drills in our Camp Spindle (Tumwater, WA), many topics of conversation would crop up. Often discussed were ways to improve the authenticity of our impressions as rangers. At one drill, our William "Major" Hibbs brought out an article from the New York Times. It was a review on a recently released book, *Confederates in the Attic*. The section of the article that captured our attention was about a group of reenactors who were featured throughout the book. These were termed "hardcore," in the sense that they tried to do everything as authentically as possible. From eating fatback and hardtack to marching barefoot into battle, accuracy was their goal.

The reviewer marveled at a moment in the book when one of the "hardcore" soldiers, sitting next to the small campfire, stopped what he was doing and looked over to see one of his comrades prone on the ground. The comrade was puffed up in an unnatural position. The first soldier hollered, "Hey, Rob! Whatter ya doin?" Rob, replied, "Ahm werkin on muh bloat!" Even that grim detail needed to look authentic! Around our own campfire this made an impression. Wow! These guys are awesome! They inspired us to raise our level of authenticity. Accuracy in our presentation was important, but not to the level of "bloating practice," and not to monitoring the thread count in the fabric of our uniforms!

In plotting the itinerary for our 2000 trek, I could see a cluster of potentially rewarding events on the horizon. Our window was the middle of October. There was a Mosby conference to consider and a preservation march/reenactment scheduled for a little later in the month, however, participating in both would not be possible.

The conference was sponsored by the Mosby Heritage Area Association and scheduled for October 13-15. The slate of presenters was an impressive collection of Mosby experts and authors: Jeffry Wert, James Ramage, Horace Mewborn, Hugh Keen, Eugene Scheel, and Marshall Krolick. What Mosby scholar would not want to attend?

The preservation march/reenactment was scheduled for October 29 in Upperville. The contact person was Rob Hodge, the "bloater" from *Confederates in the Attic* fame! The proceeds were to benefit battlefield preservation in Loudoun County and other Virginia sites. It was a worthy cause and one that fit our corporate mission. I established communications with Rob in the months prior to the trek. It promised to be an exciting event for all the right reasons. Rob was eager for us to participate but alas, we had to choose.

After weighing the pros and cons, we decided to forego the preservation march in favor of the Mosby conference. Maybe the final pro that swayed our choice was the opportunity given us to attack the conference tour bus on Sunday?

We arrived at Welbourne late Friday evening and quickly settled in because we had to be in Middleburg at the Mosby conference by 0800 Saturday. Unfortunately, the tight schedule meant we missed the usual amazing southern breakfast. Our loss was not too disappointing, however, as the conference surpassed all expectations! It was a thrill to chat with the authors, and get their autographs in their books. Yes, I lugged them from Washington State! We were able to ask questions on points that had been troubling our research. Equally important was being able to express our gratitude for the work they had done.

Knowing that we would be attacking the tour bus, I scheduled our annual Mosby Ride for the next day, Sunday. Up early, buttoned and hooked, we managed a quick biscuit and tea from Mary's kitchen. At 0730, Todd Kern arrived with horses. A rapid tacking preceded a hurried ride across Welbourne fields and over the "old Dulany Road" to Lemmons Bottom and the Goose Creek Bridge. The tour bus was scheduled to arrive at 0840 and we needed to be in position and out of sight before it showed.

Todd Kern and Mrs. Wilson at the ambush site

HMR rangers greeting the tourists at the Goose Creek Bridge

The tour crowd lined up on the historic bridge and listened to Horace Mewborn's interpretation. While all were focused on the presentation the tour leader signaled for us to begin our "attack." We began with firing a few rounds and yelling, then spurred the horses into a canter around a stand of trees to approach the tourists. They huzzahed and seemed to enjoy meeting some of Mosby's men; however, they did not like us enough to hand over their watches and greenbacks!

After the bus pulled away, we rode back past Welbourne and continued with our annual Mosby Ride. It was still relatively early in the day when we bid farewell to Todd and the horses. A quick cleanup was in order before hitting the road. As the Mosby riders had not partaken of any significant breakfast, and they were hungry, we stopped in Upperville at a mom & pop minimart.

It was a busy place sitting at the edge of Rt.50; they were known to make tasty sandwiches. As I waited behind a scruffy-looking customer at the deli, I realized he was not ordering food. He was trying to sell advertising for an upcoming event. I also noticed that he was dressed in a very thread-worn Confederate uniform. He looked suspiciously like the soldier pictured on the cover of Confederates in the Attic. In fact, he bore a close resemblance to Rob Hodge! Being a daring fellow, I said, "Rob?" He turned, eyed me with a questioning look, and replied, "Yes?"

Another serendipity moment!

Naturally, I introduced myself, then proceeded to let Rob know how much our rangers appreciated his pioneering "bloat work." An easy-going chap, Rob did not protest when I dragged him out to our vehicle to introduce him to the rest of the trekkers. Rob even tolerated the photo shoot, too. He looks better without the bloat. A pleasant, extraordinary guy, that Confederate in the Deli!

Rob Hodge and the author in Upperville, Virginia

Camp Spindle

Following the disastrous battles of the Gettysburg campaign, the Union army trailed the Confederate army southward. From Pennsylvania through Maryland and across the Potomac into Virginia, the Federals kept a wary eye on the retreating southerners. The counties of Loudoun, Fauquier and Fairfax became occupied territory. This was the field of operations for Mosby's command.

During the summer of 1863, the Rangers were almost constantly in the saddle pursuing opportunities to create havoc for the invaders. Capturing supply wagons, disabling the rail lines, gobbling up Union stragglers, liberating Federal horses and mules, and disrupting communications were effective operations conducted by the Rangers behind enemy lines.

Mosby's men were so successful in achieving their mission that it created another problem: what to do with the Federal prisoners and war materiel. With Yankee patrols ranging everywhere, Mosby needed to be cautious about moving them safely through the lines to headquarters in the south. From the beginning of the battalion, Mosby's policy had been for the Rangers to keep no camps. Having a camp would have been a great place to be captured. But Mosby needed a place to hold Union prisoners until they could be transferred to Confederate headquarters in Culpeper or the prisoner exchange in Gordonsville, VA. An isolated location in the Bull Run Mountains was set up as a temporary holding pen. Tents were set up near a spring, corrals built for horses and mules and a guard was set. This came to be called "Camp Spindle."

Surrounded as they were by the enemy, and cut off from easy communications with the Confederate command, rumors spread that Mosby and his battalion had been destroyed; however, the Rangers were still able to actively operate effectively. Mosby's captures during this time totaled 186 Union soldiers, 123 horses, 12 wagons, and an abundance of tack and accouterments.[1]

In 1990, I was able to move to rural property in Thurston County, near Tumwater, Washington. Our HMR rangers decided to drill monthly now that we had the place to do so. Our idea was that by drilling from period cavalry manuals on a regular basis we could become better horsemen, and that by "living the life" we would more accurately portray the Rangers. Eventually, we graduated from setting up tents in the pasture to building our own Camp Spindle.

Our own Camp Spindle near Tumwater, Washington

During our first drills we set up our tents in the pasture, comingling with the horses and, rain or shine (sometimes snow), we conducted drills. One morning we awoke to see that amid the frost-covered boxes and bags lying about the camp, somebody's food box had been plundered. On the ground were several oranges with horse-sized bites removed, and next to those was a can of Miller beer. The beer can appeared to have been opened by a horse tooth-shaped opener. The beer was gone. We did not think to check horse breath for evidence of orange or beer and, naturally, the horses all professed innocence in the matter. We were convinced that among our virtuous mounts, there was one that could use its lips like an opposable thumb. That experience was not the only reason for us to build "Camp Spindle," but it must have encouraged the decision.

Our camp was a more permanent affair than the original in the Bull Run Mountains, with each of our rangers constructing a platform out of foraged materials. The platforms were arranged around a central fire pit. On drill weekends, rangers fitted their canvas tents or tarps over their framed platforms, imitating the winter camps seen in wartime photos. When we were not drilling in the pasture, or practicing ranger tactics in the nearby forest, we would be found in our Camp Spindle. Our camp life must have been much like it was for Mosby's men. Commonly, we would be sitting around the fire pit, cleaning or reloading weapons (replicas of Civil War pieces), and cleaning or repairing tack or other equipment. There was much discussion about horses, tack, and tactics.

Mealtime was always an adventure. Each ranger prepared "period-correct" food over the open flames. An interesting variety of gastronomic delights was produced. It sometimes seemed to be a competition to see who could come up with the best concoction; however, there was always at least one of our rangers who persisted in bringing hot dogs, s'mores, and such, but not without chastisement from their pards.

Cooking breakfast in our Camp Spindle

Evenings around the fire were the best! We circled our camp chairs, stools or stumps. It was especially important to hold a choice spot in the winter time, so you could warm your toes and hands yet avoid the smoke. Rangers would pass around samples of their favorite elixir; some brought out cigars. There is nothing quite so conducive to time travel as these fire-lit moments. Camaraderie shone as we traded tall tales, pranked each other, and sang Civil War songs. It was in camp that our traditions were introduced. At some undetermined point in the evening – when it was just "right" - we would all stand and break out our toasting cups (required ranger equipage). Camp guests were always invited into the tradition, too. Most seemed to enjoy being included. Some even returned for more tradition.

Our tradition - an essential trekking item: travelling toasting cup; collapsing or nesting style

Tradition demanded that you poured for your neighbor in the circle, usually going in a clockwise direction. You could not pour for yourself. What was poured we called "Frog Juice," which eventually became Jaegermeister, or something else vile like Gatorade for a non-alcoholic alternative. Once all assembled had their cups ready, we would break into a rousing rendition of "Froggie Went A'Courtin'." Most of the time we only managed to get through two or three verses before fading. Our Charlie Grogan was about the only one who knew the rest of the verses. We sang before toasting because "Frog Juice" had a way of diminishing your vocal chords. When the song was finished, cups were emptied, and we would return to the reminiscing and tales, often talking about the thrill of finding Civil War artifacts. One by one rangers would retire to their shebangs, a civil war term for a soldier's shelter. The last man would bank the fire, ready for another day of drill. "Camp Spindle" life was simply grand!

When it came to researching Camp Spindle, one of our first questions was the name. Why "Spindle?" Was the camp located on the land of a family named Spindle? Was there a community called Spindle nearby? Research did not confirm property owned by a Spindle, nor did we find a Spindle community. We did find a Spindle family that lived in Waterfall, a community that sat on the eastern shoulder of the Bull Run Mountains, in Prince William County. Interestingly, it appears that two Spindle brothers, Robert and Benjamin, eventually became Rangers, but not necessarily during the utilization of the camp. The best definition we found was from local historians. In those olden days, prior to computers, when businesses needed to hold on to receipts, invoices or other important slips of paper, they would skewer them on a pointed wire spindle on the desk. Perhaps the Rangers' camp was temporarily holding important things (but without the skewer part)?

When it came to planning trek itineraries, Camp Spindle in the Bull Run Mountains came high on the list of requisite sites. It was a minor footnote in Mosby lore, but we had a personal connection. Our first attempt to locate the real Camp Spindle resulted in our finding an abundance of ticks in the Bull Run Mountains. That and an old toilet base and most of a rusted out 1950s era kitchen stove. But we did find the Bull Run Mountains Road! We were close....

After interviewing Mosby historians such as Tom Evans and John Gott, we were able to explore more purposefully. We were drawn to the area around White Rock Spring and Jackson Hollow. It wasn't until we had connected with Bob Sinclair at the Fauquier Historical Society in Marshall that we able to zero in on the location of Camp Spindle.

Bob grew up in the area and knew the neighborhood. When Bob was a boy hiking with his grandfather near White Rock Spring, his grandfather pointed and said this is where Mosby's camp was during The War. Bob's grandfather told him how *his* grandfather had pointed out the location when he was a boy. Bob kindly showed us the same spot. Exploring there became a trek tradition.

A wagon single tree connects the mule/horse to the wagon; see the wagon image next

Army supply wagon of the type captured by the Rangers

We believed that some physical evidence was necessary to give provenance to the site. When advised metal detecting was not permitted in that portion of the Bull Run Mountains, we searched for exposed artifacts that would not disturb the ground. Over time, we managed to uncover several promising relics: the iron end-piece of a single tree, part of a rusted tin can of the type in use during The War, but nothing that actually shouted, "Mosby was here!"; however, it was great sport searching.

This also opened the potential for pranks! One that I started on our first trek was to drop a previously purchased bullet in an obvious place where it would be certain to be found by one of our unsuspecting trekkers. The best "targets" were the newbies, the first-time trekkers, especially if they had heard tales around the campfire of past successes. It was a thrill to find an actual bullet; perhaps it had even been dropped by a Ranger!

The "found relic" prank was used at the Camp Spindle site a lot. It worked most of the time, occasionally well beyond expectations. One of those times was during our Fount Beattie's maiden trek. In the days before visiting Camp Spindle, we had been building up the notion of finding a relic. Discussions on the best technique for locating a treasure were casually introduced throughout the week prior. We even demonstrated the methods at other sites just to build the anticipation. Keep in mind Fount had heard and even laughed at the tales of the "found relic" prank sitting around the fire in our Camp Spindle.

As our exploration of Camp Spindle evolved, the trekkers ranged over the site deliberately, methodically, hoping against hope to find the one artifact that would conclusively confirm Mosby's campground. Fount was caught up in the fervor; however, it was difficult to plant the relic (a "dropped bullet") as Fount was so attentive. Finally, I passed the relic to Steve, our Big Yankee Ames, for him to plant. That would relieve me of any guilt should our ruse be prematurely discovered.

After an inordinate amount of time had passed, and the trekkers' zeal for the search had waned, Fount said, "Well, that's it, we should head out." With the planted object nearly touching his foot, we could not allow that.

"No, Fount, just look a little more!"

Fount was ready though, "Really, we should just go."

While Fount wasn't looking, Steve scratched the earth away from the dropped bullet, exposing it in an obvious position.

"Really, Fount, this mound looks like it has potential. We've found these before."

It took both Steve and me to corral Fount and almost place his hand on it. Fortunately, Fount saw the relic and, forgetting any previous warning regarding the prank he bit, hook, line, and sinker! Fount's reaction made it one of the grandest prank episodes in our trekking history.

Fount can actually laugh about it now.

We have yet to find physical evidence of the exact location Camp Spindle, but it will always hold a special place in our trekking lore!

A thrilled Fount Beattie with his Camp Spindle "relics"

Shots in the Dark!

Rather than setting up camps that increased the risk of being captured by the Yankees, Mosby's men typically boarded at the homes of local citizens. Sometimes young Rangers would be harbored in their own family homes. Having a safe house close by helped the Ranger to seek shelter quickly in an emergency situation. During down time, Rangers would work in the fields or mills, appearing to be civilians. Eventually, frustrated Federal commanders realized the game and would frequently send out patrols to round up Mosby men. Occasionally, Rangers would have advance warning of approaching Federal detachments and would escape into the mountains or woods. Often a Ranger would build a shanty or "shebang" in the forest to shelter in during the "hot times" when Yankees were close. If Rangers were surrounded by a Union patrol, many safe houses had trapdoors or "hidey holes" to secrete the men until the danger had passed. There are several accounts of Rangers simply blazing their way out of a trap, with some making a successful get away.

The Yankees normally sent out detachments during evenings or at night. Those were the times when Rangers would be less alert. They might be enjoying a warm meal at the supper table, or comfort and companionship in the parlor, or sleeping peacefully in their feather beds. Many Rangers were gobbled up in this manner. It became a Ranger's constant concern.

Of particular interest for me are the trapdoors. Over the course of many treks, we have been able to witness trapdoors in several Mosby safe houses. In Welbourne, it is in the back hallway, and actually now is partly enclosed in a guest room. At Belle Grove there was a door leading up into an attic, and another below the old dining room. At Seven Springs, the trapdoor was in the parlor. The trapdoor at Green Garden is now located in a closet. We found a trapdoor in the kitchen at Mt. Bleak, but the next time we tried to find it, we had to settle for stairs to the attic. The trapdoors were fairly common in the safe houses. Remodeling and modern improvements have caused some to disappear; however, we hope to continue "collecting" examples.[2]

Welbourne trapdoor

Seven Springs trapdoor

Green Garden trapdoor

One evening we were invited to supper at Doc and Annie Mitchell's in Hume. The invitation requested that we come "period correct," meaning in proper uniform. After lugging our uniforms and accouterments 2000 miles from Washington State, we look forward to any opportunity to "put on the Ritz." Properly attired, we arrived at the Mitchells' abode in good order. Doc is an auctioneer. In Hume, his business occupies an old building that long ago held a mercantile establishment. Adjoining that is their dwelling.

We entered the home into the warmth of candlelight, the glow of oil lamps, and the wonderful aroma of good southern cooking. There were five of us rangers, and Doc and Annie did their best to dress for the occasion, too. As is always true with Doc and Annie, the evening was full of tales, lies, and laughter. The meal was splendid; the company was the finest! The only modern distraction came about midway through supper when Doc excused himself to answer something called a "phone."

The repast was nearly finished. We were pushed back in our chairs around the dining table, anticipating a delectable dessert. It was a moment mindful of the many accounts I had read about cozy family evenings in Mosby's Confederacy.

Suddenly there was a loud banging from the outer door of Doc's shop. Startled, we looked to Doc who looked to Annie. Looking at each other they said, "Who could that be at this hour?"

Doc said, "Well, I should go find out!" and he quickly passed through the door into his shop, closing it after him.

The banging stopped. We presumed Doc was answering the shop's front door to see about the urgency of the summons. Just as suddenly, from the shop there was an explosion of shouting and the sound of scuffling, a general ruckus! Abruptly, Doc was at the kitchen door wrestling with Union soldiers! He was vainly trying to block their passage into the kitchen, while hollering, "Yankees! Yankees! Go!"

At this point, the rangers in the room were wide-eyed with panic. What? Yankees? Without a moment's hesitation, Annie pushed back the dining table, dishes clattering, glasses tipping over! In a flash, Annie pulled up a carpet, tugged up a trapdoor, and yelled, "Quick! Down here!"

With adrenalin surging, the five rangers scrambled down the ladder into a cellar while Annie was above in the kitchen, screaming, "Hurry! Run!"

We ran out the back into a small field next to the barn. As we skedaddled, the Union infantrymen opened fire with their Springfield muskets from the back porch. Our silhouettes were lit up by the muzzle flash. Luckily, they were not very good shots!

Before the Yankees could reload, everyone stopped, caught their breath, then let out howls of laughter!

We *knew* it was staged, but it was as *real* as any reenactment battlefield I had experienced. The lesson was clear, however! Rangers and local citizens needed to keep an eye open at all times.

Leave it to Doc and Annie to provide a fun-filled evening! The Union soldiers were Doc's brother and his buddy, reenactors of the northern persuasion. We all returned to the kitchen, full of chuckles and excellent southern food, and soon with Annie's apple pan dowdy. Always an adventure with Doc!

All in all, it was a most memorable night! Thanks to Doc and Annie and the Yankees, we now had an appreciation for what Mosby's men had experienced! Fortunately, we could gain the knowledge without the harsh penalties.

In Search of Treasures

It was June 1995. It was our first trek to Mosby's Confederacy. With The Guidebook to lead us, we had outlined an itinerary. We had no first-hand knowledge of distances or travel times. Our first day in Mosby's Confederacy was packed with surprises and epiphanies. It was in darkness that we tried to catch up with our itinerary. Finally surrendering to the lack of light, we vowed to start the next day with the sites we could not find that night.

With the best of intentions, we set out the next morning determined to catch up with the itinerary. First, we were going to return to Rectortown to recover the "lost" last night; however, on the way through Middleburg our resolve was derailed by a sign on a building in town: "The Powder Horn - Civil War Relics." Screeching to a halt and pulling into a fortuitously open parking place on the busy main street, we agreed that it would be only for a 15-minute scout. "Just 15 minutes!"

The proprietor of the Powder Horn was Bob Daly. He seemed amused at our frenzied antics as we searched his collection. After I explained who we were and the nature of our mission, Bob expressed an interest in helping advance our knowledge. After listening, he said, "Oh. You are interested in Mosby? Just a moment."

HMR ranger, Mark Liewergen, holding Ranger Johnny Lunceford's Remington

Reaching back behind him, and rummaging through a pile of "stuff," Bob pulled out a .44 New Army Remington. "This belonged to Ranger Johnny Lunceford." Our eyes bugged out; our jaws dropped. Bob said, "Here, take a look." In turn we each examined the revolver, handling it as if it was the Holy Grail. When I carefully handed it back, Bob casually *tossed* it over his shoulder back onto the shelf. A collective gasp escaped from our wide-eyed trekkers. To our delight and amazement, Bob continued to bring out Mosby-related treasures. After the fifteen minutes grew into two hours, we bid a fond and grateful farewell. It was the beginning of a long, serendipitous friendship!

Bob was not our only source of Mosby-related artifacts. Over the years, we hit any and every museum and antique shop within Mosby's Confederacy searching for treasures. With each new discovery, we felt we learned a little more about the members of the 43rd Battalion Virginia Cavalry, specifically, and about life in northern Virginia in general.

An example is the fleam in Bob Daly's collection. A fleam is an instrument that was used in bloodletting, a medical practice that was apparently and surprisingly still in use during The War. The theory was that by bleeding the patient (in a controlled manner) harmful impurities and excesses would be removed from the blood. Unfortunately, the practice actually weakened the patient. Witness George Washington's death from a sore throat after his physician removed nine pints in 24 hours.

Bob Daly's fleam came from Dr. William Dunn's medical kit. It was presented to Dr. Dunn by Mosby for saving his life, probably when Dunn attended Mosby after he was wounded at the Gooding's Tavern Fight in August 1863. Beginning in May 1863, William Dunn was surgeon for the Battalion, until Mosby had him replaced because "Dunn was too fond of fighting." The documentation with the fleam also indicated that the implement was used by Dr. Dunn in treating Mosby after the Colonel was wounded at "Lakeland" in December 1864.

Until his passing in 2007, a much-anticipated highlight for each trek was a visit with Bob Daly. Occasionally, my first stop in Middleburg would be the "Coach Stop" café to join Bob at breakfast. He always seemed to have something "new" to show us. Bob enjoyed our enthusiasm and appreciation, too. Some of Bob's collection came from John Gott, and some came from an old museum started by Ranger Dolly Richards. Several of the Mosby relics sported hand-written explanations from the Colonel. I have heard that some folks have questioned the authenticity of Bob's collection. All I know is what was presented to us, and we accepted it at face value. The following is a list of the relics that I have remembered to note. I have indicated the **source,** the location, and date viewed, along with the description of the item and its connection to the Rangers.

<u>**Mosby-related Artifacts** that we have examined during our treks</u>

<u>**Old Gaol Museum**</u>, Warrenton, VA (23 June 1995):

- ✓ Sarah Lake - <u>bonnet</u> & <u>tablecloth</u> with spots of Mosby's blood & the <u>window</u> with the bullet hole in the top, center pane (from Mosby's wounding at Lakeland)
- ✓ Ned Hurst - <u>revolver</u>, Colt .44.

<u>**Bob Daly**</u> (at the Powder Horn Shop), Middleburg, VA (24 June 1995):

- ✓ Johnny Lunceford - <u>revolver</u>, Remington .44;
- ✓ Dolly Richards - <u>carbine</u>, a cut-down Hall rifle;
- ✓ Dolly Richards - <u>daguerreotype</u>;
- ✓ James Williamson - <u>Mosby pass</u>;
- ✓ Bradford Hoskins - <u>carte de visite</u>.

<u>**Warren Rifles Confederate Museum**</u>, Front Royal, VA (27 June 1995):

- ✓ Mosby - <u>spurs</u> – cast, Texas-style with jinglebobs, embossed leather straps, engraved, "Gen. Mosby" (clearly a post-war presentation);
- ✓ John M. Lawrence - <u>revolver</u>, Allen & Wheelock .36 Navy;
- ✓ John A. Silman - <u>saddlebags</u>, oversized;
- ✓ Edward F. Wayman - <u>stirrup</u>;
- ✓ Samuel McDonald - <u>spectacles</u>, <u>pen</u> & <u>mechanical pencil</u>.

<u>**Bob Daly**</u> (at the Powder Horn Shop), Middleburg, VA (11 Oct. 1997):

- ✓ <u>Display case</u> - containing a CDV of Sarah Lake, a portion of her bonnet (3"strip of the tie) that has spots of Mosby's blood, and the bullet removed from Mosby by Dr. Dunn.
- ✓

The author holding Mosby's saber – even Jim Moyer had not previously seen it!

<u>**Mrs. Stuart Blackwell Cooper**</u>, Warrenton, VA (12 Oct. 1997):

- ✓ Mosby - <u>saber</u> (the same one shown in his late-war photo); Mosby's <u>pocket compass</u>, in wooden case with hinged lid; Mosby's <u>revolver</u>, Colt .44; and

- ✓ Two <u>letters</u> hand-written by Mosby, both in two-sided frames so front & back sides of the pages are visible:
  1. A letter written to his wife with a pen he picked up from a dead Yankee on the 1st Manassas battlefield;
  2. A letter sent to Sheridan warning the general of the consequences of any further unlawful executions of Rangers.

Mosby's pocket compass

<u>Museum of the Confederacy,</u> Richmond, VA (9 Oct. 1998):

- ✓ Ranger Norman V. Randolph - <u>revolver</u>, Colt .44;
- ✓ 43rd <u>regimental colors</u> - 1st national, oversized, wool, reversed appliqué stars (first unfurled at the Berryville Wagon Raid?).

Reproduction of the Regimental Flag hand-stitched by Chuck Kippenhan; now on loan to the Stuart-Mosby Historical Society Museum, Centreville, VA

<u>Old Gaol Museum</u>, Warrenton, VA (16 Oct. 1998):

- ✓ Cannonball fragment - from Stephenson Hill in Salem;
- ✓ Ammo box handle - from Heartland;
- ✓ James Wrenn - army blanket.

<u>Bob Daly</u> (at the Powder Horn Shop), Middleburg, VA (14 Oct. 2000):

- ✓ Bob Eastham – fiddle:
- ✓ Flag – Reunion banner, battle flag with "Col. Mosby" painted above the cross and 1895 painted below, gold satin border;
- ✓ Stick Pin – made from button Ludwell Lake, Jr. took from Sgt. Ames' uniform.

<u>Bob Daly</u> (at Welbourne), Middleburg, VA (16 Oct. 2001):

- ✓ Dr. Wm. Dunn:
    1. Revolver, Colt .44 with rolled seam Confederate holster & button-like finial;
    2. Waist belt with CS spoon buckle;
    3. Surgical kit, in wood box with brass plate on lid, kit used to remove bullet from JSM after Lakeland wounding;
    4. Mechanical fleam, presented to Dr. Dunn by J.S.Mosby for saving his life, and later used on JSM after his wounding at Lakeland;
- ✓ Tom Turner - Waist belt (partial) with MD buckle;

The author holding Welby Rector's .44 Colt Revolver

- ✓ Welby Rector:
    1. Saddle, Texas "Hope" style;
    2. Shell jacket**,** summer-weight linen;
    3. Waist belt, with CS buckle;
    4. Revolver, .44 Colt Army model;
- ✓ Dolly Richards - Revolver, Colt .31 Wells Fargo Model.
- ✓ Walter Frankland - Revolver, Colt .44;

- ✓ Mosby
    1. Revolver, Colt .44, inscribed, "To J.S.Mosby from R.H. Dulany;"
    2. Pocket watch, "Geneva", sterling silver, double-set;
    3. Binoculars with case, shown with Mosby in the late-war photo;
    4. Documents Box - with "43rd Bttn" stenciled on top, captured at Heartland, Sept. 24, 1864 by Col. Gansevoort.

Bob Daly (at Welbourne), Middleburg, VA (18 Oct. 2002):

- ✓ Lucien Love - saber, cut steel guard, wide blade, steel scabbard, maker unknown;
- ✓ Mosby - pistol, Allen pepper-pot model, JSM used this in defense from bully, George Turpin.

Bob Daly *(at his home),* Middleburg, VA (17 Oct 2003):

- ✓ Mosby - slouch hat, tan, left brim pinned up by a 5-point brass star, tan hat band & binding, 3 ostrich feathers, brown leather sweat band (2 ½-3 inches wide);
    1. hat, black felt, black binding & hat band, presented by Gen. Stuart;
    2. hat, black federal officer style slouch with gold braid tassel, embroidered crossed saber insignia, black binding, sweat band embossed in gold lettering, "R. Wallace Upperville 1863;"

Mosby hat on the left; Lucien Love hat on the right

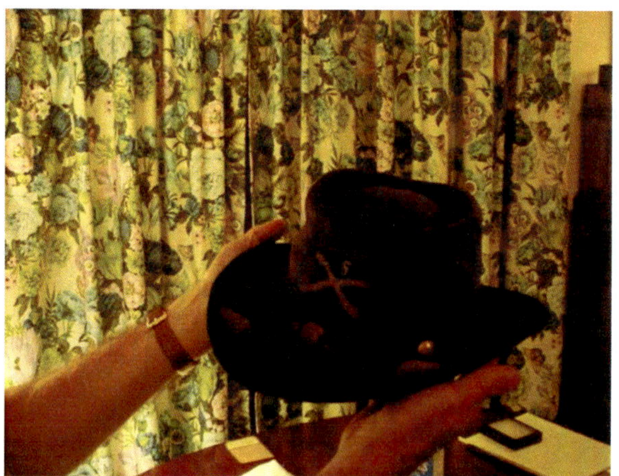
Another Mosby hat with 5th Cavalry insignia, possibly a post-war gift

3. waist belt, tarred canvas with cast brass spoon CS buckle, bullet hole from wounding at Lakeland;

4. <u>belt buckle</u>, solid brass, curved, presented by JEB Stuart in 1862;

- ✓ Lucien Love - <u>hat</u> (see photo above), black beaver, black binding, hat band & plume;
- ✓ Dolly Richards – <u>forage cap</u>, kepi-style top, cadet gray wool, gold braid, hard leather bill (not bound), stitched down in front, woven gold chin strap with brass buttons, calico liner; made by Dolly's niece who was to be wed to John Hunt Morgan;
- ✓ Aquila Glasscock – <u>kepi</u>, thick butternut wool, bound leather bill, blue piping, leather chin strap;
- ✓ Levi Waters – <u>kepi</u>, brownish-gray wool, triple gold braid;
- ✓ Dr. William Dunn
    1. <u>Ink bottle</u>, black leather case, spring release cap, oblong tin, approx. ¾" x 2" x 2" (notation: "killed some clever Yankee to get this");
    2. Richmond gray <u>broadcloth</u>, <u>cotton lining</u>, & <u>star</u>, gold embroidered, from collar of the uniform Mosby was wearing when wounded at Lakeland (note JSM's blood);
    3. <u>Brass button</u> from uniform of Wm. R. Smith;
    4. <u>Length of rein</u> from "Champ" Cpt. Smith's horse, when Cpt. Smith was mortally wounded at Loudoun Heights;
    5. <u>Knife</u>, agate handle, was brought from England to VA by Cpt John Smith and owned by the Dunn family for generations.

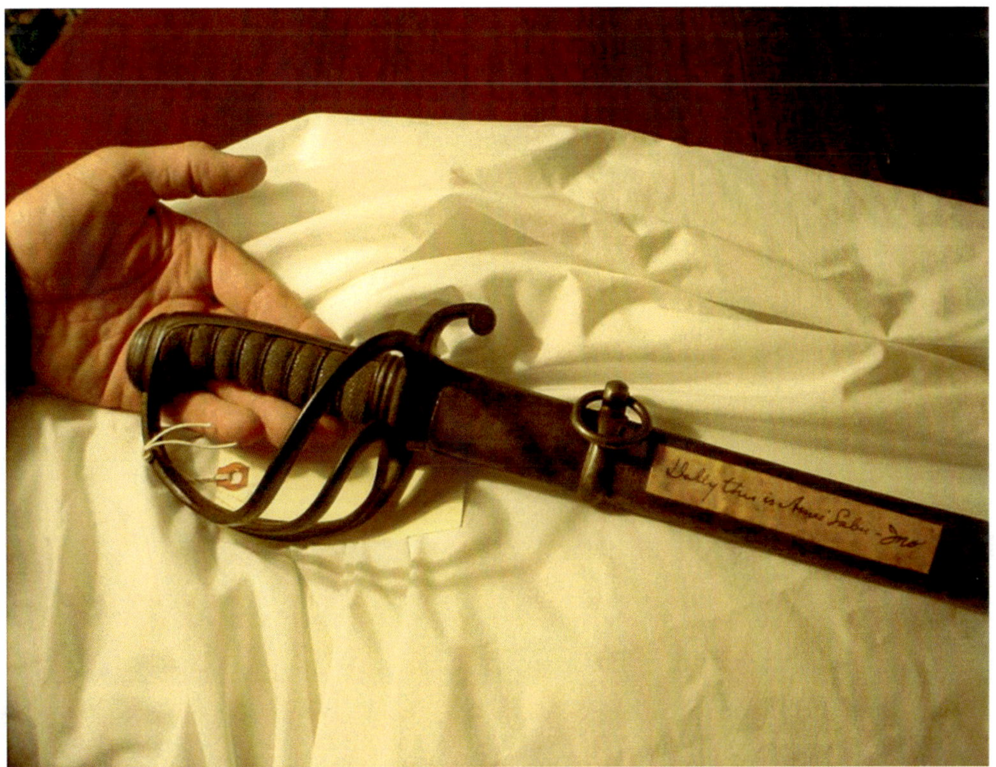

Mosby's hand-written note on the scabbard: "Dolly this is Ames' Saber – Jno"

- ✓ James F. Ames – <u>saber</u>, 1841 model
- ✓ Cpl. Kane, US, - <u>Burnside carbine</u>, used to wound Mosby at Lakeland;
- ✓ Tom Richards – <u>saber</u>, light cavalry model.
- ✓ Bob Eastham – <u>Hall rifle</u>, .58, with sling swivel.
- ✓ Willie Mosby – <u>Enfield rifle</u>, .58, cut-down for carbine.
- ✓ Richard Triplett - <u>Enfield rifle</u>, .58, cut-down for carbine.

- ✓ Tom Turner – <u>saber</u>;
  1. <u>revolver</u>, Colt .36 Navy model;
  2. <u>revolver</u>, Colt .44 Army model with broken backstrap;
  3. <u>holster</u>, rolled seam, notched for hammer;
  4. <u>waist belt</u>, leather with CS buckle; <u>hat</u>, slouch, gray felt with gray binding;
- ✓ Tom Richards

1. <u>Saber</u>, Starr model (1818-1830), cut steel "B" guard, 2" blade with blood groove.
2. <u>Battle Flag</u> – approx. 3' x 3 ½', red linen, gold-painted "43" above the cross and "VA" below the cross; written on the staff, "captured near Leesburg, Mar. 5, 1864, J. Reed, 2nd MA", in glass display case.
3. <u>Guidon</u> – Gen. Jeb Stuart's 1st VA guidon, rectangular 1st national style, 7 white stars in the blue field.
4. <u>Surrender Flag</u> – made from bed sheet for use at Millwood by Wm. Chapman, A. Monteiro, Walter Frankland, Willie Mosby, 15 Apr 1865.
5. <u>Oath Flag</u> – square, white cotton field, red linen border, blue wool 5-point star in center; hand-written note by "Jno. Mosby."

Rangers' oath flag

Bob Daly (at his home), Middleburg, VA (12 Oct. 2005):

Dr. Wm. Dunn's brass medication bottles

- ✓ Wm Dunn – medication bottles, two turned-brass "bottles" that hold glass bottles inside;
- ✓ Mosby – CSA colonel collar insignia, one set from JSM's uniform;
- ✓ Richard H. Dulany –
    1. two collar stars, gold embroidered, from the uniform of Col. R.H. Dulany, in a display case with note: "gift of the Lemmon family";
    2. guidon, swallow-tail 1st national pattern with white cotton cross appliquéd in the blue field.

Rank insignia from Col. Richard H. Dulany's uniform

Not an Artifact

Bob Daly was convinced that a large rock at the back of his property was another rendezvous spot for the Rangers. It was secluded, yet within easy access to the Ashby's Gap Turnpike and to the Plains Road. It is unlikely that it will ever be proven, but I will consider it a definite possibility for Bob!

HMR rangers with Bob Daly at his "Mosby Rock"

---

[1] Scott, *Partisan*, pp.112-113; Keen and Mewborn, *Regimental*, pp.73-74; Wert, *Mosby's Rangers*, pp.92-93; Williamson, *Mosby's Rangers*, pp.81-85
[2] Williamson, *Mosby's Rangers*, p.272

Chapter Six: *Indomitable Spirit!*

The history of Mosby's Confederacy is layered with models of courage, integrity, and resilience. Exemplary illustrations are seen not only within Mosby's command, but are abundant in the civilian population as well. I marvel at the fortitude and resourcefulness displayed abundantly throughout The War by so many people. Admittedly, Mosby's men by and large were young bucks who had no concept of fear: bravery was almost mandatory. Civilians in an occupied population will perform heroic deeds of daring and resistance. Certainly these qualities can be found in today's world but I often wonder if, overall people back then were not made of sterner stuff.

The following adventures are samples not only of youthful vim and vigor, but they are merely a few of the many instances of strength and valor found in searching Mosby's Confederacy. Perhaps there is something to be learned from their example.

The Attempted Capture of Gen. Crawford

My research leads in many directions, sometimes to all points at once. Sometimes where I want to go is not available online or any place in the remote Pacific Northwest. Often the bibliographies of my Mosby library refer to obscure sources that I could never hope to find; however, I am always scouting and sometimes I get lucky. One such occasion occurred back in the '90s. I was in Tacoma, Washington, scouring the city library for Mosby material. A pleasant surprise was finding the complete bound edition of *Confederate Veteran Magazine.* Fortunately, I had the time to dig through the index and copy the Mosby-related articles.

Among the treasures uncovered was an article in volume XXIII, 1915, titled, "The Attempted Capture of General Crawford." It was submitted by I. S. Curtis of Sherman, Texas. Mr. Curtis was one of the young, hot-blooded participants in the escapade. My attention was drawn by the inclusion of Richard "Dick" Lewis and Channing Smith, both of whom became Mosby men a year or so after this episode. One really must read Mr. Curtis's account to fully appreciate the boldness and humor of those impetuous youths, so I will not try to do more than provide a sketch of the events.

The incident occurred during June of 1863, following the battle at Brandy Station. Union General Crawford made his headquarters at the home of the Widow Lewis, who happened to be the mother of Richard "Dick" Lewis. A squad of eight Confederates was led by Captain Frank Stringfellow. Since this was Dick Lewis's home turf, the little squad decided to take advantage of the opportunity. If they could round up Gen. Crawford perhaps the authorities could arrange an exchange for their own Gen. W.H.F. Lee, who had been captured at Brandy Station.

From an elevation obscured from Yankee view, the daring crew was able to observe the General's camp guard and picket posts. A plan was plotted and hastily commenced with full confidence of success; however, Mr. Murphy of the famous law, made his presence known and a number of quirks interfered with the smooth accomplishment of their goal. The target of their mission was alerted with enough time to escape out of a back window with only his bedclothes. Actually, the daring young Confederates were very fortunate to retreat without a wound, either to themselves or to their trusty mounts. They were hotly pursued but split up and reached safety and were able to advance to future exciting adventures.[1]

Again, I must encourage reading Mr. Curtis's account for the full benefit of the telling. The nineteenth century vocabulary and phrasing is so much part of the story!

In my research, then, I became driven to locate Mrs. Lewis's house. From Curtis's article, I knew the house was located near New Baltimore. From where the farm was identified on a Jed Hotchkiss map, I could see it was north of that community. From Eugene Scheel's historic Fauquier map, landmarks were identified – the Pond Mountains (for an elevation to the east) and Hinson's Shop – but never an exact location of Mrs. Lewis's home. During several treks, I had driven along the Little Georgetown Road (Rt. 674) looking, but never finding a likely candidate. Finally, for the 2015 trek, I made it a priority. Not even high water was going to impede the mission!

After the usual false finds, and stopping to inquire of local folks, we were no closer. Don Hakenson had driven by the place a long time ago but had no recollection of its location. We were into the search about two hours. In our vehicle, frustration was growing. Remembering "Rules 4 and 5" – basically, "Do not give up!" – we persisted and went a little further.

From the road, a possible target sat afar and atop a ridge. The house was a dull gray color so it did not appear to be very large. It did not have the grand presence that one would expect from the significant history of the place. As we drove through the gateway, a sign indicated Cedar Hill. That rang a bell with Don!

We proceeded up the winding driveway. The house grew in size as we approached. The driveway divided a little below the house. Winding uphill to the left, the driveway led to some outbuildings and another smaller house. We followed the right fork as it curved around the front of the house. If it had not been for the gray paint, it would have been a grand residence. This could be Mrs. Lewis's house!

After walking around the house and knocking on the doors, we surmised that no one was home. We were snapping photos when we heard "people sounds" from up the hill beyond us. We piled in the vehicle, and drove up to the outbuildings. A man came out from where he had been working. A puzzled look greeted us. In response to our queries about the big house, he referred us to his sister in the smaller house nearby. The sister was not certain about the history of the farm, but informed us that a Smith family now owned Cedar Hill.

We left Cedar Hill and drove to Warrenton, where we dropped Don at the public library. He zipped inside and asked the archivist to investigate the address for Cedar Hill to see if it had indeed been the home of our Mrs. Lewis. After some Warrenton stops, we moved on to locate the site of the Gaskins Mill Fight – an adventure to be told another time. Later that afternoon, before we returned to Welbourne, Don received a call from the archivist who confirmed that we had indeed located the long-sought home of Mrs. Lewis!

It was only a minor incident that did not directly involve Mosby's Rangers, but it was a compelling tale that required follow-up. Another illustration of the benefits of persistence and going a bit further – ("Rules 4 and 5")!

Cedar Hill - scene of the failed attempt to capture Gen. Crawford

Notes on Channing Smith and Richard "Dick" Lewis

Channing Smith was the son and grandson of doctors in early Upperville. Active in the Black Horse Troop from the start of The War, Channing soon became a trusted scout for Gen. Stuart. Mosby requested Channing's transfer to the 43rd Battalion where he served as 3rd Lt. in Company E, Sam Chapman's company. After Lee's surrender in April 1865, Mosby sent Channing to Richmond to gain direction from authorities regarding the surrender of the 43rd Battalion. Channing Smith was a farmer and community leader following The War.

Channing Smith's grave near Delaplane, VA

Richard "Dick" Lewis served with the Black Horse Troop and became a scout for Gen. Stuart, too. Dick was captured in May 1862 and exchanged that August. At the Battle of the Wilderness in May 1864, he was wounded and his leg was amputated. He was invalided, but joined the Rangers soon after recovering. Dick was a farmer after The War and served as a member in the Virginia House of Delegates. Lt. Channing Smith considered Dick Lewis to be "the coolest man I ever saw."

Ranger Lewis's headstone, Masonic Cemetery, Culpeper, VA

Laura Ratcliffe

Think about how you would react to invaders occupying your neighborhood, town, or county. Throughout history, legends tell of depredations committed by enemy forces upon a conquered or cowering local populace. The tales also record deeds of heroic civilians bravely taking actions in resistance to illegal or harsh measures enacted by the occupiers. The War Between the States supplies innumerable examples of personal heroism.

In a Federal report, Laura Ratcliffe is described as "a very active and cunning rebel, who is known to our men, and is at least suspected of assisting Mosby not a little in his movements." Laura Ratcliffe was in her mid-twenties when she met Gen. Jeb Stuart. At the time she was nursing wounded soldiers in the general's winter camp. When Gen. Stuart decided to detail Mosby and nine 1st Virginia troopers to operate behind enemy lines, he asked Laura to assist Mosby in his endeavors.

Laura lived with her two sisters and widowed mother near Frying Pan Church. The Ratcliffe family ran a farm, so Laura would frequently be on the road selling milk and eggs to Union soldiers marching between Centreville and Herndon. What common soldier could resist the charm of a beautiful young woman? Their loose lips did not sink ships, but Laura was able to glean tactical information and pass it on to Stuart and to Mosby when he became an active partisan commander.

In February 1863, just weeks into their partisan service, Mosby's men rode into the Frying Pan Church area with a mission in mind. They encountered Laura on the road. She was actually looking for them to warn of a Yankee trap. A young Yankee soldier had bragged to Laura when he was buying milk early that morning. Obviously trying to impress her, the lad told how Union cavalry was waiting near Frying Pan Church. They were placing a few men out in the open, while the rest were concealed in the woods. When Mosby and his men came into view, they would not be able to resist the bait and would ride into the ambush. No way would the Yankees fail; this would end the Mosby problem.

Thanks to Laura's warning, Mosby was able to avoid the trap and move on to another target. Following the meeting with Laura, Mosby led his men north to Herndon Station where they captured a blockade runner. While the Yankees waited in the freezing slush and drizzle to ambush the Gray Ghost, Mosby and his men were warm and "shopping" several miles away. While procuring blockade wares, Mosby learned of a Union picket post near Dranesville. After securing their purchases, Mosby gathered his men and rode northward. They were able to return to Middleburg that night with 15 prisoners and their horses, arms and equipments, instead of themselves being made prisoners.[2]

Using *The Guidebook*, we were unable to find Laura's wartime home; however, with persistence ("Rule 4"), we were able to get to "Brookside" (or "Merrybrook"). It did require sharp eyes and making allowances for modifications to the roadway since the publication of *The Guidebook*. The entrance to Laura's post-war home is across a petite bridge over Merrybrook Run. We did not want to trespass, so we pulled up immediately after crossing the bridge. I jumped out to snap a few photos of the house. My intention to jump right back into the vehicle and drive away was suspended suddenly when a woman quietly rose up from some low-lying shrubbery. She asked, "May I help you?"

Win Meiselman chats with trekkers

Merrybrook, Laura Ratcliffe's post-war home

This was on our third trek, so I was learning to be prepared. I quickly reached through the open window of the vehicle, held up *The Guidebook* ("Rule 1"), and introduced myself and briefly explained our mission. The woman introduced herself as Win Meiselman, owner of the home. Win suspiciously quizzed us about Mosby and Laura Ratcliffe until she was assured that we were legitimate Mosby scholars.

Once we cleared security, Win gave us a tour of the place. Serendipity! She was well aware of the historical importance of her property and a knowledgeable resource on Laura Ratcliffe. After a warm visit, Win guided us to visit Laura's gravesite and "Mosby's Rock." We never would have found the gravesite without Win's help since it is in the parking lot of the Marriott Hotel fronting the Centreville Road just north of the Dulles Toll Road. In the tiny plot are the graves of Laura and the Coleman and Hanna families. The graves are surrounded by a short, wrought iron fence, which is then encircled by an overwhelming laurel hedge-done-wild. Mosby's Rock was a different story. Locating it was not easy. Even Win was not able to lead us there. Mosby's Rock was not likely called that until after The War. At the time the rock was in a remote part of the old Centreville Road. It was rumored that Laura would leave messages for Mosby hidden around the rock, and that it was also a rendezvous point for the Rangers. Who knows for certain, but it has become part of the romance of Mosby lore, and we wanted to find it!

There has been tremendous modern development in that section of Loudoun County. The old Centreville road is no longer identified as such. The rock has been nearly buried from the construction of adjacent townhouses and apartments. When we finally did locate Mosby's Rock it had lost a great deal of its visual impact, but not the historical impact. Now, nearby, there is a historical marker to help interpret the story. Do you suppose the modern neighbors ever wonder why people visit the rock?

All that remains of Mosby's Rock – the old Centreville Road was to the right

Win Meiselman was also instrumental in getting a marker placed to tell Laura's story at Merrybrook. Unfortunately, we were not able to attend the dedication ceremony, but we did contribute to the marker fund.

It was not until our 2008 trek that we found the Ratcliffe wartime farm. Tom Evans and Don Hakenson brought us there. Thank goodness! We never would have been successful on our own. The location is well off the old Centreville road and south of the Mosby's Rock site.

The only structures remaining are an old silo and what looks to me to have been the old milk house.

In the years following our first meeting with Win, stopping at Merrybrook was a frequent highlight. Win is an elegant and charming hostess, and has warmly encouraged our mission. On one memorable visit, Win prepared a wonderful southern breakfast that was ready for us minutes after we got off the redeye flight from Seattle. What a welcome! It was Andy's (our A.G. Babcock) first trek, and he exclaimed, "Wow! Is this how all the treks are?" Not quite, but yes, always full of surprises and connections! Serendipity and synchronicity!

The silo on the former wartime farm of the Ratcliffe family

Albert G. "Bone Mill" Minor

Naturally, among so many interesting characters in Mosby's Confederacy, there are many amusing tales to be told. One such tale, a favorite often told by Don Hakenson, is about Ranger Albert "Ab" Minor. Ab was a native of the Alexandria area, a farmer before The War. Before joining the 43rd Virginia Cavalry in July 1863, he had served with the 6th Virginia Cavalry since May 1861.

In August 1864, Ab was posted as guide for a Ranger attack on picket posts near Alexandria. This would be in Ab's neighborhood, and he would know his way around the area. Utilizing local men who knew the backroads and byways was one of the advantages of Ranger-style tactics.

Having accomplished their mission, the Rangers turned to Ab Minor to guide them back to Mosby's command. Mysteriously, Ab became confused. It had grown dark, and the deeper they rode into the woods, the more confused their guide became. Ab kept reassuring his Ranger colleagues that he would lead them out safely. He just needed to find the bone mill, then he would have his bearings; however, Ab's confusion only increased. He would pull up his horse and say, "If I could only find the bone mill, it will be all right."

Don interpreting the "Bone Mill" Minor site

This kept up all night. Ranger Minor never found the bone mill, but the Rangers managed to make their way back to the command the next day in spite of Ab's "guidance." As is common among friends, the episode became a pretty good source of ribbing by Ab's comrades. He came to be known as "Bone Mill" Minor, at least until a young, greenhorn Bill Trammell taunted Ab with the new name. Ab took offense and shot him! It seems no one referred to Ranger Minor as "Bone Mill" after that. Well, not to his face anyway![3]

Site of the elusive bone mill on Accotink Creek near Franconia, Fairfax County, Virginia

It's a great story when Don tells it, and even better when Don has you standing at the site of the elusive bone mill. Through diligent research, Don was able to locate the site. It is much easier to find today than when Ab Minor was searching. In 2013, Don took us to the site that is in a park on Accotink Creek near the Franconia-Springfield Parkway. The mill is gone, of course, but some of the foundation stones exist.

Apparently the lesson to be learned in this case is to not tease anyone named "Bone Mill."

Roberta "Bert" Pollock

From the multitude of episodes of Southern patriotism and courage, a shining example comes in Miss Roberta "Bert" Pollock. Accounts of Bert's story come from Alexander Hunter, *The Women of the Debatable Land*; from V. C. "Pat" Jones, *Ranger Mosby*; and from Major John Scott, *Partisan Life with Col. John S. Mosby*. The three versions differ in many respects, but the underlying message is one of decisive heroism. For now, I will lean heavily on Hunter's interpretation since he indicates that he actually interviewed Miss Pollock shortly after her adventure.

Roberta Pollock was the third daughter of Rev. Abraham D. Pollock. Her maternal grandfather was Charles Lee, Attorney General during the Washington and Adams administrations. By all accounts, Roberta was intelligent, charming, and spirited. The Pollock family lived at Leeton Forest south of Warrenton.

On a cold December day, Roberta walked into Warrenton to visit a friend. Earlier that day, the friend had witnessed Federal officers escorting a stranger, a slave man, to the office of the provost marshal. The conclusion was that there would be some damaging information passed to the Yankees. Miss Pollock decided to find out. She approached the house where the provost marshal was situated. At first the guard would not let her into the building, but succumbing to her charms and possibly some discretely deposited coins, Roberta entered. She secreted herself in a cellar directly beneath the room where the interrogation was proceeding. Roberta clearly heard the slave telling the officers that he could guide them to Mosby.

Bert knew she had to get word to Mosby or his men. All accounts say she walked into town that day, yet somehow Roberta obtained a horse. She rode back through the Union pickets at the edge of town, using her pass to return home; however, she turned instead toward the north, to get to Salem (today, Marshall) to reach Mosby. It was already late in the day as Bert headed out. Before long darkness fell, the temperature fell, and the cold wind picked up.

Roberta pressed on, determined to find her way regardless of the hazards. After hours of plodding through the freezing dark night, a voice rang out, "Halt! Who goes there?"

Summoning her quick wit, Bert answered in a voice raspy from the cold, "Surrender!"

To her surprise and great relief, the next sound Roberta heard was galloping hooves retreating into the night. Among the Union troops, Mosby inspired a fear of nighttime attacks!

Continuing on her quest, Bert came to a spot where she could finally get her bearings. Unfortunately, she had been riding in roughly a circle around Warrenton, lost in the dark cold forest. But now she knew in which direction to proceed. Salem was still miles away! For Roberta there was no question of turning back. The Rangers must be warned!

Passing several more miles, Bert was suddenly halted by another Federal guard. Grabbing her horse's reins, he informed her that he was taking her to the picket reserve. Roberta responded, "I will not go! You may shoot me, but I will not go!"

The trooper replied, "It is my orders."

The staunch response came, "I am willing for you to do your duty, but I will either die here or go free!"

The soldier said that to detain her would be cruel, and then escorted her around the reserve camp to a nearby farmhouse. The occupants warmly welcomed Roberta. She turned to thank the soldier for his kindness. He responded, "I have three hours yet of picket duty, and I will spend the time in thinking of the half-frozen Virginia girl." He then turned his horse and vanished into the darkness.

At that late hour, with Union pickets alerted, it was impossible for Bert to continue her mission. Before she left the farm family the next morning, a gaggle of Yankee troopers came to the farmhouse. In cheerful spirits, they bragged how they had outsmarted Mosby the night before when he had sent a lone Ranger ahead to lure them into a trap. Too smart for Mosby, they quickly advanced to the rear!

Miss Pollack rode on to Salem and successfully delivered her information. That evening, Christmas Eve, the Federals raided Salem looking for a reported-by-a-reliable-source Ranger celebration. Not a Ranger was to be found![4]

I like the story of Bert Pollock's ride because it shines brightly on the resilience, determination, and spirit of the Southern soul. The devotion to the cause demonstrated by a 17-year-old woman stirs the heart! Tracking Roberta's courageous adventure has been an active objective for me ever since my first encounter.

Since Roberta's home was Leeton Forest, that was a good starting point. While I am not a great fan of the internet, I do admit that it does at times provide a beneficial utility. A search for Leeton Forest turned up a couple useful hits. One was a photo of the historic marker noting the importance of Charles Lee, U. S. Attorney General, and the location nearby of his home Leeton Forest. Have you ever noticed that the historic markers are seldom planted at the real location? I suppose there is a reason for that, but it frustrates me in a minor way. It simply means additional research.

The other online link was for a real estate office that had listed for sale Leeton Forest. Photos and an address were provided. Somewhere in my research I came across information that the Pollock home had been lost to fire long ago. The current home replaces the original, but is still impressive, and the property at least provides an anchor for Miss Pollock's journey.

The path of Bert's ride is difficult to identify. Except for View Tree Mountain and Watery Mountain, landmarks are not mentioned in the accounts. From her home south of Warrenton, it would have been logical for Roberta to ride west, then north to avoid contact with the Federal pickets that encircled the town. Riding in that direction eventually would have brought her to the mountains in the stories. With 150 years of modern development, it would be impossible to duplicate Roberta's route today. Apparently, View Tree Mountain was known by the locals as "lovers' lookout" as it presented a romantic view of Warrenton. This may have been the spot during her ride from which Roberta was able to see the lights of the town and get her bearings.

I was able to locate View Tree Mountain (elev. 1084 ft.) on a map. It is northwest of Warrenton. The map shows ruins of a Civil War signal tower atop the mountain. Local folks may have a better notion of how to arrive at the objective. After driving a circuitous route along barely passable roads, through a water hazard and past hidden houses, we finally came onto Bear Wallow Road. Believing this was going to deliver us to the desired vista point, we soon encountered another obstacle. Some kind of military installation (Warrenton Training Center) blocked our way. Although we were unsuccessful in sharing Roberta's view of Warrenton, at least we now have an idea of the terrain she covered that night. We appreciate that travelling in that area on a freezing dark night would have been a major challenge. We had difficulty driving in broad daylight!

The view from "Leeton Forest"; Roberta's goal was north of the far ridge

As for the Watery Mountain reference, it further makes sense that Roberta would have continued in that direction from View Tree Mountain. It lies nearly in a direct path toward Salem (Marshall), which was Roberta's goal. Watery Mountain Road looks much like it must have at the time of her ride. She could have ridden along other back roads to Salem, or followed the Winchester Turnpike (Rt. 17) straight into town. Given the number of Union pickets and patrols swarming the area, back roads would have made sense.

The only other clue is from the accounts given by Hunter. In the morning, Miss Bert continued her ride from the farmhouse, but "Mrs. Marshall's boy, a lad of some ten years" went by an alternate route also. The warning must get through! Perhaps deeper research would locate the farmhouse of the Marshall family. We would then have an additional piece of the puzzle in place.

Henry C. "Cab" Maddux

Cab Maddux is one of the most colorful Rangers, among an entire battalion of such characters. At the ripe age of 15, he joined the 43rd, apparently on an impulse during a running fight through Upperville, past the academy he attended. The stories differ but each variation is an entertainment, and all agree that Cab was at school at the delicate moment of commitment. The first version I encountered, provided by Jim Moyer, was that Cab saw and heard the skirmish running through the town, jumped out the window, grabbed a riderless horse as it ran by and joined the chase.

Another version, told by eyewitness Ranger John Munson, is that when the fight came raging through town the students were at recess. Cab realized the situation, leaped on his own horse and joined the fray, textbook in hand.

Shortly after The War Cab Maddux, 4th from the left, posed with his Ranger comrades

Cab's wild enthusiasm did not end that day (February 20, 1864) with the fighting near Blakely Grove School. From that day until the unit disbanded on April 21, 1865, Cab was considered by his fellow Rangers to be spirited, quick-witted, and among the bravest warriors. Cab was the perfect choice of Ranger for my son, Tyler, to portray.[5]

Tyler grew up in our Historic Mosby's Rangers (HMR) unit. I always believed that our crew was a positive influence on the development of desirable traits in our own circle of children, as well as in other reenactors. Because of our qualities as gentlemen, and expertise as horsemen and historians, we mentored several cavalry units over the years. Tyler benefited from the modeling of our rangers and became a fine ranger and gentleman himself.

Author's son, Tyler, AKA "Cab Maddux," at the charge

Tyler's journey was not always smooth. Like Cab Maddux, Tyler was spirited and quick-witted, and a rebel during his teens. On our reenactment battlefields he was fearless. Even though there was no physical resemblance (Cab was short and stocky, Tyler was tall and lean), Cab must have chosen Tyler, as Tyler did not finish high school, either. The U.S. Army made Tyler wait until he turned 18 and completed his G.E.D. Tyler ended up serving in the 1st Cavalry Division, earning his spurs during two tours in Iraq.

With the experience overseas and the influence of the HMR rangers, Tyler returned to civilian life a fine young man. He completed his A.A. degree, then a self-designed B.A. with a double major, and is now gainfully employed. Like Cab Maddux and many of Mosby's men following The War, Tyler is making a positive contribution to his community.

Following the Cab Maddux story was interesting enough in itself, but especially because of Tyler's connection. For an in-depth account of Cab's life, please refer to Eric Buckland's *Mosby's Men II*, pp.102-110. We knew that during The War Cab's family resided at Llangollen Farm near Upperville in Loudoun County, and that Cab attended school in that town. Naturally, locating these sites became a goal in our early treks.

Finding Llangollen Farm proved to be another serendipitous moment. It is located across the road from another farm we were seeking, Ayrshire, which was the wartime family home of Ranger George Ayer, and a favorite back door where Col. Mosby could count on getting a cup of real coffee.

Llangollen Farm is an imposing estate. At the time of The War, it must have covered several thousand acres. The main house sits on the eastern shoulder of the Blue Ridge (not too far from today's Mt. Weather). The wartime house must have been much smaller, but still impressive, with an incredible view across the countryside to the east. We were thrilled to locate Llangollen, but were intimidated by the mile-long drive from the road up to the house. Until the fall of 2015, only once did we brave the approach to the house and then it was only for a very quick drive-by. This is when I measured the length of the drive.

The Llangollen manse sits a mile from Trappe Road on the eastern shoulder of the Blue Ridge

The author on the front lawn at Llangollen

For the September 2015 Mosby bus tour, Eric Buckland had arranged for the bus to drive up to the house, legally, much to the satisfaction and enjoyment of the "tourists." Of course, Eric's presentation included poignant anecdotes about Cab Maddox and several of the other Rangers who used Llangollen as their boarding or safe house. The sun was warmly glowing. It was another perfect moment of synchronicity!

The location of Cab's school has been more of a challenge. Various accounts place it in the town of Upperville, which straddles the line between Loudoun and Fauquier counties. On one of our early treks, Jim Moyer pointed out a building as the school. It is now a residence, located on the main street of Upperville. At the time of The War, this was Columbia Street or the Ashby Gap Turnpike. Today this is Route 50, also named the John S. Mosby Highway.

The former Armstrong Academy – possibly Cab Maddux's schoolhouse

From Eugene Scheel's Fauquier County historical map, I found two schools nearly next door to one another – the Upperville Academy and Armstrong's Military and Classical Academy. My current research is attempting to find the enrollment records of both schools to determine the place where Cab's Ranger career began. The Upperville Academy was founded several years prior to The War by an act of the General Assembly of the Commonwealth; however, I have not found much more than the names of the trustees and that the Upperville Baptist Church met in the academy building until 1840. The academy was located across the street from the current location of the church.

Unfortunately, and within possibility, so is the Armstrong Academy. The Armstrong Academy was located on Lot 45 in a large stone building. Started by an Irishman, James J. Armstrong, it was an academy for boys and girls from 1854 until The War. At the beginning of The War, Armstrong entered the Confederate service, was commissioned captain of his company, and was killed in his first battle in January 1862.

It appears that the Armstrong Academy was not in operation when Cab joined the Rangers in 1864. The building pointed out by Jim Moyer is a better fit for the location for the Upperville Academy. Until we can confirm Cab's enrollment, the question remains: where was Cab attending school on that day when he charged into battle, textbook in hand? It is puzzlements like this that keep me coming back. The journey's the thing!

Mrs. Waters' Son and His Pard

Some of the most entertaining reading on Mosby lore was written by former Rangers. For anecdotes, phrasing, and vocabulary, my favorite Ranger memoir is John Munson's *Reminiscences of a Mosby Guerrilla*. One story that captured my attention for further research merits exposure here. Because it is such a pleasure to read, the temptation is to copy the entire episode, but instead I will direct the reader to Mr. Munson's book to enjoy the amusement firsthand.

Munson's narrative takes place during the winter of 1864-1865, an especially icy and snowy season. As was common practice of Mosby's men, Munson boarded at fellow-ranger Hugh Waters' family home. The Widow Waters' farm, Edgewood, was located a short distance south of Middleburg.

The tale begins with word that Yankee patrols were nearby, so Hugh and John camped out on the farm property. Their campsite was close to the Plains Road, but they were hidden from view by a rocky cliff and surrounding trees. Hoping that the Yankees would not come out in the inclement weather, the young Rangers slept peacefully that night. In the morning, they were informed that Yankees had stopped at the house looking for them. The Federals then rode on to Middleburg.

Rangers were always on the lookout for action, so Munson and Waters proceeded toward Middleburg to gather information. Along the way they met up with Lt. Fount Beattie who likewise had been roused early from his slumbers. At Middleburg the trio found both information and action when they were spotted by the Union camp.

After exchanging shots of greeting, the chase was on. The Rangers galloped away on the Salem Road and seemed to be making a clean escape; however, at a rise in the road they saw another detachment approaching from the opposite direction. Being pinched between pursuing forces, the Rangers knew they faced the need for dramatic action. They were being squeezed from both ends, and they were hemmed in by imposing stone fences on both sides of the road.

As resourceful Rangers are known to do, they back-trotted to a gap in the fence, pushed through and were making a successful getaway across a field. Much to the Rangers' surprise the Yankees had made it over or around or through the stone fence, too, and closed in on the Rangers from two oblique directions. The three Rangers spurred their mounts even harder in an attempt to reach a hill on the far side of the open field.

At this point, the story becomes a greater adventure for Munson. His recently "acquired" horse did not seem to share the same sense of urgency the circumstances merited. In fact, the horse clearly slowed his gait, contrary to Munson's fervent desire to escape the clutches of the fast-closing Federals. Beattie and Waters had reached the target hill. As they sat protected among the trees, they shouted encouragement for Munson to come along quickly. But Munson's stubborn equine partner actually halted in apparent protest. With Munson sitting on his idle horse, and Beattie and Waters sitting in the woods atop the hill, the Yankees halted, too, wondering what the trick was here.

The Union troopers began yelling, and cajoling Munson. Today, it would be termed trash talk. He was wearing a new greatcoat of especially fine quality. The Yankees may have presumed Munson was an officer, and hearing his fellow Rangers hollering to come along, may have feared another Ranger ambush was waiting for them on the backside of that hill. The brave Confederate "officer" looked to be luring the pursuing troopers into the trap. When Munson's horse finally decided to calmly stroll toward the woods, and the other two Rangers commenced firing, the entire Yankee force turned away. They were not going to fall for that tired old ruse – again! The three Ranger comrades quietly dropped over the far side of the hill, and rode on without further Yankee interference.[6]

This episode captures the spirit, fortitude, and competence of the Rangers. It creates in my imagination a typical Ranger event, maybe encountered daily during The War. And, therefore, I wanted to track the location of the tale.

Typical terrain features near Middleburg and Edgewood Farm

It was easy enough to find the Plains road at least I thought so at first. Munson gives the description of Mrs. Waters' farmhouse as being about midway between the Plains Road on the east and the Salem Road on the west. In my early research, my thinking made modern-day Zulla Road (Rt. 709) the Salem Road and the Halfway Road (Rt. 626) the Plains Road leading generally south from Middleburg. So my first site study brought me to Hickory Tree Lane. Located there on a rise was a fine old Greek revival style house. A dignified structure surrounded by an expansive park of lawn and trees, it looked to me to be an appropriate candidate for Edgewood. Although it was located between the roads identified by Munson, the distances did not fit. A survey of the area did not provide a rock cliff, either.

Explorations with expanded parameters on subsequent treks did not bring satisfactory results. I even drove partway down Sullivan's Mill Road (Rt. 807), but rejected that as a possibility. It was leading to the Middleburg Experimental Station (established for agricultural research), which is too far east to fit Munson's description.

Finally, progress was made in a conversation with Don Hakenson. He told how he had recently driven into the experimental station, and inquired about Mrs. Waters' home. Don was informed that the experimental station had indeed been Edgewood Farm. The original Waters house has been demolished, but there are several structures on the property from the time of Munson's tale. This was good news; however, this location was not quite right, either. It put The Plains Road (Rt. 626) to the west of the farm instead of on the east as Munson described.

On the 2015 trek, we drove into the experimental station to look around. Don was adamant about the connection, but I still was not convinced. We searched for a rock cliff. It must be still there, right? Nothing popped out as a possibility for the Rangers' campsite. We will continue the search on the next trek.

Mrs. Waters' Edgewood Farm, today's Middleburg Experimental Station – courtesy LRRHD application

It was only after returning to my office that I discovered an amazing online resource, the *Little River Rural Historic District (LRRHD) application to the National Register of Historic Places*. Among many treasures, I found the solution to my conundrum about Edgewood. On page 100, the summary of a deed indicates that the road now known as Hulberts Lane (Rt. 627) during the 19th Century was known as the *Plains Road*. Hulberts Lane runs north to south along the *east* side of the experimental station.

What was then known as the *Salem Road* is now Burrland Lane (Rt. 705), located *west* of the experimental station. With these new pieces of the puzzle in place, the location of Edgewood is satisfactorily confirmed. We still want to explore for the rocky cliff campsite location, just to complete Munson's story!

John Tyler Waller

Approximately three million combatants, North and South forces combined, fought in the War Between the States. That translates into nearly one in ten Americans that went off to war. It truly was a domestic fight with brother against brother, father against son, families divided and, predominately in the South, soldiers defending their homes and families. It is not surprising that so many personal stories have survived. It is the continuing discovery of new stories and information that propels me along this journey.

Among the many episodes that have captured my imagination, one stands out. It may be another minor event in the grand scheme of Mosby lore, but it is a tale that not only illustrates the character of the young members of Mosby's command, but also plucks at the heartstrings.

For all the chaos and disruptions of war, people still live a daily routine as best they can. People continue to grow food, chop firewood, and fall in love. The story of John Tyler Waller has several versions, but I will try to relate only the basic information.

John Tyler Waller turned 16 a few days after the Battle of First Manassas. His grandfather was former President John Tyler. John Waller was small in physique, 5'3" in his stocking feet, but he was huge in spirit and devotion to Virginia and the Southern cause. Before he turned 19, John had served in the infantry, was seriously wounded at Williamsburg, and had served as a midshipman aboard ship before joining Mosby's Rangers in the spring of 1864. Among Mosby's young "hot bloods," Waller was considered the wildest; fearless, he loved danger for danger's sake.

But apparently John Waller was passionate in the affairs of the heart as well as those of battle. Some accounts claim he was courting the sister of Rangers John H. and James "Willie" Foster, while other accounts report that the two lovebirds were engaged to be married. Two stories actually involve Waller and his darling.

The first incident is recorded in Alexander Hunter's *The Women of the Debatable Land.* John Waller was on his carefree way, almost daring the Yankees to interfere with his ride. The young Ranger was chased to his sweetheart's home by a Yankee patrol. She exhibited amazing composure as the Federals searched her home. She calmly indicated that the "rebel" ran out the back as the Yankees came to the front door. The young woman stood demurely in the foyer while the search continued. After the Yankees departed, petite-framed Waller came out from under her voluminous hoop skirts, where he had safely hidden.[7]

Alexander Hunter wrote that John Waller was a cousin, so maybe he heard the story from Waller himself. But one has to wonder, given Waller's gallant nature, how he would have accepted the ribbing from his comrades had the story come out about him hiding behind (or under) a woman's skirts?

As recorded by James Williamson, the second incident occurred about a year later. On March 14, 1865, John Waller and Ranger Harry Sinnott were surprised at the house of Mr. Fishback, near The Plains. They ran out the back as the Yankee patrol, a detachment from the 8th Illinois Cavalry, approached. Sinnott jumped his horse over a fence and escaped. Waller turned and charged the Federals with revolvers blazing. A volley from the Union troopers dropped John Waller from his saddle, dead before his body touched the ground.[8]

We will never know what Waller was thinking when he decided to take on the entire patrol formed up and facing him. One possibility is that he did not trust being treated fairly if captured, so it would be better to stand and fight. Perhaps he was hoping to delay the Yankee pursuit of his comrade? Not surprising would be that he believed he could successfully blast his way through and make his escape. After all, when we are young and full of vim and vigor, we like to believe that we are invincible!

One version of the Waller story has Cornelia Foster as the sweetheart who had hidden him under her hoops. She would have been about the right age, 18, to fit the story. Her family home was Glenville, just west of The Plains. Waller and Sinnott had visited Cornelia at Glenville, but were trapped by a detachment of the 8th IL Cavalry in Fishback's lane, north of The Plains.

Glenville - the home of the Thomas R. Foster family, including daughter, Cornelia

The various conflicting versions of the John Waller story present a compelling reason to dig deeper. On the 2015 trek, it became one of the priority incidents to pursue. The details were confused. Who was Waller's sweetheart? Where was the house where Waller hid under her skirt? Where was the site of Waller's death? What is the true version?

The initial attempt was on a Tuesday when we were actually enroute to sites in the south. We were passing through The Plains and stopped to fuel our rental vehicle. While fueling was in progress, Cousin Carol went in to inquire about the location of the Fishback place or the Foster place. Carol was directed next door to a shop, where Mark might know something; however, Mark was not open for business because Tuesday was his day of rest. We made a note to return on another day when Mark would be open for business.

After invoking "Rule 2 – Go with the flow," that day arrived the next day. It was Wednesday, Mark was in and his shop was open. Mark chuckled when informed that we were sent to him for answers. He pleasantly sent us across the street to the ZigZag Gallery, because "Henry knows these things." Unfortunately, Henry was out and not due back any time soon; however, Henry's sister, Roberta, determined what we needed, and quickly ascertained a solution for us. While we waited in her shop, Roberta ran down the street. She returned several minutes later with a diminutive woman in tow. Roberta introduced Marcia "Marci" Markey, a Ph.D. historian and journalist who had been a colleague of the late, legendary historian John Gott.

The Turner home in The Plains: site of the hiding-in-hoop incident?

Marci is a longtime resident of The Plains, and was able to address some of our questions. Local legend has the hiding-in-hoop incident occurring in what was then the Turner home on Main Street. Mary Foster Turner owned the home, but it was a refugee from Alexandria under whose hoops it was that a youthful Confederate soldier had hidden. The young woman refugee has not been identified in local legend. Only Alexander Hunter has identified the "hider" as John Waller.

Trekkers conferring with Marci Markey

An interesting side note on this Turner home: carved on the inside of the door to the smokehouse is an image of a monkey-like character with the inscription, "Lincoln is an ape." As he began his first term of office, this was a widely viewed opinion of Lincoln, both in the north and south. The Lincoln-ape concept often appeared as cartoons in newspapers, but to have it saved for posterity in an old smokehouse is unique!

With a new twist being introduced, the refugee woman, the story becomes a bit more complex. It is possible that she was a relative of the Fosters, or perhaps Cornelia had been staying with relatives in Alexandria before seeking safety in The Plains. It is also possible that Waller's hoop-hider was another sweetheart apart from the Foster sister.

The Turner's smokehouse, location of the "Lincoln is an ape" artwork

If the shooting death of Waller took place in Fishback's lane, where exactly is that location? Marci's maps and books did not answer that question. Don Hakenson and I returned to The Plains a couple of days later to continue the search. We stopped to visit Marci, but her husband could not locate her. He took us down Main Street to the Grace Episcopal Church where Marci volunteers. After not finding her, we thanked her husband and were walking up the street when Marci, in her stocking feet, found us. She had been on the back porch knitting. We walked back to her home. Marci is a treasure, giving us more time for further clarification of the Waller story.

After leaving Marci, still in her stocking feet, Don and I drove north on the Halfway Road seeking a likely location for the Fishback place. We did find a possibility to the west of the road and north of the town. Driving up to the main house only supported our suspicions. The original portion of the house was mostly hidden by modern improvements and landscaping, but it definitely was at least war era. No one answered our door knocking, but as we started to pull away, a young man came out to begin his daily run. He was a guest at the house so he did not know its history. He ran and we drove away.

Without finding resolution to all the Waller story questions, I returned home at the end of the trek. It was such a burning issue for me that I devoted additional time and energy to seeking the answers. Some help was provided by the 1860 U.S. Census. It confirmed that Cornelia, 14-year-old daughter of Thomas R. Foster was living at Glenville. Cornelia was definitely sweetheart age by the time of the romance with John Waller.

The real jackpot came in the form of the *Little River Rural Historic District (LRRHD) application to the National Register of Historic Places.* From the LRRHD manuscript, we found that Isaac Foster and his descendants have, over time, owned the Whitewood, Byrnely, and Glenville farms. Before the Fosters, the Fishback family owned the Whitewood and Byrnely farms. At the time of The War, the Farmington (New Whitewood) farm was owned by John Nelson Fishback, (Old) Whitewood was owned by Josiah T. Fishback, and the executors of William Byrne's estate owned Byrnely. Byrnely is now owned by Robert Duvall. While still incomplete, I believe we are closer to solving the puzzle.

I have been able to confirm that the farm off the Halfway Road that Don and I visited that afternoon is indeed Farmington (New Whitewood). So now we are trying to confirm which Whitewood (Old or New) saw the gallant, but fatal, charge of John Tyler Waller only weeks prior to the end of The War.

Either the Turner place in town or Glenville could have been the home of Waller's sweetheart. Both homes offer lanes leading to the Fishback farms. Now all we need is to dig up new evidence to confirm the identity of John Waller's sweetheart and, maybe, we will have the rest of the story! The reader may wonder why does it matter? Well, the journey's the thing!

---

[1] I.S. Curtis, "The Attempted Capture of General Crawford," *Confederate Veteran*, vol. XXIII, 1915

[2] Scott, *Partisan*, pp.29-31; Jones, *Ranger Mosby*, pp.81-82; Wert, *Mosby's Rangers*, pp.122-123; Hakenson and Mauro, *Fairfax*, pp.19-24, 28-32

[3] Hakenson and Mauro, *Fairfax*, pp.109-111

[4] Hunter, Alexander, *The Women of the Debatable Land.* Pp.215-228. Washington, DC: Corden Publishing Co., 1912. Reprinted by Ulan Press, San Bernardino, California, 2015; Ramey, Emily G. and Gott, John K., eds., *The Years of Anguish: Fauquier County (Va.), 1861 – 65*, p. 55, Warrenton, Virginia: The Fauquier Democrat, 1965. Jones, *Ranger Mosby*. Pp.155-160. Welton, J. Michael, ed., *My Heart is So Rebellious: The Caldwell Letters, 1861 – 1865.* P.253n2, Warrenton, Va.: TheFauquierNationalBank

[5] Munson, *Reminiscences*, p.83; Williamson, p.200, 285, 306

[6] Munson, *Reminiscences*, pp.131-135

[7] Hunter, *Debatable*, pp.60-64

[8] Williamson, *Mosby's Rangers*, p.354

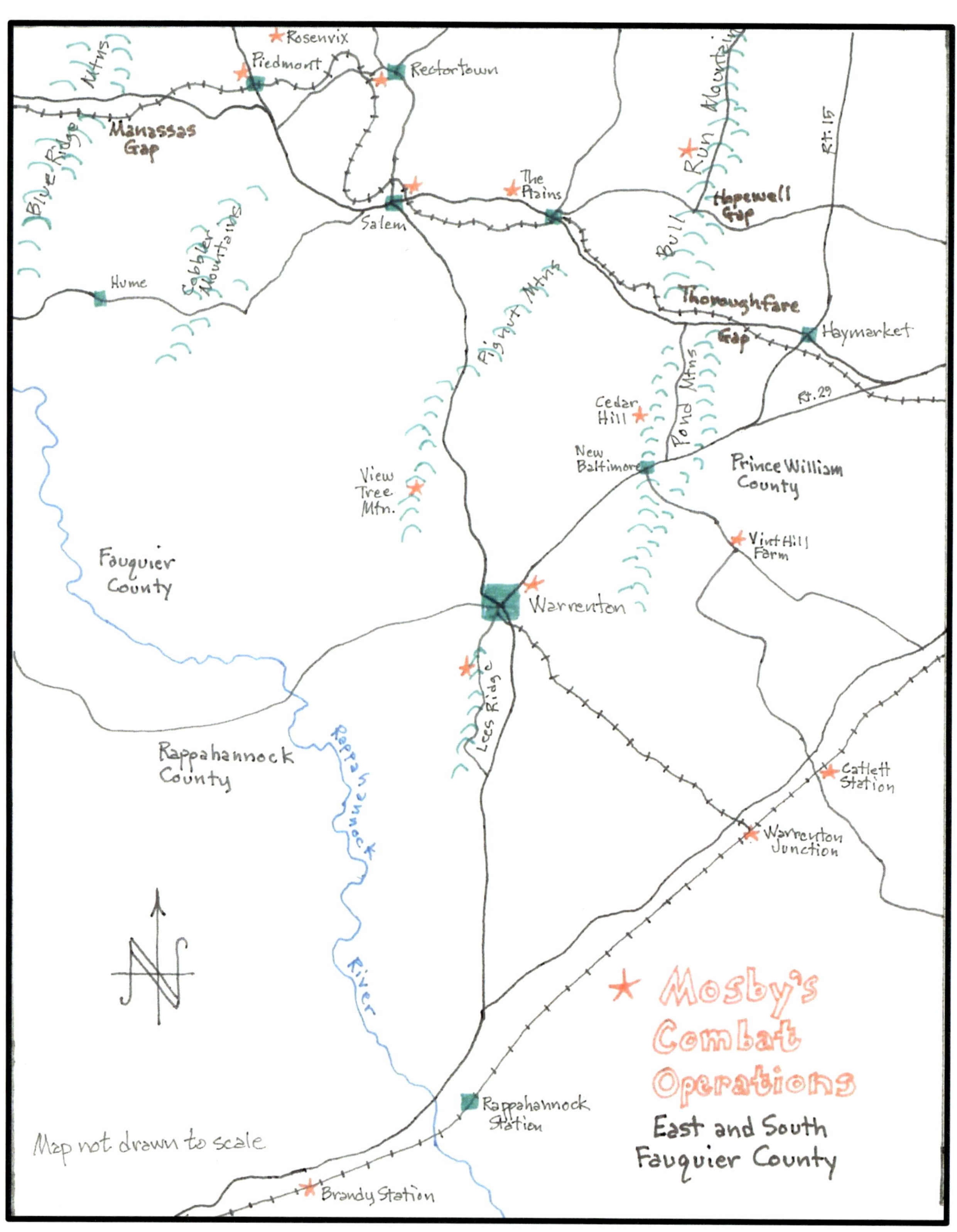
Rosenvix
Piedmont
Rectortown
Blue Ridge Mtns
Manassas Gap
Salem
The Plains
Cobbler Mountains
Hume
Bull Run Mountain
Hopewell Gap
Rt. 15
Thoroughfare Gap
Haymarket
Pignut Mtns
Pond Mtns
Cedar Hill
Rt. 29
New Baltimore
Prince William County
View Tree Mtn.
Vint Hill Farm
Fauquier County
Warrenton
Lees Ridge
Rappahannock County
Rappahannock River
Catlett Station
Warrenton Junction
Mosby's Combat Operations
East and South Fauquier County
Rappahannock Station
Map not drawn to scale
Brandy Station

Chapter Seven: *The Journey's the Thing*

For some folks, reaching the end is the goal. For me, the goal is to experience everything before reaching the end. Ideally, there is no end. One of the splendid things about our treks is the more we dig the more we find out we need to dig deeper. There is no finish line in sight for our journey!

Of course, it matters that we grow our knowledge base of Mosby lore. Sometimes we find that what we thought we knew was not exactly accurate. That often opens new, expanded avenues of research. Stumbling across an obscure point or a recently discovered reference, and then researching, often reveals another new adventure. There is always more to learn.

Our research and treks frequently leave questions unanswered or generate additional mysteries that demand further investigation. Not finding the solution is all right. The quest is the mission. The journey's the thing!

In this chapter, several examples of "the journey's the thing" are presented. For some, the questions were resolved; for others, mysteries remain open to continue the journey.

Back Roads

One of the pleasures of our trekking is to drive on the back roads of Mosby's Confederacy. There exist a surprising number of roads that essentially have not changed over time. An impressive amount of mileage can be covered over "original" roadbeds. Driving them helps us get a feel for the land as it existed in wartime, and can help us interpret actions of the Rangers.

Sometimes it is simply a thrill to navigate a road, imagining Mosby's men riding to the fight. Many accounts tell of Rangers meeting obstacles in the midst of a foray where they were required to jump their horses over a high stone fence, across a chasm or ford a raging stream. One such road presented a memorable challenge.

It escapes my memory why we decided to take this "shortcut." That morning we may have been exploring around Unison, or we might have been visiting the old county "poorhouse" which is where "Major" Hibbs died and his nephew became superintendent. What objective was next on the itinerary has long been forgotten, but from the St. Louis Road, Rt.611, we knew that Jeb Stuart Road would cut down our travel time, giving us more time for interviews and exploration!

Jeb Stuart Road starts off as a pleasant country lane. Not far along, though, it loses any semblance of a modern road. The macadam surface dissolves into a rutted, muddy, tree-lined pathway. We were thinking, "This is great!" We were transported back to wartime, even half expecting General Stuart himself to ride up, cape and plume fluttering in the breeze. Unfortunately, the road suddenly disappeared when the grade sloped down to what looked like a large puddle of water. We halted to reconnoiter the situation.

The ford across the North Branch of Beaver Dam Creek

Our rental vehicle for this trek was a Chevy minivan, front wheel drive, room for six trekkers, good for most back road driving, but good for fording bodies of water? Being the driver, I turned to our trekking crew to ascertain their desires. Should we about face and find an alternate route, or should we take a chance that the puddle is shallow and the ground is solid beneath the water? On horseback, there would not be any doubt. The minivan was no horse. After a few moments of discussion, the unanimous thinking was to apply "Rule 3 – Go for it!" After all, the journey's the thing!

After backing up a bit to build up forward momentum, we plunged ahead. The roadbed immediately dropped dramatically lower, the water abruptly deeper! The minivan plowed forward, pushing the water up and off to the side. About halfway across, the water came about halfway up the doors. This was becoming exciting! The distance across the water obstacle seemed like it was at least 50 feet, but it probably measured only 20 to 30 feet. The minivan did not let us down. We chugged across and up the far slope safely with the engine still running and no water leaking in around the doors. The flushed faces of the trekkers belied the sense of confidence displayed prior to the "running of the waters." Nobody expressed disappointment for the adventure, although no one said, "Hey! Let's do that again!"

Later, we determined that the "puddle" actually was the North Fork of Beaver Dam Creek. Really? The journey's the thing!

"Lost" Roads and Old Maps

Even as a young lad I held a fascination with maps. I do not know why. Maps are just engaging for me. I can recall visiting my Buntain grandparents and being drawn to my grandfather's stack of *National Geographic* magazines. I would go through the stack and pull out the maps and study them. They showed wonderful places all over the world. Sometimes he would let me take a map home with me. Treasure! One map that particularly interested me showed the United States with Civil War battles and campaigns marked on it. I would trace the flow of action across the paper and imagine the terrible fights.

HMR rangers resting their mounts in Gap Run

Many of the resources used in our Mosby research have been maps. Especially valuable have been wartime and historical maps. Not always easy to obtain, wartime maps have helped locate roads now lost, property owners and boundaries, railroad lines, landmarks, and local names. My collection is expanding and now includes a series of S. Howell Brown maps of the lower Shenandoah Valley (reproduced by the Jefferson County Historical Society), and an 1863 map of western Fauquier County (obtained from the Virginia Historical Society). In addition, the series of historical maps from Eugene Scheel and the historical map of northern Fauquier County from Curtis Chappelear's *Maps and Notes of Upper Fauquier County, Virginia,* have provided significant contributions to our research. For locating water bodies and identifying terrain features, I collected a set of topographic maps from the USGS. For just getting around Mosby's Confederacy I rely on the ADC atlases of the northern Virginia counties. All of them usually accompany me on a trek. I do not travel light!

From various accounts we learned that it was not unusual, and not a little unnerving to the invaders, for Mosby and his men to be seen sitting on horseback at an elevation, sometimes silhouettes just watching. We learned that the Yankees rarely traveled except by the main roads due to a reasonable fear of a Ranger ambush. It also became clear to us that the Rangers could engage the enemy at a particular spot on the highway. As the Yankees fled along the route of the turnpikes toward the safety of their camps back in Fairfax, the same contingent of Rangers could strike again on the road further east. How was that possible? The Rangers had the home field advantage. The local Rangers knew the back ways and pathways to use as convenient shortcuts to strike swiftly with surprise and force.

Silhouetted HMR rangers

In our study of the maps, comparing old and modern, we could see several examples of roads that would certainly have been utilized by the Rangers, but did not seem to exist in present day. One war-era road led from Fleetwood Mill on the Winchester Turnpike (Rt.17) over a hill down into the Gap Run Valley, turning uphill and coming out at Bollingbrook. The old road eventually connected to Ashby Gap Turnpike (Rt. 50) in Upperville. Using this road definitely would give the Rangers the "bulge" on a Federal patrol. (Getting the "bulge" on the enemy was a term used by the Rangers, as in "we got the drop on them first"). We decided to see if we could locate this road.

There is no better way to find a "lost" road than from the back of a horse, "Ranger style." On our 2004 trek we arranged to ride on property leased by the Virginia Beef Association. We met Todd Kern, with the horses; Gray Coiner, our permission; and Jolly de Give, moral support at the Fleetwood Gate on Carr Lane. Carr Lane is another slightly "improved" road that meanders along the edges of Gap Run. It easily transports one into the past with no visible modern improvements for almost its entire length. Once we were through the gate and onto the cattle land, riding in uniform on Todd's properly tacked mounts, we were Rangers scouting for Union patrols!

The first part of our ride was over the land of Ben Lomond. This was a farm that first had been occupied by Isaac Henry and his wife Judith Carter Henry. Judith later moved to Prince William County, where she became the first civilian killed in The War when the Henry house was destroyed during the First Battle of Manassas. At the time of The War, Ben Lomond was owned by the Armistead family. General Walker Keith Armistead died in 1846 and is buried in the family plot on a bluff above the creek. General Armistead was the father of General Lewis Armistead who was killed in Pickett's Charge at Gettysburg. The graveyard is entirely overgrown, but we were able to find the headstone for the father.[1]

The overgrown Armistead family cemetery

Continuing the ride, we forded Gap Run, then turned westward uphill past the ruins of the old Carr place. The fields are fenced much like they were in the 1860s. We traced a path over the crest of the hill where we stopped to view the Winchester Turnpike below. The remnants of a road led uphill to our position from Fleetwood Mill, so we designated this location "Fleetwood Gap." Even here the Rangers had an excellent vantage point for scouting Yankee activities in the Crooked Run Valley.

We about-faced and explored, looking for traces of the road that the map showed to connect with Upperville. The traces were faint but did exist. We followed as best we could back across Gap Run to Carr Lane. A bit of ranging about revealed what looked to be a good possibility. Exploring a few yards up the hill into the trees, we found the evidence we needed: old stone retaining walls spaced about far enough apart for a big wagon to navigate. Eureka!

Definitely overgrown, but not so much we couldn't ride through with minimal effort, the "lost" road ran directly uphill. The map showed the road ran almost straight past Bollingbrook into Upperville. By the time we reached the summit of the hill, a modern fence stopped any further progress. On the other side a lush pasture stretched northward to a copse of trees that stood at the backside of Bollingbrook!

Looking at the backside of Bollingbrook from the summit of our "lost" road

After several minutes of reflection, savoring the moment and maybe a bit of gloating, we turned our mounts to the south and began our return. Before we reached the "Fleetwood Gate" and the modern vehicles, our ride brought us to an outlook. From our vantage point, we could see across the Gap Run Valley and the Ben Lomond fields to our Fleetwood Gap. The clouds parted with sunbeams smiling over all we viewed. We smiled, too, and sat on horseback in quiet contemplation. Mission accomplished! As "Rangers," we sat silently soaking in the glow.

HMR rangers looking over Fleetwood Gap and the Gap Run Valley

Rosenvix

Tromping through the woods and tangling with the wicked Virginia briars is not the best way to spend a day, at least until one actually discovers a "lost" site. This has happened for us on occasion, and then the cuts, bruises, gashes, and sweat are worth the pain. It is not always so foreboding, however.

Rosenvix was the home of Clotilda Carter. After the destruction of his home, Heartland, Ranger Joe Blackwell stayed at Rosenvix, home of his aunt, Miss Carter. At this home, on December 21, 1864, Col. Mosby attended the wedding of Ranger Jake Lavinder and Judith Edmonds, Miss Carter's niece. That evening Mosby was informed that Yankee cavalry was advancing nearby toward Rectortown. Mosby, with Ranger Tom Love, left to investigate. Later that night, Mosby and Love were taking supper at Lakeland, the home of Ludwell Lake, when a shot blasted through the window. Mosby was wounded. The Union patrol did not realize who the wounded soldier was, and Mosby was left to die. Tom Love was taken prisoner.[2] This story is best told elsewhere! Back to Rosenvix…!

Jim Moyer at the ruins of Heartland, Ranger Joe Blackwell's home

On the first trek with Jim Moyer guiding us, he brought us to the ruins of Heartland. This was Joseph Blackwell's home, which had served as a kind of headquarters for Mosby until destroyed by the Yankees in 1864. Heartland was never rebuilt, and today all that remains are the stone foundation walls and chimney. They are surprisingly not much overgrown. The site is beautiful, but now is under private ownership. No trespassing!

Heartland chimney on the left; Big Cobbler Mountain in the right background

After Heartland, we drove about half a mile northward on Rokeby Road (Rt. 623). Jim instructed me to turn in at the sign, "Bear's Den." This was not a moniker I would expect in Mosby's Confederacy. Did Jim have the right place?

We pulled up to a modern house, got out of the vehicle, and approached the front porch. Here's where Jim first demonstrated "Rule 1: Smile and show 'em the book!" A large man (he must be "Bear!") answered our knock. Jim held up *The Guidebook*, and introduced himself. "Bear" listened politely while Jim explained that we would like to explore in the woods to find the ruins of Rosenvix. "Bear" smiled and consented to our request: "No problem!"

So we hiked down the field along the edge of the woods. Jim told how he had located the ruins once, about 15 years previously, but he had a pretty good notion where they were. We poked around in the brush and the brambles. We even improvised a grid system, but after an hour, no luck. We hiked back toward Bear's house and delved into the wilds again. I have to say, the Virginia version of briars is more shredding than anything we have in the Pacific Northwest!

Underneath the brambles it looks suspiciously like a stone wall!

Another hour passed with nary a stone footing. About to toss in the towel, or to grab it to dab the sweat, I noticed something under some brambles that looked suspiciously like a stone wall. Reaching in to lift away the camouflage, I was rewarded with an entire wall! I hailed the other seekers. We basically were surrounding the foundation walls. If we had walked toward each other just a few more steps, we would have skinned our shins on the stonework! Phew! It was a hard-earned victory, but worth it!

In October 2004, we returned to Bear's Den. Steve and Burke had not been to the site, so it seemed like a good idea. I used Jim's approach at the front door, and used "Rule 1." "Bear" did not answer our knock this time. It did not seem appropriate to inquire as to his whereabouts. The woman who answered the door looked at *The Guidebook* in my hand, and listened to our request to look for the ruins of Rosenvix. For a moment she regarded us with a skeptical eye. Perhaps it might be a bit too odd to look for ruins? However, she granted permission, and off we marched. Now it had been less than 15 years since I was here with Jim, so I was feeling quite confident in my ability to take us directly to the ruins.

Do you realize how fast Virginia's briars and brambles can grow in a very few seasons? I had not anticipated that. I assured the guys that we would find the stonework in short order. It was not until an hour later that Steve tripped over something that revealed itself to be a stone footing. It is amazing how difficult it is to locate a large stone object under the protection of nature!

This also provided another example of the benefit of applying "Rule 4: Persistence – and a bit more."

Steve, Burke and the author finally re-discover the ruins of Rosenvix, 2004

St. Bernard

When new reference materials surface from time to time, they serve to jump start research. Renewed energy flows into the journey. Sometimes a key piece of information only jumps out with the second or third reading. I believe that it is a lot like finding an agate on the beach; actually, it calls to you when it is ready to be found.

An example of the agate finding me was in the October 2001 issue of *Blue & Gray Magazine* featuring a splendid article by Horace Mewborn that succinctly described Mosby's late war operations. Included are maps, endnotes, and an especially valuable list of Ranger safe houses (compiled by Hugh Keen). Mewborn's article is so packed with detail that one needs to read and re-read because otherwise interesting items, keys to further research may be overlooked. Something that I did not pick up until a couple of years ago was the discussion of Mosby's boarding at Brookside following the Federals' destruction of Heartland. Mosby's boarding at Brookside was not new information but my memory was refreshed.

Much of the detail for the information on Brookside was provided by Ranger J. Marshall Crawford, who published his memoir, *Mosby and his Men,* in 1867. I like Crawford's book, even though his recollections sometimes are a bit mixed up. He included anecdotes that only Rangers would know - little things like the time near Waterford that Bob Walker, after having had his horse shot from under him, escaped capture by sitting in an apple tree.

Here is the agate. The exciting discovery for me was Mewborn's mention of an "intercepted rebel letter" dated November 28, 1864. The letter confirms Crawford's claim that Mosby moved his headquarters to Brookside with Holland's factory. The letter points out that Mosby also boarded at St. Bernard, Ranger Dick Buckner's home. This was news to me! I had never known about the "rebel letter" before as I had not paid attention through the initial readings of the article. With this new knowledge, the location of St. Bernard became a new priority!

A side note about Brookside/Holland's factory: John R. Holland was a Union man who operated a woolen mill adjacent to his home, Brookside. Mr. Holland had been spending most of his time in Washington City. Whenever his factory had produced a sufficient quantity of wool, Mr. Holland would return with a detachment of Federal soldiers. The wool would be dumped out onto the road, then set on fire. The soldiers would depart, the fire would be extinguished, the burnt wool returned to the factory, and Mr. Holland would subsequently bill the Federal government for the loss of his entire stock. Sometimes the claim was for much more wool than was destroyed. He apparently even bragged about his scam to local folks.

Maybe this Mr. Holland's attempt, on the sly, to do his part to break the North and thereby gain independence for the South.[3]

Brookside – site of Mosby's unofficial headquarters after Heartland was destroyed

Since this was a new development for me, I had to dig for more explicit information about St. Bernard. My wartime map of western Fauquier County identifies some farms, but does not show a location for St. Bernard. Online I found an appendix to a Fauquier County historical sites map. St. Bernard is indicated by a number on the map, and is a little west of Marshall (Salem). Perhaps the folks at the Fauquier Historical Society reference library in Marshall could help?

On the 2015 trek, Don Hakenson and I were driving and exploring. As we approached Marshall, we discussed a book that I had found online: *A Pride in Place.* In the book there was more information on St. Bernard. Don happened to have the book with him. As we entered town, Don read about a connection between the O'Bannon place to the west of town, and the burial site of Ranger James M. Lawrence at Dick Buckner's St. Bernard! Boy howdy! Synchronicity strikes again!

With a quick about turn, we proceeded to the O'Bannon historic marker west of town. Never ones to turn away from a potential discovery, Don and I climbed the gate next to the marker. The old roadbed leading to the O'Bannon place was seriously overgrown. We were fairly confident of success as we both had been to the ruins of the house/gravesite a long time ago. It was not so difficult a path back then!

Overgrown road that leads to St. Bernard ruins and grave of Ranger James M. Lawrence

Don's recollection was that the ruins were located about one hundred yards from the highway. Blazing a trail through the jungle of briars, brambles and poison ivy, we did not find anything resembling our goal. Even using "Rule 5 – Go a little further" did not produce the desired result. After searching to the far tree line, approximately 300 yards, nothing resembling ruins of a house or a graveyard had revealed itself. We reluctantly and with no small amount of puzzlement turned back. We returned to the car scratched, sweaty and determined to apply "Rule 4 – Persistence, and a little more." The search continues!

The Lottery Site

One of the more tragic episodes in the history of Mosby's command is the hanging of his men captured in Front Royal and Mosby's subsequent retaliation. On September 23, 1864, about 120 Rangers under the command of Capt. Sam Chapman attacked a Federal train near Front Royal. Upon perceiving that the Federal column was indeed a full brigade, Chapman attempted to call off the attack and ordered his men to fall back through Chester Gap. Unfortunately, Ranger Capt. Frankland had by this time already engaged the enemy, who then proceeded to challenge the Ranger assault and retreat. A body of Federals under Lt. McMaster attempted to block the Rangers' avenue of escape through Chester Gap. In doing so, McMaster was mortally wounded in the ferocious fighting. All but six of the Rangers fought through superior numbers of the enemy and made a successful, scattered flight to safety.

The Lottery scene by A.V. Erickson

Adding to the calamity of the day, the dying McMaster alleged that he had surrendered before he was shot multiple times and ridden over by the Rangers' horses. Understandably, Yankee emotions ran high. Rather than appropriately being treated as prisoners of war, the six captured Rangers were ordered to be executed by the Union command present in Front Royal. The grim details are told in other sources, but of the six Rangers murdered that day, three were shot and two were hanged. The sixth, 17-year-old Henry Rhodes was a Front Royal resident and was not even officially an enrolled member of Mosby's command. As the Rangers charged through town, young Rhodes grabbed an old horse and joined the melee. Before being executed, Rhodes was dragged through the streets of town tied between the saddles of two Union cavalrymen and taken outside of town and shot. Rhodes's body was delivered to his frantic mother in a wheelbarrow.[4]

The last chapter of this tragic episode occurred November 6, 1864, when Mosby retaliated for the executions of his men in Front Royal. Mosby had determined that it had been Gen. George Custer who sanctioned the executions of the Rangers. Therefore, during the time between the disaster in Front Royal and the beginning of November, Union soldiers from Custer's command who were captured were held prisoner by the Rangers. In addition, another fiasco took place October 13 when Ranger Albert G. Willis was illegally executed by order of Col. Powell near Flint Hill. Mosby was compelled to take drastic action in an attempt to halt the Federals' brutal executions. During the interim, Mosby had received authorization from the Confederate War Department to conduct executions of an equal number of Custer's men. It was hoped that such draconian measures would put a stop to the Federal high command-sanctioned executions.

Between 500 and 600 Rangers met near Rectortown for the drawing of lots to determine which of the prisoners would be executed, measure for measure. A total of 27 men from Custer's brigade were lined up. The drawing was solemnly conducted by Rangers who had no heart for this type of activity. Seven numbered slips were drawn, with those seven to be executed and the others sent south to prison. In an oversight, a Union drummer boy had been placed in the lineup and had drawn a numbered slip. A quick conference determined that the drummer boy would be removed from the lottery, and another drawing would be conducted for the final numbered slip of paper. It was a painful scene to witness.

The condemned men were being led into the Valley under guard of Rangers commanded by Lt. Ed Thomson. The column met Rangers returning with additional prisoners. Capt. Montjoy exchanged one of his captives for one of the condemned men, who happened to be a fellow Mason. The executions were to take place as close to Custer's headquarters as possible. The night was dark and rainy. Thomson selected the spot near Berryville off the Winchester Turnpike. During the ride, one of the prisoners had escaped. Of the six remaining prisoners, three were hanged and two were shot. The sixth man had been able to untie his hands and when Thomson aimed his revolver at the prisoner, the man jumped Thomson, knocking him to the ground and escaping into the darkness.[5]

While extreme and not entirely successful, the executions served to convince Grant and Sheridan to halt further such measures against Mosby's men. The Rangers generally felt that they were not in The War to be executioners and were greatly relieved to be done with that duty.

A piece of the tree used by the Rangers to hang Union soldiers captured from Gen. Custer's command

Because of the extreme nature of this episode, it became a focus of our study. Of course, the Lottery became a priority for our treks. On our first trek, everything seemed to take longer than the itinerary provided. That was a good thing! We learned early on that "Rule 2 – Go with the flow" was going to be the guiding custom for our treks. We met several people on this first trek that had not been anticipated in the planning, so it was dusk by the time of our first entry into Rectortown. Using *The Guidebook* for directions, we found the Woodward Store, a three-and-a-half-story red brick structure now a private residence in the center of the town. Its windows glowed a warm, soft light, except in the one window where a white marble bust of George Washington brilliantly shone out at us. Leaving the Woodward Store, we were not able to discern much more in the way of Mosby sites. We vowed to return in daylight for better results.

The Guidebook is vague about the location of the Lottery site. From the Woodward Store, directions say, "Continue on Rt. 710 for .1 mile. Here the captured Union soldiers drew lots to determine who was to be executed." Following those directions leads to the parking area for the Post Office and a building that looks like it was a store at one time. Our vision of the Lottery was that the prisoners were lined up here and the Rangers were scattered about the immediate area where homes are now situated. It seemed a bit strange that the Lottery would have been conducted so close to the main part of the town.

The Guidebook lists the Rectortown Railroad Station without giving directions to the site. We accidently found the station and the stationmaster's house. At least that's what we believed them to be at the time. It seemed to me that the station would have been a better site for the Lottery to be held. Fewer homes were nearby and no trains were coming through as the Federals had discontinued the campaign to rebuild the Manassas Gap Railroad.

Over the course of many treks, we wavered on the location of the Lottery site between the old store parking area and the RR station. On the 2000 trek we inadvertently broke a cardinal rule of trekking: Respect Private Property! It was nearing the end of another busy day of exploration. We had stopped to contemplate the Lottery episode and to consider the options for the site. Being a bit weary from the long dusty trail, we decided to review the day and discuss matters while resting on the porch of the old store building. I do not recall why it was in my mind that the building was unoccupied. Maybe it had been a feed store, a mercantile or something similar. After several minutes of discussion, it occurred to me that we actually might be sitting on somebody's front porch. Not moving from my comfortable position, but feeling a smattering of guilt, I said, "You know, someone might be inside here wondering, 'What are these people doing on my porch?'" At that very moment, a woman's voice said, "Yes! What are you doing on my porch?"

Yikes! You can imagine our collective shock and remorse! I stammered, "We are following Col. Mosby's trail."

Through the screen door the voice said, "Have you found him?" She could have been irate; could have brought the sheriff; could have brought out the shotgun!

My response was, "No, but we are getting closer. Have you seen him?"

"No, but you better get back on his trail. I will let you know if I see him."

"I apologize for encroaching on your property, and violating your space!"

"Good luck finding Mosby!"

We quickly hopped in the vehicle and exited the scene of our crime. It was an important lesson, cheaply bought, and a lesson not easily forgotten: RESPECT PRIVATE PROPERTY!

Private property! Do NOT do what we did!

The 2015 MHAA Mosby Ride journeyed cross-country to the Lottery site. Our guesses were close, but not quite accurate. The actual Lottery site is removed from the town about a half mile northwest of the post office and nearly a mile north of the RR Station. It is located in a hollow near Goose Creek, not quite visible from the Rectortown Road. It is a relief to finally know where it is. It only took twenty years!

We have not yet found Mosby, but we are getting closer!

A view toward the Lottery Site from Rectortown Road

On our 2015 trek, we stopped at the Rectortown post office. The old building that was the site of our transgression on the 2000 trek, was no longer there, not the slightest trace. Was it ever? We never did see the person behind the screen door - the voice. A ghost from the past? The trekkers on that day will swear it really did happen!

Mosby's Cavern

Another persistent mystery is the existence of "Mosby's Cavern." The cavern is only reported by Virgil Carrington Jones, but mentioned four times in his esteemed book, *Ranger Mosby*. On page 240 in *Ranger Mosby*, a description of the cavern is provided. When a Union trooper's horse crashed through the charred remains of a trapdoor in a burned-out building, stairs leading down were discovered. With the aid of torchlight, troopers went down the stairway and came into a huge cavern. The space was large enough to conceal 200-300 horses. Makeshift stalls had been built. At the far end of the cavern, a narrow opening led to the Shenandoah River. From the outside, the entrance was only wide enough for one horse at a time, and only after wading through three feet of water. Bushes and rocks at the base of a high cliff face disguised the entry as well.

Jones includes three other references to the Rangers being chased by the Yankees only to disappear without a trace at the edge of the river (pp. 170, 185, 200). One time was in the aftermath of the Loudoun Heights Fight. The cavern was purported to be several miles upstream from the confluence with the Potomac River.

If this was indeed a hiding place for the Rangers, why was it never mentioned by Mosby or any of the Rangers? If it was a temporary Ranger hide-out, would there not have been horse equipment, military accouterments, evidence of food and personal items to be found? None were mentioned in *Ranger Mosby*.

The cavern is another minor tale in the Mosby lore, but it is an enigma that has captivated our imagination. Locating the cavern has been a primary objective since the time of our earliest treks. The search has provided interesting adventures.

Our initial research revealed geology for the region that was conducive to cave formations. We learned that there were several spelunker organizations active in the Shenandoah Valley. The most notable caves are the Luray Caverns, a popular tourist attraction. Our target needed to be within a few miles of Harpers Ferry. We were not certain on which side of the river the cave would be located. We also realized that the river course most likely had changed over the intervening 150 years. We knew we faced a bit of a challenge!

On one trek, Steve and I explored the area between the Shenandoah River and Chestnut Hill Road, on foot and through the tangle. There were some towering rock-faced cliffs across the river on the west bank, upriver from Harpers Ferry, but maybe not far enough. There were modern structures sitting above the cliffs. That could have been the location of the burned-out building with the charred trapdoor. Sometime after I had returned to Washington (the state), Steve stopped at a yard sale above the cliff, when he realized where he was in relation to our earlier exploration. He asked the local folks there about a cave, but they could not confirm a site.

Another trek brought us to a site on the opposite side of Harpers Ferry, along the Potomac River. Tom Evans and Don Hakenson guided us to the cave after an elderly local man showed it to them previously. The local man, Frank Angelo denied any relationship with the notable Ranger Frank Angelo, which seemed like too much of a coincidence to me! This was definitely a cave, and Mr. Angelo had it on good authority it was Mosby's Cave! The top of the cave had been blocked off with heavy steel plating. We tried to squeeze through a small opening for a better look inside. We didn't fit. The bottom of the cave was near river level, but it was blocked off by about a 20-foot height of ballast that supported the B & O Railroad tracks. A survey of the land above the cave showed very little sign of structure ruins. Fortunately, no trains came by during our exploration.

Analyzing John Brown's Cave, Harpers Ferry

Mr. Angelo's word aside, this site does not fit the parameters of Lozier's and Jones's description. First, it sits at the edge of the Potomac, not the Shenandoah. Second, I have never read anything to indicate that the Rangers fled in the direction of the cave. Third, the USGS map has the cave identified as "John Brown's Cave" as do several other sources. Caverns exist all over the Shenandoah Valley.

Another time when Steve was talking with a local gentleman about our search for Mosby's Cave, the man seemed well versed on the topic. He said that there is a power substation upstream from Millville. The substation was built over a huge cavern and the power lines run from the dam on the Shenandoah through the cavern. It is sealed off, but it might be the cave we are seeking.

On the next trek, we made it a priority to investigate the dam site. Francesca Edling and her two sons joined us for the exploration. Francesca is in possession of a journal by a Loudoun Heights old-timer whose great-great-grandmother was sister to Mosby's mother. The old-timer mentions Mosby's Cave and knowing where it is located. Francesca is trying to track it down. We found the dam and spillway on the Shenandoah. The water level is high enough along the base of the adjacent cliff that we could not identify the depth or possibility of fissures in the rock for an entrance to the cave. It appears that a crossing of the river could have existed near the dam, so the Rangers could have forded and then ducked into the cave, if it existed. This was our most likely location to date.

Rock face at the dam powerhouse on the Shenandoah, near "Keys Ferry" – Perhaps Mosby's Cavern is here

When we were exploring, looking for the east end of Myers Ford further upstream, we met a local fellow. He was a river guide and claimed to know the location of several caves along the Shenandoah between Keys Switch and Berry's Ferry. As we were not prepared to go river rafting at that time, the idea was filed away for future reference.

Finally, on the 2015 trek, we met Jim Glymph, who lives at Kabletown. Jim is a historian who spent his youth in the Kabletown-Myerstown area. In phone conversations before the trek, Jim acknowledged that he knew Mosby's cavern, and as a lad had seen the cave. Jim told how local homes trying to put in wells would drill through earth and then about 75 feet of air before hitting dirt again. Inside the cavern one could see all the water pipes dropping from the ceiling. Several years ago the local farmers, finally tired of losing their cattle inside the cave, dynamited the entrance closed.

Jim Glymph interpreting Mosby's Cavern and Myers Ford

On the trek, Jim took us down to the river and pointed out the actual location of Myers Ford. Then he showed us where the former entrance to the cave was located. It is on private property, so we could not inspect it close up. It is a distance from the river now, and that can be conceded to the river course changing over time and periodic flooding. It fits the distance requirement, and Rangers riding hard to escape the Yankees could easily scramble across the ford and into the cavern. Now we have a new, best solution to the mystery!

The author with Virgil C. "Pat" Jones

From Jones's end notes, the cavern description is based on a newspaper clipping saved in a scrapbook of Mrs. Elizabeth Iler Fisher of Shreveport, Louisiana. The information in the undated newspaper article was provided by John Lozier of New York, assistant surgeon for the 1st New York Cavalry. Perhaps Lozier's article gave evidence that there was indeed a Mosby's Cavern. When I met Mr. Jones at his home, I was too much in awe of the man to remember to ask him about the cavern. Unfortunately, he passed before I was able to return and interview him regarding the cavern. Mr. Jones had extensive notes kept in ledgers, but they were damaged beyond redemption by a flood in his basement. If I were an ace investigator, I would find John Lozier and/or Mrs. Fisher. Presuming Dr. Lozier was an eyewitness to the cavern, he may have indicated its precise location.

Mosby's Cavern may or may not exist. I am not sure what we will do if the cavern is finally proven to be a reality. Move on to another mystery I suppose. After all, the journey's the thing!

Mosby's Hollow

Mosby lore is replete with intriguing and dramatic incidents. Among my favorite is the tale of Mosby's Hollow. It is another example of Ranger resilience and youthful ability to create entertainment in stressful times. The day was spent scooping up Yankee prisoners in keeping with Mosby's strategies to disrupt Federal supply and communication lines, and to wreak havoc on Union morale.

The only Ranger to describe the episode was John Alexander in his memoirs, *Mosby's Men*, p.106. Various accounts agree that Mosby, with about 80 Rangers, was in the Valley on October 12-13, 1864. They were scouting for opportunities along the Martinsburg-Winchester Turnpike. According to Alexander, the Rangers spent the 13th in "high-rolling sport" on the turnpike. The command was secluded in a convenient wood, while scouts were posted on a nearby elevation. The scouts would report the movement of Yankee squads on the road. Rangers would then advance to the road to meet the enemy and turn them back toward their starting point. The fleeing Federals would then ride into another squad of Rangers at their rear. The intercepted Yankees would surrender and the Rangers would prepare for the next unsuspecting targets to approach on the turnpike. This routine carried on for the greater part of the day until one group of Yankees decided to flee rather than surrender. Alexander and his fellow Rangers chased the Yankees for some distance before finally shooting one and overtaking another. The reason the Federals had spurred away was that they were "Jesse Scouts," Union soldiers disguised as Confederate soldiers – spies, basically, who would be executed as such. The wounded Jesse scout died in Alexander's arms. Alexander said that it was the only wartime death that "left a haunt in my head." It was a sad ending to a day of sporting.

That evening, Mosby marched the Rangers to the rail line near Brown's Crossing, about two miles east of Kearneysville. In the wee hours of October 14, the westbound train was derailed in what became known as the "Greenback Raid."

The Rangers' day of sport is referenced in James. E. Taylor's *Sketchbook*, p.481, in connection with a report by exhausted Federal troopers who had chased the Partisans to "Mosby's Hollow." Taylor describes the hollow as a "secluded woods, in which flowed a Sulphur spring, three miles to the eastward, near Opequon, a favorite rendezvous of the band, when working the pike in this section."

Jordan Springs, the former seminary and one-time resort-spa buildings in the background

The story is captivating. I wanted to locate the mysterious Mosby's Hollow and the elevation used by the Rangers to spot Federal patrols on October 13. A study of old maps showed several springs north of Winchester and east of the turnpike: Helm's, Rocktown, Ross's, and Whetzel's Springs. Only one Sulphur spring showed up, Jordan White Sulphur Springs, which is located about three miles southeast of Stephenson's Depot and approximately five miles northeast of Winchester. We found Jordan Springs on the 2004 trek. Over time, it has been the site of a resort-spa, a seminary and private foundation offices. The current grounds are a peaceful, park-like setting. The surrounding terrain is heavily wooded and it is easy to visualize the Rangers using it as a rendezvous.

We drove up and down the turnpike from Stephenson's Depot to the West Virginia state line in search of a likely candidate for the scouts' elevation. Modern development has not modified the landscape in any significant degree; however, no hill in the area seemed to be high enough to fit the description. After considering that where I come from the east coast notion of mountains falls into our category of hills, maybe even foothills, my expectation for an "elevation" was reexamined.

Burke and the author evaluating the possibilities for "Mosby's Hollow"

What we found were low-lying "elevations" around Helm's Spring, just a stone's throw east of the turnpike and about half a mile south of Stephenson's Depot. We spent some time exploring around the spring and evaluating the merits of the surrounding "elevations." None of the "elevations" around Helm's Spring seem to have enough height for an adequate observation post. Neither Alexander nor Taylor mentions the depot, so we may need to explore into West Virginia for the location of the "elevation," which is fine! We will apply "Rules 4 & 5" and persevere. It is one little mystery that keeps us trekking!

Helm's Spring – watering hole for Rangers' horses – in a possible Mosby's Hollow

An elevation at a possible Mosby's Hollow

Parkins Mill

The Thanksgiving Day Raid was another favorite of reminiscing Rangers. Early on November 24, 1864, William Chapman led a detachment of Rangers looking for opportunities in the Shenandoah Valley. Several Union soldiers were captured and sent back to Fauquier with Ranger Frank Angelo. Mosby and additional Rangers met up with Chapman. Further recon brought the Ranger force into striking distance of a train of Union foraging wagons under guard of infantry and cavalry. Upon eyeing the plum target, the Rangers initiated a spirited attack and chased the Yankees all the way into their camp at Parkins Mill on Opequon Creek.

In the Federal camp that billeted Gen. Tibbets' brigade, the soldiers were leisurely sitting around campfires cooking turkeys and their Thanksgiving meals. The Rangers blasted through the camp disrupting the preparations and gathering a little plunder in the process. Though totally unprepared, the Yankees hastily reacted and in various states of impairment, began a pursuit of the retreating Rangers.

For their part, the Rangers fought a delaying action as they withdrew toward the Shenandoah. It became a lively chase as the Yankees followed closely. The Rangers gave up their captures along the path back to the river. Col. Mosby's young horse became unmanageable when its bit broke. Two Rangers came to the Colonel's aid and they made off safely; however, Capt. Chapman's horse was shot. Ranger John Kirwin gave up his horse to Chapman and jumped on behind another Ranger to escape the fracas. Now you know where Hollywood got the idea for their movies!

After the Yankees gave up the chase near Millwood, and the Rangers lost all their captures, Chapman's horse and Frank Angelo were the only Ranger casualties. Ranger Angelo had not yet reached the river when he encountered the Union squad under Maj. Otis. Angelo lost his prisoners and became a prisoner himself.

Back in the Union camp, under interrogation, Frank Angelo entertained Gen. Tibbets and Maj. Otis with his wit and charm. The Federal commanders decided to send Angelo north to the jail in Martinsburg until he could be transported to the Old Capitol Prison in Washington City; however, a wager was made between Tibbets and Otis. Otis bet a basket of champagne that Angelo would never get to Washington.

Clever Angelo made his escape from the Martinsburg jail the first night and was safely back in Fauquier the next day. Gen. Tibbets lost the bet and I never discovered if he actually paid up.[6]

A side note about Frank Angelo: His Ranger nickname was "Mocking Bird" as he was quite the mimic. He was known to have escaped tight situations by imitating animals. In the dark of night, who could tell that the "pigs" in the swamp were actually a human?

While not a major engagement, the Thanksgiving Day Raid provides a good example of Ranger tactics and a vision of a raid or skirmish. After scouting the target, then deploying the force, one of the Rangers' strengths was in the charge. With regards to the charge, it was considered better to give than to receive. In most Rangers actions, the chaotic struggle seldom lasted more than a few minutes. By then the damage was done and the Rangers would disappear.

It was not until the 2013 trek that I was able to locate Parkins Mill and visit the site. On that day, Don Hakenson and I were studying various sites in the Valley. Don had never been to the site, either. One of the first pearls I learned was how to properly pronounce Opequon, as in the Creek. Oh-PECK-un. It's important to know how to blend in!

It was not difficult to get to the site of the old mill. At first, we approached from the west side of the Opequon. A winding, unpaved road led us to the creek side. Scouting around, we did not see any sign of old mill ruins, nor would we have placed a cavalry camp in the bottomland.

We drove around to the east side of the Opequon, only to find the road down to the creek blocked off. There is a large old-but-refurbished home surrounded by farm fields adjacent to the old mill road. It appeared that folks were home, and as we were not certain who owned the old mill road, we drove up to the home. I approached the door with *The Guidebook* in hand ("Rule 1"), and rang the bell. A woman answered, listened to my speech, and asked me to wait a moment while she went to bring the mistress of the house.

The lady of the house was very receptive to our mission. She informed us that the old mill road was not on their property, so we could hike on down to the creek. Her son and daughter were curious, too, and asked meaningful questions about our trek. We presented SMHS pens and First National Flags to the kids. As Don and I began exploring the old mill road, we could see the mom driving a garden tractor over their fields. The two children, riding in an attached trailer, were holding their new flags high in the wind. The sight of their simulated Ranger charge made me smile!

The old mill road, long out of use, was much overgrown and weather-rutted. The deciduous trees lining the road are "new" growth, 40 or 50 years old at best. So we tried to envision the terrain as mostly treeless at the time of the raid. About a quarter mile of bushing it we found the Opequon. Again, the undergrowth was so thick that we did not see any sign of mill ruins.

The old mill road leading down to the east bank of the Opequon

As we hiked back up the old road, we kept an eye out for potential camp sites. Keeping in mind that Tibbets' camp was brigade size, and that the creek was the only source of water for men and mounts, we decided that the most logical location for the camp would have been in the farm fields around the "big" house on the east side of the Opequon. Also, none of the period accounts mention anything about the Rangers splashing through the creek at any point in the raid. The camp would have been positioned to protect the Federal access to the Winchester-Front Royal Turnpike and to launch patrols to counter Mosby's activities in the Valley. Now that we had a site orientation, the details of the raid become clear! What a sight it must have been!

It was not until after I returned home and was discussing the trek with Steve Boudreau that he informed me that Don and I had been on Todd Kern's property. Our friend's stables are located on the west bank of the Opequon, where the old mill site was. Next time we will stop in for a visit!

Picture Gen. Tibbets' brigade camped in the fields surrounding the "Big House"

There is so much more to learn about Mosby, his Rangers and his Confederacy. Our treks are the path for the mission. Like Susan Sontag said, "I haven't been everywhere, but it's on my list." After all, the journey's the thing!

[1] Chappelear, *Maps and Notes*, pp.4, 6, 17

[2] Williamson, *Mosby's Rangers*, pp.222, 245, 250; Keen and Mewborn, *Regimental*, p. 180; Jones, *Ranger Mosby*, pp.175, 212, 245

[3] Horace Mewborn, "Operations of Mosby's Rangers: Railroad Raids and the End of the War." *Blue and Gray Magazine*. Vol. XIX issue 1, p.20. Columbus, Ohio: October 2001; Crawford, *Mosby and His Men*, p.307

[4] Williamson, *Mosby's Rangers*, pp.239-241; Scott, *Partisan*, pp.317-320; Keen and Mewborn, *Regimental*, pp.175-178; Jones, *Ranger Mosby*, pp.209-212, 222, 226-227

[5] Williamson, *Mosby's Rangers*, pp.288-294; Scott, *Partisan*, pp.356-360; Keen and Mewborn, *Regimental*, pp.209-212; Jones, *Ranger Mosby*, pp.221-228

[6] Scott, *Partisan*, pp.371-373; Keen and Mewborn, *Regimental*, pp.224-225

Chapter Eight: *Mosby Tactics*

Any discussion regarding tactics employed by Mosby and his men rightfully begins with a reference to the many histories of the regiment. For an in-depth review of the record of the 43rd Battalion Virginia Cavalry, recommended would be the published works of modern day authors Keen and Mewborn, Wert, Ramage, and the grand mainspring of contemporary Mosby studies, Virgil C. Jones. Of course, the premier expert on Mosby tactics was the Colonel himself. Mosby's thoughts on tactics were defined in his various writings following his military career.

What is clear about Mosby is that his tactics were ideally directed to achieve his command's mission. The Rangers operated almost entirely within enemy occupied territory to disrupt lines of communication and supply. Usually outnumbered against forces using manuals developed during the Napoleonic wars, the Rangers utilized strategies seen with Francis Marion, the "Swamp Fox," in the American Revolution.

Mosby realized early on that he would need to hit the enemy when and where they least expected it. A Ranger assault normally included only the number of men necessary to achieve the mission. Smaller numbers were more mobile, easier to conceal and fit the surprise mode of the fight. When the battle approached, Mosby and his men believed that it was better to give than receive. A full-tilt skirmish generally was accomplished after several minutes.

Knowing that their encounters with the enemy would usually be close quarter fights, Mosby demanded that his men use revolvers, with a pair of Colts recommended. Although a few instances are noted where a Ranger used a saber, they were basically useless in Ranger-style actions. It is also noted that some Rangers carried carbines as well, which occasionally came in handy. There are frequent references in Federal after action reports about the advantages of the Rangers' revolvers.

Mosby was a fast thinker, quickly responding to the situation in the field. He was a good judge of leadership and selected his officers accordingly. Mosby's men followed him with confidence and it paid dividends on the battlefield.

There are numerous examples of Mosby tactics that demonstrate the uniqueness and success of the Rangers' record, too many to include in this book and outside its scope. Some good examples to pursue in further reading are the Cub Run skirmish, the Herndon Station raid, Miskel's Farm fight, the Five Points fight, Anker's Shop fight, the Guard Hill fight, the Big Poplar fight, the Fairfax Station fight, and the Gold's Farm fight.

The events presented in this chapter are included to illustrate the adventures we experienced in tracking the stories of Mosby and his tactics.

Seneca Mills Fight

The 43rd Battalion conducted several incursions into Maryland. The first came on June 10, 1863, with the official organizing of Company A. Following the signing of papers, the swearing in of men, and the election of officers, the Rangers set out from Rector's Crossroads on the inaugural operation as a formal unit in the Confederate army. The objective was the camp of Union cavalry sitting at Seneca Mills, Maryland.

As the Rangers rode toward the Potomac, darkness came. Their guide got them lost during the night, so they did not reach the river until dawn. Mosby's plan for a night raid was dashed. Mosby sent three Rangers across Rowser's Ford to capture the Union picket. Three more men waded across to reinforce the first detachment. They proceeded up the C&O Canal towpath where they captured additional Yankee troopers and a canal boat. Meanwhile, Mosby brought the remainder of the company across the Potomac.

Alerted by shots fired, the Union guard at the Seneca Locks turned the bridge that crosses the canal. Mosby's men managed to return the bridge to its position, then charged north into the enemy's camp. The Federals fled at the Rangers' attack. The momentum was with the Rangers who were flush with the scent of victory. The Yankees were pursued across a bridge over Seneca Creek. Even though an effort was made to stand their ground, the Yankee resolve melted quickly under the relentless onslaught of the Rangers. After chasing the Federals for about a mile toward Poolesville, the Rangers returned to the Union camp. The abandoned camp was quickly destroyed and the Rangers re-crossed the Potomac with 17 prisoners and 30 liberated horses. Not a bad launching for the new company![1]

One of the first sites we visited on our first trek was the Rector house at Rector's Crossroads (today's Atoka). It was dark and we were not able to see much besides a for sale sign, but we were thrilled because it was the anniversary of the night that Gen. Jeb Stuart stayed there in 1863. That was shortly after Company A was organized in the parlor and nearly two weeks after the Seneca Mills Fight. The Mosby Heritage Area Association (MHAA) offices are in the building now. We have been to the Rector house many times since, visiting and helping with MHAA programs.

At this point, there is no way to positively identify the route taken by the Rangers. We only know they started from Rector's Crossroads and arrived at Rowser's Ford the next morning. I determined a path for us to get to Rowser's Ford. I love the old maps and the ADC Road Atlases! In 2004, with Don Hakenson along, we drove east on the Leesburg Turnpike (Rt. 7) and turned north onto Seneca Road (Rt. 602). At the end of the road we parked the rig and found a trail that led to the Potomac.

The Rector House in the background with its historic springhouse in the foreground

The trail leading to the river was easy going until we came upon a trickle of a waterway. Through the trees and scrub brush on the other side of the water hazard, the Potomac was visible. We were not prepared for wading through swampy creeks that day. Fortunately, there was a mossy log stretched across that we interpreted to be a primitive bridge. One by one, and hoping that the soles of our sneakers would provide solid traction we carefully inched our way across the providently improvised bridge. Unfortunately for Don, his shoes and the mossy log were not compatible. Midway across the bridge, Don's step turned into a fast-dance slip and slide. For a brief moment, it appeared that Don would be saved by an overhanging branch; however, the safety of that possibility vanished with a snap. In a slow-motion ballet, Don and his branch landed in the slimy embrace of the waterway. It was not deep water, but it was cold. Don managed to extricate himself from the mire and continued to the river. Don is a true trooper! He shivered through the rest of the itinerary that day without complaint.

Later, in checking the maps, I discovered that the waterway we had crossed was likely the old channel of Sugarland Run. We had reached the Potomac at the eastern tip of Lowes Island. Rowser's Ford was off to our right as we looked across the river to the Seneca Aqueduct. This is where Mosby and his men crossed the Potomac to attack the Union camp at Seneca Mills!

The day after we located Rowser's Ford in 2004, our itinerary led us into Maryland. Being soaked and chilled at Rowser's Ford the day before did not dissuade Don from joining us again, and we guaranteed no encounters with mossy logs and water hazards. Also, Don was curious about the mill site we had found in 2001. The journey's the thing!

Trekkers studying Rowser's Ford while Don tries to dry out; the Seneca Aqueduct is visible across the river

The Seneca Aqueduct on the C&O Canal; the Union camp was on the far side of the canal and to the right of the creek

After exploring Mosby sites at the Point of Rocks, Adamstown (both raids), Noland's Ferry, Monocacy, and Poolesville, we arrived at Seneca Mills, site of the June 11, 1863 fight. The lockkeeper's house is restored and stores park department equipment. The bridge over the canal is rebuilt, and the aqueduct across Seneca Creek is still functioning as it has since it was built over a hundred years ago. We did not see any canal boats, however.

Seneca lockkeeper's house; the C&O Canal and the bridge over the canal are to the right; the Rangers' approach was from the right side of the house; the Union camp was to the left

The Seneca Aqueduct carries the C&O Canal over Seneca Creek; the bridge over the canal is to the left

Before exploring the possible location of the Union camp, we hiked westerly along the towpath until we came to the path that leads to the red sandstone mill ruins. The former Seneca Stone Cutting Mill might be in ruins and losing the battle with the native flora, but it is an impressive sight. Nothing in our research has indicated Mosby activity at the mill itself.

Exploring the ruins of the Seneca Stone Cutting Mill

The mill was a major operation for many years, including 1863

At the time of our explorations, we were not aware of the history of the mill. Until we determined its function, the mill remained a mystery. Eventually, we learned that the mill produced building material. Red sandstone was quarried nearby and processed in the mill. Stone from the mill was used in constructing the Smithsonian "castle," as well as the aqueducts, locks and adjunct buildings for the C&O Canal, and many other buildings in the area.

Following a satisfying survey of the mill ruins, we hiked back to the aqueduct and the Seneca locks. From this position, we could see Virginia across the Potomac and Rowser's Ford. It was an easy leap to visualize Mosby's men advancing up the towpath to where we then stood the subsequent gunfire, and the retreating guard turning the canal bridge. Thankfully, the bridge stood in place for us and we advanced toward the Union camp as we imagined the Rangers might have done in 1863, minus the deadly firefight!

Looking easterly across the Potomac from Seneca Locks; Rowser's Ford is on the far side center moving to the left

Unless some local folks have metal-detected and determined the location of the camp, it could have been anywhere to the right of the path that leads up to the highway (Rt. 112) and Poole's General Store. A modern bridge crosses over Seneca Creek just south of the store. Without knowing the history of the bridge, one might believe the old road would have crossed a bridge at or near the same place. There is definitely an old road that runs roughly parallel to and north of the modern highway. It would have run directly past the store.

Looking at where the old road crosses Seneca Creek; the modern bridge abutment can be seen beyond in the center of the creek; Poole's General Store is uphill to the right

South, across the old road from Poole's is the site of another old mill: Darby's Mill. North, behind Poole's feed store, is the site of a grist mill. Looking now one might be surprised to realize this intersection was an important center of commerce at one time!

According to the various accounts of the fight, the Union troopers retreated on the old road, now River Road. The Rangers gave chase for about a mile, returned to the Union camp, completed their mission and re-crossed the Potomac into Virginia. It took us two days, but once we walked the ground, the Seneca Mills Fight became clear.

We were fortunate to be able to time our 2005 trek to coincide with the annual SMHS Mosby Tour. Tom Evans, Don Hakenson and Gregg Dudding were the tour leaders. I arranged to attack the tour bus at the Seneca Locks. At the appointed time, the bus pulled up to the lockkeeper's house. From our concealed positions, we launched the ambush. Don had to convince the bus driver that it was all part of the show before he was willing to open the bus door! Once on board, we attempted to relieve the tourists of the burden of their greenbacks and watches, but the entire assembly was satisfied to maintain possession of their encumbrances. After a good bit of fun verbal exchanges, we all dismounted and Don asked me to do the interpretation of the fight. I must confess to being nervous. To be on the stage for my mentors and their audience was an exemplary honor!

Catlett's Station Raid

In the spring of 1863, Gen. Stuart suggested to Mosby that the Rangers could do some damage to the Union campaign by harassing the Orange and Alexandria Railroad. Maj. Mosby suggested to Gen. Stuart that the Rangers could indeed do as the General asked if they were in possession of an artillery piece. Arrangements were made to address the request.

On May 29, the Rangers assembled at Patterson's Mill south of Middleburg. Much to their amusement, there sat a two-and-a-half-inch mountain rifle. According to Ranger John Munson, the men thought that "it was too big to fit into a holster, but too small to be called a cannon." Because Sam Chapman had previously served in an artillery unit, he was detailed to drill a few men to become the cannon crew.

Patterson's Mill was located near this site at the confluence of the Little River and Barton's Creek

After a few hours of drill, the crew was deemed sufficiently ready. With fifteen rounds of ammunition loaded on the limber, Mosby led the command south and east to camp near the O&A rail lines. In the morning, Rangers were sent out to scout a suitable spot to attack the train. The selected point was about a mile north of Catlett's Station near the home of Squire Stone.

The Rangers derailed the train and Sam Chapman's crew fired rounds, first into one of the cars and then into the engine, causing the boiler to explode. This attack was not exactly subtle with Union camps within a mile in both directions! The Yankee guard and crew fled into nearby woods. The Rangers proceeded to ransack the cars, taking whatever appealed, and set torches to the cars. Knowing that they needed to retire with speed, the Rangers did their grand skedaddle.

The 5th NY and 1st VT cavalry pursued the Rangers in what became a hotly contested running fight. The Rangers plotted a course northwesterly, and planned to unlimber the gun and toss a round when Mosby felt the Yankees got a bit too close. Finally, in a lane near Grapewood Farm, Sam Chapman set the mountain rifle at the top of the lane. With the high-banked sides, the sunken lane forced the Federal attackers to advance in closed files, four abreast. The Yankees charged several times, only to be repulsed with point-blank canister rounds. At last the little rifled gun ran out of ammunition. The last charge by the Yankees was met with Sam Chapman defending the gun with the rammer.

At the last moment Mosby escaped along with Fount Beattie, George Turberville and the rest of the unwounded Rangers. Sam Chapman was seriously wounded but eventually recovered, Richard Montjoy was captured, and the Englishman, Bradford Smith Hoskins, was mortally wounded.[2]

When Gen. Stuart received word of the skirmish, he remarked that Mosby could sell a gun for such a high price anytime. Mosby was able to procure additional artillery pieces periodically, and in the summer of 1864 he formed an artillery company. Knowing that Mosby had artillery options put a further twist in the anxiety knots of the Federal command in northern Virginia. The Point of Rocks Raid, the Mt. Zion Church Fight and the Berryville wagon Raid are several examples where Mosby employed his artillery to good effect. While Mosby was engaged in the Greenback Raid and its aftermath, the Yankees captured four of the battalion's guns that had been hidden on Cobbler Mountain. In November 1864, the artillery company was disbanded and reorganized as Company G.

On several treks, we attempted to locate the site of the Catlett Raid. Based on field study and research, we identified two possible locations. We decided the key would hinge on being able to positively place the house of Squire Stone, which has been elusive so far! We have not taken Don Hakenson or Tom Evans to our tentative site, and they may have the definitive answer on a future trek.

For the interim, we looked at a site off of Gaskins Lane and another off Dumfries Road. The Dumfries Road location is generally accepted as the site of Squire Stone's house. There are modern – 20th century modern – structures in place near the junction of the road and the tracks. While the terrain features may have been modified through intervening farming practices, they do not quite fit the various accounts of the raid. Also, it is over two miles to Catlett's Station whereas the descriptions indicate "about a mile." The Rangers' exit route would have been shorter from this site, however.

The traditional site of the Catlett's Raid is a hundred yards from this point; the cannon would be on the left

A view of the field where the cannon would have been deployed; RR tracks are to the right; the traditional site

Alternate site for Catlett's Raid off of Gaskins Lane; Catlett's Station is about 0.6 mile to the west around the bend

Possible site of Squire Stone's home on Gaskins Lane; ruins are in the trees; tracks are to the right

We favor the Gaskin Lane option at the site for the Catlett Raid for several reasons. First, the terrain at Gaskin Lane is closer to the description in the accounts we have studied. Second, the elevation is more advantageous for the placement of the mountain rifle. Third, there are structural ruins near the junction of Gaskins Lane and the railroad tracks. Fourth, across the farm fields to the northwest is a clear avenue of escape. And last, on the

NW side of Rt. 28 there are signs of an old road that would have connected to the Burwell Road (Rt. 604) at that time.

We understand the Rangers were in a grand skedaddle, meaning that each man made his escape as best he could. Mosby did manage to rally some of the Rangers to act as a rear guard and to delay the Federal pursuit. Those Rangers traveled along Burwell Road. We followed that route until it met Fitzwater Drive (Rt. 652), where we turned left. Fitzwater Drive comes to a "T" at Rogues Road (Rt. 602) with Vint Hill Farm across the intersection. Today one must turn left here onto Rogues Road and drive a short distance before a right turn onto what was then Grapewood Lane. We found evidence of an old roadbed a little before reaching the "T." It made sense to us that retreating Rangers with Yankees hot on their trail would not stop at the sign and then turn left. The original road had to lead directly into the lane. From our experience as rangers on horseback, it also seemed that fleeing to Greenwich, as some accounts report, would make less sense than a more direct route to the Grapewood Lane. We are not certain, just saying….

On our 2005 trek, our Sam Chapman and Fount Beattie reenacted the final stand – sort of….

Burke Nebeker (Fount Beattie) and Dave Surowiec (Sam Chapman); the cannon placement was to their right, aimed down the lane

The location of Patterson's Mill, where the Rangers were introduced to the mountain rifle, remained a mystery until the 2015 trek. It was actually not so difficult a task as I had anticipated. Combining readings from Scheel's historic Fauquier County map; the ADC road atlas; the USGS Middleburg, VA map; and the *Regimental History*, Patterson's Mill site is precisely where it should be, southeast of Middleburg on the Barton's Branch of the Little River. We were able to drive to it directly without getting lost even once!

The epilogue to the Catlett Raid story is the fate of the little bronze mountain rifle that was captured at Fitzhugh's Grapewood Lane. After The War, the 5th NY post of the GAR purchased the gun. In 1872, the post cut two inches off the barrel to make a key to the city for a visiting dignitary. The old gun is now on display in the 45th Infantry Division Museum in Oklahoma City, Oklahoma.

Mosby's first cannon on display in the Oklahoma City museum

The Greenback Raid

One of the favorite raids among Mosby's men became known as the Greenback Raid. In the wee hours of October 14, 1864, the Rangers de-railed a westbound train on the Baltimore & Ohio line a few miles east of Kearneysville, WV.

Deep into Yankee controlled territory, the raid was consistent with Mosby's mission to disrupt the enemy's line of communications and to cause chaos within the Federals' area of operations. The results of the derailing were celebrated in the Confederacy. The engine was destroyed, the cars were burned, Union soldiers were captured, but most importantly, widespread panic and dismay swept the north.

The Rangers swept down from their hiding site above the cut to quickly empty the nine cars of passengers and anything of value. Among the crowd were two Union Army paymasters who were promptly relieved of their burdens. Over $170,000 in greenbacks were taken back to Loudoun County where the money was divided among the participating Rangers the next day at Ebenezer Church in Bloomfield. Each man received around $2100, a princely sum in those days. It also explains why in the months afterward many of the Rangers were finely attired.[3]

It is not my purpose to re-tell the details here. The reader may refer to the many excellent accounts written by others. See V.C. Jones, J.J. Williamson, J.W. Munson, Keen & Mewborn, and Col. Mosby. There are many accounts, varying in interpretation, but all are entertaining.

Because of the fame of the Greenback Raid, and because it provides a clear example of the effectiveness of Mosby's tactics, it was another site/story that commanded our interest. Using *The Guidebook* we attempted to locate the site on our first trek.

Quincy's Siding west of Brown's Crossing, B & O RR

The Guidebook got us to Brown's Crossing, and we hiked along the tracks 200 yards west to what we believed to be Quincy's Siding; however, the terrain did not fit the descriptions in the various accounts. The land fell away from the tracks into low fields of crops instead of being a cut through the rolling farmland that surrounded the area. The accounts describe the derailing taking place where the tracks passed through a deep cut. The Rangers waited above the cut for the train to arrive, where the engine fell over against the bank of the cut.

For many of our early treks, we re-visited Quincy's Siding trying to find ways to make it fit the accounts. I even knocked on doors of houses sitting near Brown's Crossing, asking if this truly was Brown's Crossing and if that was Quincy's Siding 200 yards to the west. The only responses were blank expressions and "I dunno." But we kept coming back each trek. Finally, it occurred to us that we should apply "our rule 5 – When you can't find the place: go further." It's a pretty good rule and has paid off many times, including here.

On a later trek, Steve, our unit's sergeant and "Big Yankee" Ames, hiked another quarter mile west and found the missing cut! Go further! There we found the rail line running through a deep cut. Clambering up the cut, we could see a copse of trees a short distance to the south where Cab Maddux would have stood guard over the mounts with a couple other Rangers while the plundering of the train proceeded. At least it was a vision in our minds that helped convince us that we had located the actual derailing spot.

The Rangers used the cut visible in the distance as the site for their attack

The cut was approachable by driving further west than Brown's Crossing (Go further!). Easy access was by a dirt track across a farm field next to a home off the highway. We were pleased with our progress, and on our next trek we brought Don Hakenson to the cut for his input. Until Don could conclusively verify information, his usual response would be, "It's possible." When we showed him the cut, smiling, he said, "You just might be right! It all fits!"

To the best of our knowledge no one before had made this connection for the raid site. A trek or two later I met a fellow in Harpers Ferry and described what we do and our theory about the raid site. He explained that he had grown up in the Harpers Ferry-Charlestown area and knew the farmer who owned the land at the cut.

The rumor was that during the raid a Ranger had dropped a box containing gold coins. Sometime in the past, the farmer had given permission to a man to metal detect over the ground near the cut. Several gold coins were recovered. Because of their dates, the thought was the coins were connected to this raid. Reportedly a dispute over the recovered treasure ended the farmer's future cooperation. I have not yet found any more to verify the gold coin story but "it's possible!"

Trekkers hiking to the top of the cut where the Rangers would have been waiting – the RR tracks are to the right

After showing Don our site for the raid, he began to take his Mosby bus tours there. On one occasion, he brought a group of National Guard officers to the site as part of a Mosby Staff Sortie. The aggregate members agreed with our interpretation. Don said he had already accepted that this is the "true" location of the Greenback Raid, but with the endorsement of the military strategists, there was no question. Now on his Mosby bus tours, Don announces that this is the site of the Greenback Raid and that it was brought to his attention by these guys from Washington State, "And, I agree with them!"

Looking toward the woods to the south, from the top of the cut where the Rangers left their horses under guard

Unfortunately, a few years ago the state built a freeway through the site. At least the southern portion of the cut, the Mosby part, was removed. Only our photos remain to show an important location in the Mosby lore. The message for me is that it is imperative that we continue to preserve the past before it falls to progress and modern development.

We were distraught to see "they" built a freeway through it!

Manassas Gap Railroad Campaign

As the Federal army under Gen. Sheridan advanced up the Shenandoah Valley, the supply line grew longer and more susceptible to Confederate incursions. Chief among the Union's antagonists in this arena were Mosby and his Partisan Rangers. With his ranks steadily expanding, Mosby was able to keep almost steady pressure on the Federals in the Valley from mid-1863 on. Almost at will the Rangers repeatedly and successfully attacked Union patrols and wagon trains and gathered valuable reconnaissance. To the Yankees, it seemed no patrol was large enough to keep Mosby's men at bay.

On August 12, 1864, over 500 supply wagons made up a convoy on its way to Sheridan from Harpers Ferry. The convoy was guarded by three regiments of infantry and some cavalry strategically interspersed among the wagons. The train stretched into a long, slow, dusty spectacle, often with wide gaps in the line of wagons. About a mile north of Berryville, the segments of the train pulled into a field, a wagon park, off the turnpike to water, feed and rest the teams, teamsters and guard. Throughout the night and into the morning of the 13th, wagons rumbled into the park, unhitched, re-hitched, and rolled on toward Winchester.

Mosby was in the Valley near Berryville with about 350 Rangers. As dawn approached, his scouts returned with confirmation of the supply train. Mosby deployed two squadrons with one regiment held in reserve to support the artillery. They had brought two howitzers, but one broke a wheel en route and was unserviceable. As the Rangers in the gun crew set the cannon in position, they were attacked by an army of hornets whose nest was disturbed by a wheel of the gun. The gunners quickly recovered their piece and set up in a position far away enough that the hornets were no longer interested in pursuing. A good thing! The third round from the cannon was to be the signal for the Rangers to initiate the attack.

The cannon was set on a hill about 200 yards across the turnpike and creek from the wagon park. Due to the early morning fog drifting over the creek and the pike, Mosby's deployments were not noticed by the Federals. The thunderous cannon shots caught the Yankees entirely off guard, momentarily causing a frozen shock in the wagon park. When the Rangers charged into the train, chaos reigned and most of the Union soldiers fled. A lightning strike caused shock and awe among the teamsters and the few Union soldiers who remained offered weak resistance.

As with most Ranger operations, the attack evolved quickly. Rangers unhitched teams, leading 10-12 mules or horses together. Wagons were plundered, then set on fire. In short order, the Rangers were pointed back to Loudoun County. The Rangers conducted their own raucous, dusty train, a cacophony of braying mules, bellowing cattle, moaning prisoners, and jubilant Rangers. One can imagine Sheridan's reaction to the report about the attack and the loss of 75 wagons burnt, over 500 mules and horses and more than 200 head of cattle lost, and approximately 200 prisoners taken.[4]

An interesting story about the Raid is told by Samuel S. Moore in *Through the Shadow: A Boy's Memories of the Civil War in Clarke County*. Young Sam witnessed the Raid from his family home located on the corner of Buck Marsh Road (Rt. 340) and the Winchester Turnpike (Rt. 7). The Union supply wagons coming south from Harpers Ferry made a sharp right turn at the corner where the Moore house stood, then headed west toward Winchester. When the Ranger attack commenced, many of the teamsters left their wagons on the road. Some wagons crashed in the chaos of the melee.

An 11-year old Samuel Moore watched the Berryville Wagon Raid from the back porch of this house

Sam and two of his young comrades were recruited by Rangers to help un-hitch the teams and torch the wagons. Sam also tells how one of the wagons near his house was loaded with barrels. At first the boys were not much interested, but soon townsfolk came out of their homes to liberate whatever treasures they could find among the ruined wagons. It turned out the barrels in question were full of sugar, a substance not available in town for some months. The sugar wagon was soon emptied of its burden. Sam's family ended up with a full barrel thanks to the kitchen servant.

When the Yankees came around following the cessation of the Raid, they made it clear that anyone found with plunder from the wagons would suffer dire consequences. The clever servant in Sam's home emptied the contents of the barrel into a pantry bin, broke up the barrel for fuel in the kitchen stove, and then demurely returned a bag full of sugar to the Yankees with an apology. Hard times demand tough measures![5]

The Berryville Wagon Raid influenced the Federal command's decision to re-build the Manassas Gap Railroad. It would provide a shorter supply line from the Washington City supply depots to Sheridan in the Valley. The main drawback would be that the line needed to be constructed through the middle of Mosby's Confederacy. The construction crews needed to be protected by a heavy guard. At the beginning of October 1864, the Federals commenced efforts to re-establish the Manassas Gap Railroad.

On October 3, Mosby's attacks greeted the advance work details on the east side of the Bull Run Mountains near Haymarket. For most of the month, the Rangers were constantly in the saddle harassing the Union endeavors, not just along the Manassas Gap line but also in the Valley. The Gray Ghost seemed to be everywhere!

Looking east across Salem toward the rail line from Mosby's artillery position on Stevenson's Hill

Advancing into Salem on October 5, Mosby deployed two howitzers on Stevenson's Hill. With 200 Rangers pushing through town toward the Union camp, the artillery opened fire. The Yankees determined that an immediate withdrawal was the prudent course of action. The Rangers plundered and then destroyed the abandoned Union camp.

Over the next several days, the Rangers kept up continuous attacks to delay the Federal construction crews. Mosby made good use of his artillery pieces with constant shelling of the track and the Union camp and entrenchments around Rectortown.

With every assault by the Rangers, the Federals increased the number of troops to defend the track construction. The Rangers in turn carried out clever tactics to impede the Yankees. On one occasion the Rangers dislodged a few rails and allowed a train to pass slowly with Union infantry marching along beside the cars. After the train had passed, the Rangers fired into the rear car, which induced the engineer to throttle to full steam ahead, and into the loosened rails and destruction.

With the Rangers constantly badgering the railroad guard and crews, progress was slow, but the Federals were determined and resorted to extreme measures to counter Mosby's efforts. The Yankees began placing captured Rangers, then local civilian prisoners in the cars to dissuade attacks by the Rangers. The strategy failed to achieve the desired results.[6]

When planning the project at the end of September, the Federals had estimated it would take two days to complete the track from Thoroughfare Gap to Piedmont, approximately twenty miles. It did not get completed. By the end of October, the Federal command ordered cessation of the project. Of all Mosby's wartime accomplishments, he believed the most important strategically was the prevention of the rebuilding the Manassas Gap Railroad.[7]

Our exploration of the Manassas Gap Railroad Campaign took us from the train depot in Rectortown, to the artillery position on Stevenson's Hill, to the Plains and Thoroughfare Gap in the Bull Run Mountains. On different treks, we were guided by Jim Moyer, Tom Evans, or Don Hakenson. A lot of exploration was carried out on our own.

We were with Jim on our first visit to Stevenson's Hill. From the position of Mosby's howitzers, we could make out the location of the railroad tracks. By peering through the distance across the village, the grain elevators could be seen standing next to the original depot. Jim told us that somewhere on the Stevenson property there was an artillery round embedded in rock. The property was vacant and for sale at the time. We felt comfortable searching for the rock, but a cursory search revealed nothing. Perhaps it was merely another Mosby legend?

A legend that has gained traction in Salem (today's Marshall) concerns the "Frye House." Located on Main Street east of the intersection with the Warrenton Road, John Frye's house became the recipient of an errant round fired from Stevenson's Hill. The cannon ball crashed through the roof and landed in the Frye's kitchen. The story tells how John retrieved the unexploded round and tossed it out his front door into a group of marching Union soldiers. Quickly realizing the potential hazard of the situation, the Yankees broke ranks and skedaddled in every direction. Nothing in the legend indicates whether or not the round ever detonated, but the image of marching soldiers suddenly inspired to scramble by the appearance of the cannon ball brings a smile. The Frye House survived the ravages of war and it eventually it became a low-key tourist attraction. Alas, the house was gone by the 2015 trek, a victim of old age, neglect and/or or modern development.

We wanted to visit Rawlingsdale, a farm located to the west of Rectortown. There on October 7th, Mosby placed four cannon and commenced shelling from the farm's rolling elevation to the tracks below and to the Union fortifications around Rectortown. Rawlingsdale was also known for horse races, hence a popular Ranger hangout. The farm is privately owned, so we have not yet conducted a field study.

Another study on the back burner is to locate the Union camp and fortifications at Rectortown. The one person who most likely knew the answers, John K. Gott, has passed on, may he rest in peace. I had discussed several research topics with John, but my research had not yet reached Mosby's railroad campaign.

During this time, the Rangers were constantly active in their pursuit to carry out Gen. Lee's order to disrupt the railroad construction. Another interesting event occurred October 11 near The Plains. Mosby, with Company D, was again harassing the track-laying crews and their guard. Concealing the greater part of the Rangers in the forest on Whitewood Farm, Mosby led a dozen of his men toward the Union cavalry camp. Upon seeing the Rangers, the Yankee troopers quickly mounted their horses to engage the enemy. Mosby and his men rode into the woods for better cover from the Yankee carbine fire. Believing the Rangers were fleeing, the Federals gave chase. By this time in the conflict, the Yankees should have learned that Mosby was the master of the "bait and switch" strategy. With the Yankees in hot pursuit, Mosby about-turned his men and charged the Union cavalrymen. The Yankees broke and fled back to their camp. In the midst of the foray, Mosby's horse was shot and fell, pinning the Colonel's leg. The Rangers continued the fight while a few formed a cordon around their leader until he could gain his release. It was another close call![8]

We have attempted to find the location of this event. We have identified the Whitewoods Farm property, but without more precise information the event could have taken place anywhere over several hundred wooded acres. It will help narrow the search when we find the location of the Federal camp.

Whitewood Farm fields and woods – possibly where the October 11, 1864 skirmish took place

Oakley - the Dulany Farm Fight

Oakley Farm is an amazing site! Located on rolling hills and scattered woods south and east of Upperville, it sits adjacent to the Upperville Horse and Colt Show. The property has been in the Mellon family for several decades. Today, it even boasts its own airport, but that's not our main interest here.

In 1857, Oakley Farm had been purchased by Henry "Hal" Grafton Dulany and his wife, Mary Eliza "Ida" Powell Dulany from his cousin, Richard Henry Dulany of Welbourne. At that time, Oakley encompassed over 800 acres and, in the manner of the time, was a self-sufficient agricultural enterprise. Hal (27) and Ida (25) were young parents of three children when the hostilities commenced in 1861. Hal joined his cousin Richard's unit, the Dulany Troop, as an officer. The Dulany Troop was incorporated into the 6th Virginia Cavalry. After Hal went to the cavalry training camp in Ashland, he was not home much until the end of The War. Young Ida was left to raise the children, care for her extended family, maintain the household, and manage the farm on her own. By all accounts, Ida did well keeping everything together during a most difficult time. To learn her story and the hardships suffered at Oakley, it is recommended to read her journal, *In the Shadow of the Enemy*, published by the University of Tennessee Press, 2009.

The Oakley Farm manse faces north toward the Ashby Gap Turnpike (Rt. 50)

Our interest in Oakley is because of a fight here on October 29, 1864. In Mosby lore, the action here is usually known as the "Dulany Farm Fight." The accounts will vary, but the basic outline suggests a fight that should not have happened. Walter Frankland, Captain of Company F, and about 100 Rangers were following a force of about 200 from the 8th Illinois Cavalry. At the Goose Creek Bridge on the Ashby Gap Turnpike, Mosby left Frankland with instructions for the Rangers to continue toward Rectortown and to set up an ambush like they had successfully done earlier at Dranesville. Mosby rode on to Green Garden Farm to raise more Rangers for the fight. They were just leaving Green Garden Farm with Dolly Richards when they heard gunfire off to the southeast. Mosby and Richards arrived at Oakley after the damage had already been done.

What they found was that the 8th IL had been aware of the Rangers following and the troopers were taking appropriate measures. Frankland had spotted the 8th IL setting up a defensive position around the Oakley house. Rather than scouting the ground, Frankland determined to attack. He divided his force. There would be no surprise element.

Lt. Ab Wrenn, with about 70 men, attacked the Yankee front, while Lt. Grogan hit the Yankee flank with about 30 Rangers. Several problems developed from the start. Wrenn was charging across about a mile of open ground into the Federal position on high ground at the house. The Yankees were armed with Spencer repeating carbines. Well-aimed, rapid volleys from the Federal lines halted Wrenn's charge almost immediately. Meanwhile, Lt. Grogan's detachment encountered a surprise in the form of a deep ditch with steep sides and then a stone fence before they could even face the Yankees. Wrenn's Rangers had been repulsed, badly damaged, before Grogan tried to attack the Federal flank. By then, the Yankees were able to focus their fire on Grogan's Rangers to devastating effect.

After the fight at Loudoun Heights, the Dulany Farm Fight was Mosby's most grievous defeat. According to John Alexander, "We selected our ground and then failed to know it, and that ignorance was fatal to us." The Rangers' loss was significant, but it could have been much worse. Mosby relieved Frankland of command and never forgave the man.[9]

The Dulany Farm Fight demanded our attention. Mosby's defeats were few. We were curious about the ground and how Frankland could have believed his hastily conceived attack could hold promise of success. Mosby believed Frankland was driven by a quest for glory. Was a victory against the intrepid 8th IL really possible? A field study was definitely on our list of required sites.

The Oakley Farm manse as seen from the west

Until we had a number of treks under our belt, we merely drove by the entrance to Oakley. We were conscious of the privacy of the owners and respected their property rights. The house is not visible from the turnpike. The long driveway, bordered by groomed lawns, is imposing, and we really wanted to get closer. Finally a trek presented us an opportunity. There were workers busy the length of the drive. It appeared that vehicles were moving in and out. There was no sign posted to stay out, so we drove in close enough to see the house. It was an impressive structure, a kind of rusty pink in color. Was that the historic shade? It seemed rather modern to me. We snapped photos then scooted back out.

We still had not been able to find the field of the fight. So on the following trek we bravely drove in as far as the sign that pointed to the farm manager's office. We proceeded further and turned into the office parking area. Rather than all of our crew piling out when we might not be allowed to stay, Don and I went into the office. The farm manager was not present, but we explained our request to look over the field where the charge occurred. As long as we were not a tour bus, he did not seem too concerned and told us to go ahead. Back at the minivan, the jubilant trekkers climbed out. We walked across the parking area to a fence that bordered the field we suspected was the battle site. As the six of us were studying notes, snapping photos, and discussing the merits of the ground, a vehicle drove up to the office. A woman stepped out and strode into the office. I glanced over my shoulder and could see a heated conversation zipping between the foreman and the woman. I recall wondering what could be the big issue; maybe a domestic dispute?

It did not take long to find out the reason for the heated exchange. The foreman came marching up to me, with a flushed and pinched facial expression, and said, "You need to leave! Now!" I inquired why? "I did not realize you had a tour group. The manager said you need to go. NOW!" Naturally, we were a bit perplexed, but made a hasty departure.

Later that week, while sitting in the Welbourne parlor, we were reviewing with Nat Morison some of our adventures. When I told him about getting kicked out of Oakley, Nat chuckled and said, "Why didn't you tell me you wanted to go there? My cousin is the farm manager!" Yes, why indeed!

On the very next trek, I asked Nat to smooth our way into Oakley to be able to actually walk out on the fields to study the ground. He assured us it was cleared. On the appointed hour, we drove right in – we had permission! – and parked at the manager's office as we had the year before. Nat's cousin greeted us cordially. Reminded of our indecorous departure the previous year, she said, "You did not mention you were friends of Nat's!" Once again, Nat came to the rescue!

Even with modern, superficial changes to the setting, it is easy to visualize the fight. What still does not make sense is why Frankland ordered the charge. It was contrary to proven Ranger tactics. Notwithstanding the physical obstacles hidden on the Yankees' flank, a frontal assault across the long expanse of open ground runs contrary to established Ranger tactics. At this point in The War, frontal assaults in general had become outmoded. Unless long-lost letters of Walter Frankland surface someday, we may never fully understand his motivation on that day at the Dulany farm.

Oakley Farm fields over which the Rangers charged into the guns of the 8th Illinois Cavalry

Myerstown Fight

From the beginning of our journey, the Myerstown Fight was a captivating example of the effectiveness of the Rangers. The fight occurred November 18, 1864, in Jefferson County, West Virginia, south of Charlestown. By this time, Mosby's command had grown to seven companies, able to actively attack Yankee positions over a wide region. To facilitate his operations, Mosby had built a cadre of officers, each man carefully selected for his courage and ability to think quickly through the chaos of battle. On any given day, Rangers could be attacking points from Alexandria to Winchester, VA, and from Poolesville, MD to Warrenton, VA. This amplified the legend of Mosby as the Gray Ghost: he was here, there, everywhere! As Melville's epic poem, *The Scout Toward Aldie*, timorously lays out, "…as glides the seas the shark, Rides Mosby through green dark…!"

During 1864, Mosby conducted a series of actions to help counter the Federal advance up the Shenandoah Valley, the "bread basket of the Confederacy." The Union forces were under the command of General Phillip Sheridan, who became increasingly frustrated by Mosby's activities. Mosby had been a persistent thorn to Sheridan's Valley Campaign, inflicting critical defeats, from the no-shot-fired capture of Duffield Station on the B & O rail line to the "no mercy" rout of Custer's "barn-burners" in Col. Morgan's Lane. Mosby's attack on the Union's supply wagon train at Berryville caused Sheridan to pull his lines back toward Harpers Ferry.

Buck Marsh Spring; the wagon park was in field beyond the trees

Mosby's artillery was posted on the hill; fired across the Winchester Turnpike into the wagon park

In response, Sheridan fielded a company of scouts, 100 handpicked men, armed with Spencer carbines to "clean out Mosby's gang." Under the command of Richard Blazer, these scouts proceeded to track the Rangers. On September 4, 1864, Blazer's Scouts surprised an element of Company A of Mosby's battalion at Myers Ford on the east side of the Shenandoah, soundly defeating the lounging Rangers.

Of course, this stung the Rangers. They were used to inflicting the damage; however, over the next few months the Rangers continued to pursue their harassment of the Union forces occupying northern Virginia. The Scouts and the Rangers played cat and mouse without much actual contact. That changed suddenly on November 16, when Blazer's men hit Company D of Captain Montjoy's Rangers who were returning to Loudoun from a raid near Berryville, VA. The Scouts attacked near Clay Hill, the residence of Frank Whiting. A running fight with the Rangers continued to The Vineyard, the residence of John Estes Cooke. The Rangers briefly rallied before withdrawing to Loudoun County via Berry's Ferry. Blazer's Scouts had gotten the bulge on the Rangers, again.

Clay Hill, where Blazer's Scouts met the Rangers in a running fight

The fight ran down this road 2-3 miles to The Vineyard

It now became clear that the Scouts and the Rangers could not occupy the same territory. When Mosby heard of this latest episode, he sent Captain Dolly Richards across the Shenandoah with Companies A and B to eliminate the troublesome Scouts. Several Rangers reported that Colonel Mosby salted his order with some rather disparaging remarks about their manhood. Now, that's quite a bit of background, but it's necessary to understand the importance of the Myerstown Fight.[10]

On November 17, about 110 Rangers set out from Loudoun to find and engage Blazer's command. The Rangers learned that the Scouts were in the vicinity of Kabletown, WV. It might seem strange that two groups of combatants could ride across the same ground and not find each other, but it wasn't until the following morning, the 18th, that the Rangers found the still smoldering fires of Blazer's camp outside the village of Kabletown. Blazer's tracks appeared to be turning in a southerly direction. Richards turned the Rangers south as well, but on the road toward Myerstown, the next village.

Based on artifacts found by Jim Glymph, Blazer's camp was located in the closest copse of trees

What happened next is classic Mosby tactics. Richards chose the ground to the best advantage of the Rangers. He led his men through a stand of trees into an open field, and then positioned them behind a swell that concealed them from Blazer's view. Blazer, not wanting to miss a golden opportunity to hurt the Rangers, pursued and dismounted some of his men at a fence line to use their Spencer carbines. Richards had Harry Hatcher with Company A begin tearing down a fence at the far, south end of the open field. Blazer, perceiving this move as an attempt by the Rangers to escape, had his dismounted men begin breaking down a hole in their fence so the remainder of his squad could charge the fleeing Rangers. No way would Mosby's men get away!

This was the moment Richards had anticipated. He charged with Company B, while at the same time Hatcher wheeled Company A and slammed into the Scouts' flank. It was a perfect trap! Vicious hand-to-hand fighting resulted in the complete destruction of Blazer's command. Mosby's Colt revolvers prevailed over the Spencer carbines of Blazer's men in the close-in fighting.[11]

This fight has always been fascinating to me, not only from a tactical point of view, but because the site is so pristine. Not much has changed in Myerstown since the fight. Farm fields and scattered stands of trees roll across the terrain. The Shenandoah is only about a mile to the east at Myers Ford. We used *The Guidebook* to locate the site on an early trek. From the directions provided, we identified the battlefield. It was beautiful to behold: sun glowing in the southern sky; rolling fields crusted in corn stalk stubble; a weathered wooden rail fence at the far south end of the field; wooded hills rising up from the river off to the east; no power lines in sight; and the unimproved gravel road meandering through the fields. Pristine!

As much as I liked the setting, it was difficult to make the fight fit the site. Succeeding treks never helped resolve the questions. Over the years, I arranged with the farmer who owned the fields to interview him and explore the entire ground. The farmer had never plowed up any evidence of the fight. For the 2004 trek, I even shipped my metal detector back so we could try to locate spent Spencer cartridges. If we could locate cartridges, we could establish Blazer's line and clarify the orientation of the fight. That would provide the information to satisfy our persistent puzzlement. We did use the metal detector one afternoon, probing along a tree-fence line. The only thing of interest dug up was an old wrench, which the farmer pronounced to be for use with Model T Fords.

Spenser carbine cartridges – brass casing with lead minie' ball projectile – of the type employed by Blazer's Scouts

A side note here describes the camaraderie among our trekkers. Pranks are open field on the trek, usually to the immense amusement of all participants. On the 2004 trek, we were headquartered at Welbourne as was usual by then. Boarding at Welbourne was Connie, Miss Constance. Our Sgt. Ames, recently released from an unhappy alliance, became immediately smitten with the winsome Miss Constance, and who among us would not be charmed! Miss C joined on our daily explorations, always hanging near the dashing Sgt. Ames. This was fine with the rest of the crew. They made an endearing couple. Also, Miss C was an exceptional researcher in her own right, and was in tune with our Mosby mission.

The conflict came toward the end of the trek when Ames came to Fount and me and asked to be released from the day's exploration. He wanted to have one last day in the company of Miss C. Being the brothers that we are, Fount and I gave Ames a wee bit of flak, but understanding the notion of true love, or at least of twitterpation, released him from duty. However! A ranger never abandons the mission! So Fount and I decided that Ames would have to pay. After leaving Welbourne, we stopped in Upperville at Cliff Sophia's relics shop. Cliff happened to have a decent Spencer cartridge casing. Perfect! Fount and I continued on with the day's itinerary. Later, when Ames caught up with us, he was appropriately disappointed to learn that we had "returned to the Myerstown site to continue metal detecting and had found the Spencer casing necessary to orient the fight on the field." Being the good brothers that we are, Fount and I presented Ames with the casing. Nothing more was said about Ames's abandonment.

That is, nothing was said until the 2005 trek. We had some newbie trekkers with us, along with Ames and Miss C. A side note to this side note: Ames and Miss C were married during this trek. It was a beautiful, Mosby-style ceremony on the historic Lemmons Bottom Bridge across Goose Creek. The bride was radiant and the groom arrived on horseback in dress uniform accompanied by his fellow rangers.

As the assembled trekkers stood on the Myerstown field, Fount interpreted the fight with Blazer's Scouts. In a perfectly natural tone, Fount concluded the story by revealing the prank that we had played on Ames the previous year, with the purchased casing. The punchline was delivered so perfectly that it took several moments for everyone, especially Ames, to fully absorb what had happened. Of course, it achieved the lesson: a ranger never abandons the mission! A great laugh was enjoyed by all; well, maybe not Ames. Eventually Ames recovered, mostly. Your brothers wouldn't do these things if they didn't love ya!

Back to the Myerstown interpretation. It wasn't until the 2015 trek that we finally made progress in resolving our questions regarding the field. Prior to the trek, Steve had chatted with a gentleman at a meeting in Winchester. Jim Glymph was an acquaintance of our mentor, Don Hakenson, and had lived in the Kabletown-Myerstown neighborhood for several decades. After hearing from Steve of our continued questions about the Myerstown field, Jim agreed to guide us on his interpretation of the fight.

JimGlymph interprets the Myerstown Fight for the Trekkers

The clincher for us was that back in the '60s, Jim had metal-detected the field and found a line of Spencer casings! Jim took us to the site of Blazer's camp. He knew that it was the site from the relics he had found there. At the campsite, it became clear how the Scouts and the Rangers had missed one another.

The route that Blazer's men had taken to the south was through a deep draw in the farm fields, completely hidden from view from the road. The Rangers and the Scouts could not see each other, but they had to sense the presence of the other.

Myerstown battlefield; the Rangers feigned escape tree line is to the right

On the road leading from Myerstown to the river, not too far from the village, a draw cuts across the road. This point is where Blazer followed the Rangers through the trees to the fence to attack into the open field. It is easy from this perspective to see how Richards' squad was concealed behind a swell, and the fence line at the south end of the field where Harry Hatcher wheeled Company A to charge Blazer's flank. Finally! It all fit! It was in the field west of the one we had always believed to be the battlefield. Thank you, Jim Glymph!

Summerhill Farm – Mt. Gilead

Sometimes the smallest mention of an event will provide the carrot to dig deeper. A few years ago I found an intriguing anecdote in an obscure source, Asa Moore Janney and Werner Janney's *The Composition Book: Stories from the Old Days in Lincoln, Virginia.* During the 1930s, the Janney lads recorded stories told by the local old timers as they sat around the pot-bellied stove in Janney's store/post office. It's a fun read just for the accounts of the old days, with a lot of humor, but there were a few entries connected to Mosby that grabbed my attention. Most of the Mosby stories were relayed by "Cousin" Charley Hoge. He was a young boy during The War. He grew up on his father's farm, Summerhill Farm, so he witnessed the scenes he described for the Janneys.

Summerhill Farm sat in a valley below Mt. Gilead in Loudoun County. William Hoge, Charley's father, was a Quaker, as were most of the neighbors in that neck of the county. William was for peace and not exactly pro-Union or pro-Confederate; however, due to unavoidable circumstances, William found himself boarding several Rangers at any given time late in The War. He also occasionally sold fodder to Union soldiers who had encamped above at Mt. Gilead.

One night, Mosby watched Mr. Hoge load corn into several Yankee army wagons. Before the wagons returned to their camp, the Rangers attacked, ran off the wagon teamsters and burned the wagons. Next morning Mosby stopped by the farm and told farmer Hoge, "…I saw you measuring out the corn…. I could have attacked the Yankees then, but I held off, because I knew you were a Union man and it would get you in bad with your own side."[12]

Mosby could have watched the corn shed from this field

There are other stories, but this one appealed to me. It demonstrated the wisdom of Mosby and shows that he was not the ruthless demon portrayed by the northern press.

Of course it demanded further investigation! Where was/is Summerhill Farm? Is it still in ownership of the Hoge family? Where was the Union camp located? Where were the wagons destroyed? When did this episode take place? Did any Rangers ever write about this?

It wasn't until the 2013 trek that we made any progress on finding answers to our questions. Burke (our Fount Beattie) and I drove up to Mt. Gilead to see what we could uncover. Neither of us had been there prior to this. Mt. Gilead had been only a name on the map, and a side note. (Also, Ranger William "Major" Hibbs was a blacksmith there.) The only approach is on a road that appeared to be much the same as it was during The War. There were lots of ruts, and it was crowded by overhanging trees with occasional peeks at farm fields. The tiny village appears much the same, too, with mostly, "period" houses and not much in the way of modern development.

We drove the length of the village snapping photos of interesting houses. But where was the site of the Union camp? Where was Summerhill Farm? As we sat in the car, pondering, we noticed a woman jogging, accompanied by a dog. When she neared our vehicle, I hailed her, introduced ourselves and posed the questions that had brought us there. She laughed in a friendly way and said she was relatively new to Mt. Gilead and did not have knowledge of these things. But she went on to say we needed to talk with her neighbor, Bill, as he knew everything about the history of the area.

I asked where we might find Bill, and we were directed to a home about 100 feet away. Not wanting to burst in on anyone, I asked if she happened to know Bill's phone number. Surprisingly, she gave us both Bill's cell and landline numbers. We thanked her profusely. She returned to her jog, dog happily in step.

Burke and I drove the short distance to Bill's driveway, stopped and debated whether or not to call him to proceed with our search. A brief discussion resulted in applying our "Rule 3. When in doubt, go for it! Maybe you're only here one time!" Burke made the call.

After listening to Burke explain our mission, Bill said we just needed to come up to the house. Following greetings and introductions, he invited us into the parlor. Bill is a civil engineer, former army, a historian and author. Indeed, Bill (William C. Ray) had published *Mount Gilead: History & Heritage*. Another serendipity moment!

Bill guided us through his book and a few maps, attempting to find answers for us. After a pleasant session, Bill was not able to identify the Hoge farm, but he offered to give us a driving tour of the community. We were able to identify the locations of the camps, and the basic layout of the wartime village.

Historian Bill Ray describes Coe's Mill site at Mt. Gilead

A bonus side trip took us through a gate and down a private path to the site of Coe's Mill on the North Fork of Goose Creek. Some ruins remain of the old mill (originally built in 1772), and the site is pristine, thankfully protected from development. Across the creek, a short distance to the west, is the North Fork Baptist Church. Due to its remote setting, this was the site for the organizing of Company H of Mosby's command, April 5, 1865. The bridge that used to cross the creek to connect to Mt. Gilead is long gone, so the road into the church from the west is also the road out. The church sits on a graceful and peaceful slope. The small cemetery is an appropriate resting place for Rangers John W. Holmes and John C. Kirkpatrick.

Bill is a treasure! I bought his last copy of the 5th edition of his book. We said our thank yous and good-byes and drove on to another site on the day's itinerary. We were buoyant with our progress and optimistic for more discoveries.

After returning home, I kept up correspondence with Bill. He kept researching the Hoge farm. He is a very precise, experienced researcher. Eventually, through deeds and titles, Bill located Summerhill Farm and was able to dig up some history on the Hoge family. The bonus was that he identified the current owners, Warren and Sarah Marion. Bill did not know them but provided an address. In preparation for the 2015 trek, I wrote to ask permission to visit the farm. Sometime later I received a response from Casey Marion, the daughter, excited about our research and learning that their home had some significant history to it. Arrangements were made!

Steve, Burke and Bill look toward Snicker's Gap from Mt. Gilead

We met first at Bill's home in Mt. Gilead. This day our trekkers included Don Hakenson, my cousin Carol Jeffords, Burke Nebeker and me. Again led by Bill, we looked over the village, including a vantage point where in the hazy distance we could see Snickers Gap through the Blue Ridge. Then Bill drove onto a private road that was the wartime road taken by the corn-filled Yankee army wagons. Today there is no way to determine the location of their destruction, but the road certainly gave us the feeling of the event.

Casey Marion and the author at Summerhill Farm

The Hoge farm, now named Sycamore Bend, is within easy access of the Union camps up the hill at Mt. Gilead. Farmer Hoge's house, granary and barn are nestled in a hollow on 43 of the original 172 acres. Walking through the farm's fields, it is easy to visualize that night when the Rangers watched the loading of corn. We enjoyed a longer-than-intended, amiable visit. It would be a challenge to find any hosts more cordial than the current owners.

Bill has included the Mosby-Hoge episode in the newest (the 6th) edition of his book. I bought the last two copies he had at his home, one for my research and one that we presented to the Marions, our Sycamore Bend family. Fortunately, Bill was able to locate additional copies for the rest of our crew at the Willowcraft Winery just down the road.

Basking in the glow we bade farewell and drove back "home" to Welbourne!

[1] Williamson, *Mosby's Rangers*, pp.69-71; Scott, *Partisan*, pp.99-101; Keen-Mewborn, *Regimental*, pp.66-67
[2] Williamson, *Mosby's Rangers*, pp.64-68; Scott, *Partisan*, pp.92-96; Keen-Mewborn, *Regimental*, pp.59-62; Jones, *Ranger Mosby*, pp.122-129
[3] John S. Mosby, "With Mosby's Men in '64," *The Illustrated American*, vol. XX no.1, June 27, 1896; Alexander, *Mosby's Men*, pp.104-115; Scott, *Partisan*, pp.334-338; Ramage, *Gray Ghost*, p.207; Keen-Mewborn, *Regimental*, pp.191-198
[4] Munson, *Reminiscences*, pp.102-111; Scott, *Partisan*, pp.274-279; Taylor, *Sketchbook*, pp.284-287; Keen-Mewborn, *Regimental*, pp155-159
[5] Ned Burks and Mary T. Morris, eds., "Through the Shadow: A Boy's Memories of the Civil War in Clarke County," by Samuel Scollay Moore, D.D. *Proceedings of the Clarke County Historical Association*, Berryville, Virginia: December 1990
[6] Williamson, *Mosby's Rangers*, pp.247-257; Scott, *Partisan*, pp.324-327, pp. 333-334; Jones, *Ranger Mosby*, pp.212-213; Keen-Mewborn, *Regimental*, pp.183-191
[7] Adele Mitchell, ed., *The Letters of John S. Mosby*, p.99
[8] Alexander, *Mosby's Men*, pp. 104-106; Keen-Mewborn, *Regimental*, pp.190-191
[9] Alexander, *Mosby's Men*, pp.128-139; Munson, *Reminiscences*, pp.168-172; Scott, *Partisan*, p.356; Williamson, *Mosby's Rangers*, pp.284-287
[10] Williamson, *Mosby's Rangers*, p.302; Keen-Mewborn, *Regimental*, p.207
[11] Alexander, *Mosby's Men*, pp.116-128; Munson, *Reminiscences*, pp.119-125; Scott, *Partisan*, pp.364-371; Williamson, *Mosby's Rangers*, pp.300-309
[12] Asa Moore Janney and Werner Janney, *The Composition Book: Stories from the Old Days in Lincoln, Virginia*, pp.7-8. Lincoln, Virginia: privately published, 1973

Chapter Nine: *Returning the Favor*

An Important Mission

Our annual Mosby Rides have provided a unique perspective in experiencing the lore of Mosby and the 43rd Battalion Virginia Cavalry. The insights gained into Ranger tactics and into the lives of the inhabitants of northern Virginia are so much enhanced when viewed from horseback. When describing our mounted forays through the unspoiled Virginia countryside, listeners are fascinated and delighted. Many have expressed admiration for what we do and others want to tag along. We are not interested in becoming a tour company, charging for public horse rides; however, we are intent on giving back to the Mosby community. Innumerable people have been so supportive in our perpetual quest that we decided early on that we would return the favor whenever possible. In fact, it is a big part of our mission as an organization, and a significant personal goal.

In this regard, we have been successful. Historic Mosby's Rangers (HMR), as a non-profit corporation, has raised funds and in turn has made annual donations to various historic and preservation organizations. At times we have donated to the Brentmoor group for restoration of Mosby's post-war home, and we have donated to the Piedmont Environmental Council, too. We even contributed to the effort to lower the speed limit on Rt. 17 through the Crooked Run Valley.

A major project for us was to sponsor the historical marker for the fight at Loudoun Heights. We worked with Francesca Edling and her neighbors, the Virginia State Office for Historic Markers, Don Hakenson, and Tom Evans to research the fight and word the marker. We raised the funds to cover the costs and organized the dedication. It is one of our proudest achievements.

There are other more personal ways we have reciprocated. Several times we have made presentations to neighborhood gatherings and provided support for various ceremonies. Exchanging Mosby lore with others is another less formal and more frequent activity.

Since its formation, we have been donors to the Mosby Heritage Area Association (MHAA). We have supported various MHAA projects. In 2013, I was pleased to be able to assist in the observation of the 150th anniversary of the official organizing of Mosby's Partisan Rangers, 43rd Battalion Virginia Cavalry. MHAA had a number of events planned. As a participant, I helped with the Ranger Descendants Reunion. At Belle Grove, Eric Buckland and I volunteered as interpreters, and I was period-correct color for whatever was needed at the reenactment of the Battle of Upperville off of Trappe Road. It was my honor to be able to give back!

We are also proud of two ideas we brought to the MHAA that became reality. The first idea was the need for a Mosby descendant gathering. There are many valuable family stories that slip away but should be preserved. We suggested the idea to Judy Reynolds, who was the MHAA executive director at the time. Maybe it was not a new idea, and maybe they had already considered it, but we feel that it was at our spurring, in 2008, that MHAA began its annual, then semi-annual, reunions for the descendants of Mosby's Partisan Rangers. The reunions are now held on the odd-numbered years and have proven a great success.

The second idea we brought to MHAA was to conduct a ride through portions of Mosby's Confederacy. Mosby's Confederacy encompasses the finest horse country in Virginia, perhaps in the nation. Combine that with Mosby history and you have a fabulous opportunity! Also, in hunt country, it would be easier to arrange an informative, picturesque ride from farm to farm. The ride could even be a fundraiser for MHAA. Each year the ride could focus on Mosby events specific to the location of the ride. We volunteered to lead the rides and provide interpretation to the sites!

The first "Mosby Ride" was held in 2005. Franny coordinated the event for MHAA, and we coordinated the interpretation sites with her. Members of MHAA, as well as non-members, were offered the event for a reasonable fee. We were excited to be involved, as the date of the ride coincided with our annual trek. On the day of the event, participants arrived at Walter and Franny's farm north of Willisville where there was plenty of room for all the rigs to park the trailers. Tacking up was a festive event in itself. Since we did not bring our own mounts from Washington State, which would have been a logistical nightmare, we had to borrow horses from MHAA members. This is hunt country, so we were mounted on hunter-jumpers. For our group of rangers, the smallest horse was 17 hands! In our unit at home, the largest horse was 16 hands, maybe 16.2. What a thrill for us!

HMR rangers interpreting the Blakely Grove Fights for the MHAA "Mosby Ride"

We rode out with Walter and me on point. Crossing scrub brush fields until reaching Millville Road, we trotted along a path south of and parallel to the road. A congenial group, it reminded me of the accounts of Mosby's men riding to a raid: laughing, joking, chatting, carefree; no "form fours" here!

Our first site was the Blakeley Grove School. The Rangers collided with the Yankees here on two different occasions. On May 6, 1863, fifteen Rangers chased Union cavalry toward the Blakeley Grove School where the hidden Union infantry fired upon their own cavalry. When they discovered it was an ambush set for their benefit, the Rangers declined the offer, turned about and galloped back toward Upperville. The Yankees suffered casualties and made a half-hearted effort to pursue the Rangers, but finally gathered up their dead and wounded and returned to their camp across the Shenandoah near Berryville.[1]

On an interesting side note, Ranger John Charles Buchanan was wounded in the skirmish here on February 6, 1863. John was the first cousin of Gen. James A. Buchanan who, in 1909, purchased Ayrshire Farm, where this failed ambush took place.[2]

The second clash came on February 21, 1864, when Yankees under the command of Major Henry Cole had been raiding in the Piedmont area and scooping up Rangers. Cole halted his men in Upperville to feed, water and rest their horses. Mosby had gathered about 50 Rangers by then and attacked the Yankees, throwing them into confusion. A running fight raced through the main street in Upperville. It was at this moment that young Cab Maddux quit his academic career and joined up with the Rangers. The Rangers pushed the Yankees overland across Green Garden Farm. Cole's men finally took a defensive position behind stone fences at the Blakeley Grove School crossroads. Mosby seized the opportunity to flank the Yankees, and routed them from their stone protection. The Rangers pursued the Yankees in a wild race as far as Bloomfield.[3]

After this skirmish, the schoolhouse was used as a field hospital for the Union wounded. One Union trooper who was wounded in the head, lingered for a while, then expired. He was buried along the stone fence. Many years later, the rumor of a dead Yankee at the schoolhouse was a source of speculation and fear for the neighborhood children. When they were little girls, Nat Morison's grandmother and her sister would sing a little ditty and run as fast as they could to get beyond the grasp of that Yankee ghost at the schoolhouse.

While trying to interpret the events here, we were all still mounted. My borrowed horse apparently did not like to stand too long, and kept up a steady dance. Nothing like a samba, but enough that I felt like I was the bouncing ball on the screen and the assembled audience was trying to follow my narrative with rhythmic nods.

We moved off toward the next site, Green Garden Farm, at a leisurely stroll. Again, the ride resembled Mosby's men, meandering down a rutted lane back in time. It is only about a mile from the Blakeley Grove crossroads to Green Garden Farm. We rode up the tree-lined lane, hardly changed from wartime, to form up at the front steps of the red brick house. This is one of my favorite sites because of its significance in Mosby lore and because of its pristine condition.

Green Garden Farm was the family home of Rangers Tom and Adolphus "Dolly" Richards. The older brother, Tom, became Captain commanding Company G, while "Dolly" became Major of the regiment, third in command after Mosby and William Chapman. In antebellum years, the brothers were members of a local militia led by Turner Ashby. Games were hosted at Green Garden Farm where the young men would race and joust and run at the heads. Legend has it that it was here, in the fields west of the house that raucous cheering and taunting evolved into the "Rebel Yell." I realize that other sources claim the distinction. I am not presenting it as other than a story that goes with the place and I like it!

On February 18, 1865, the Yankees set out from their camps west of the Shenandoah to conduct another nighttime raid through the Piedmont-Upperville area. Splitting their force at Paris, Major Gibson, with about 100 troopers from the 14th PA Cavalry, took the road toward Markham, while Captain Snow, with about 100 men from the 21st NY Cavalry, moved toward Upperville. Their mission was to capture as many Confederates and as much plunder as possible before dawn.

Major Gibson's detachment was fairly successful, rounding up 18 Rangers and 50 horses. At Upperville, Captain Snow was not as fortunate. He had left a detachment in town to search for Rangers there while he took another detachment, under the guidance of a deserter named Spotts, to Green Garden Farm where the informant reported Major Richards was at home. Snow's troopers surrounded the house and proceeded to search for Richards. I like this story because staying with Richards were two other Rangers, John Hipkins and Bob Walker, who is my ranger. The Rangers were surrounded but they had enough warning to grab their weapons and disappear through a trapdoor into a hidden space under the house.

After two hours of futile searching, the Yankees ransacked the house, taking whatever they wanted. Snow called off his men and returned to Upperville. What he found was about one third of the men roaring drunk. Apparently two barrels of apple brandy had been captured, and the Yankees partook of some to relieve the suffering of the bitter cold night. It must have been exceptionally cold! Captain Snow decided it might be safer to return to their camp in the Valley rather than rendezvous with Major Gibson. He left six of his troopers who were too drunk to ride, taking their weapons, horses and accouterments. It appears to me that Captain Snow believed the drunkards deserved to be captured!

While the debacle played out in Upperville, Richards, Walker, and Hipkins found borrowed clothes, mounted up and rode out to raise Rangers to pursue the departing Yankees. Bob Walker roused J.J. Williamson at Ayrshire, then rode on to spread the alarm, and then to meet up with Richards on the Ashby Gap Turnpike.

In the meantime, Major Gibson, realizing that Captain Snow was not going to meet the rendezvous at Piedmont, turned his men and captures back toward Ashby Gap. The Yankees were well along the path back to Shepherds Ford on the Shenandoah when the Richards-led Rangers struck the rear of the column near Mt. Carmel Church. The Rangers' attack was so sudden and fierce that the fleeing Federals were simply overcome. The story of the fight itself is best saved for another chapter, but you should know that the Rangers recovered all the prisoners and horses that had been swept up by the Yankees.[4]

Now, because of my dancing steed, I was not able to relay all of the above to our audience standing in the front yard of Green Garden Farm, but we knew it was time to ride out. We took a path from Pantherskin Creek, through the bottom, and came out of a stand of woods into an open field. As we rode folks began to spread out, about thirty of us. By the time we reached the crest of the ridge above the creek, all were nearly at the trot. Without any command or signal, we suddenly broke into a canter, basically in a line of battle! I looked over to our Sam Chapman and Fount Beattie, drew my .44 Remington and hollered, "Hey! Rangers at the charge!" They laughed and drew their revolvers, too. Another magical moment, but within a flicker of another moment the other riders, all hunters, hollered back, "don't shoot – don't shoot! The horses will go berserk!" The moment was exciting, but fleeting, as we were quickly approaching the end of the field. Our revolvers were not loaded by the way!

The remainder of the ride was pretty low-key compared to the "charge," but was pleasant. As we pulled up to Walter and Franny's farm, Judy Reynolds was there with a smile and a table spread with refreshments. After some chatting time with folks and a grand thank you to Walter, Franny and Judy, our first MHAA Mosby Ride was finished.

The second MHAA Mosby Ride was scheduled to take place during our next trek. In 2006, we were coordinating with Franny again. For this ride, the rendezvous point was in Atoka, in the field adjacent to the MHAA headquarters in the Rector House. On magnificent borrowed horses, we again led the assembled riders over fields, and except for crossing a paved road, through sun-blessed pristine landscape. Our destination was Lakeland, site of one of the more significant stories in Mosby lore.

HMR ranger Burke Nebeker presents the Lakeland interpretation

Lakeland is a large farm situated south of Rector's Crossroads and north of Rectortown. At the time of The War the proprietor was Ludwell Lake. The Lake family was friendly to the southern cause. With Ludwell, Jr. and four members of the Lake family serving with Mosby, Lakeland was a hub of Ranger comings and goings.

We knew that visitors were seldom allowed at the house. A while back I had tried a cold-call request but was denied, and I had heard about tour buses being turned away. The MHAA Ride opened the door for us. To actually be able to ride over Lakeland ground and right up to the house, "Ranger style," was an incredible opportunity eagerly anticipated by our crew!

The story begins at Rosenvix on December 21, 1864. Ranger Jake Lavender was getting married at his aunt's home. A number of Rangers were present for the celebration, including Col. Mosby. Early in the evening word came that a Union force was trolling the area and approaching nearby on the Salem road. Mosby quietly left the festivities with Ranger Thomas Love to reconnoiter. They observed the Yankees building fires, and presumed they were going into camp for the night.

After making arrangements to engage the enemy in the morning, Mosby and Love rode northward. It was an icy and snowy night, so they decided to stop at Lakeland for warmth and a good supper. It was widely known that gentleman farmer, Ludwell Lake, enjoyed a well-supplied table and real coffee.

Suddenly, there was the tramping of many horses around the house. As Mosby was looking out at the Union troopers surrounding the house, a shot was fired. The bullet crashed through the window, wounding Mosby in the belly. Always quick to analyze and act, Mosby stashed his colonel's uniform jacket out of sight. He dabbed blood from the wound to his mouth to simulate a mortal wound. Before leaving, the Yankees examining the wounded soldier asked who he was. The Lake family avowed that he was a stranger, and the wounded man gurgled that his name was Lt. Johnson of the 6th Virginia. Assuming that he was soon to expire, the Yankees took Love, as well as Mosby's boots, hat and cloak prisoner, and rode off into a dark and frosty night.

A while later Mosby staggered out into the main room, shocking the Lake family who supposed he was dead. Ludwell's daughter, Sarah, used her bonnet to staunch the flow of blood while Ludwell made arrangements to transport Mosby to a safer location, knowing the Yankees could return at any moment, and sent word to alert the Rangers of the Colonel's wounding.

The family wrapped Mosby in blankets and quilts for warmth, then loaded him into an oxcart and sent him off into a cold, snowy, sleety night. Daniel, one of Lake's servants, guided the oxcart by way of back paths to Aquila Glasscock's cottage at Rockburn, a few miles to the south.[5]

As we gathered the horses around the house's back patio, Burke, our Fount Beattie orated. Because he was participating dismounted this day, he became the only member of our trekking crew ever to have the honor to visit the inside of Lakeland.

Leaving the Lake house, our entourage rode away on a back farm road. The old road meandered through farm fields and woods, sloping downhill over its length. As we progressed down the tree-shrouded path, it struck me that we could be riding on the very route Daniel used to deliver Mosby to Rockburn. All that was needed was sleet, snow, ice, and the dark of night. Oh, and an oxcart!

At the bottom of the farm lane, we joined Crenshaw Road. This is one of my favorite original-road-bed-pristine back roads in Mosby's Confederacy! Unimproved and hardly changed in 150 years, it is easy to envision cavalry, gray or blue, at the trot or faster, searching for the enemy! No Yankees were sighted so our column moved southward on the old road.

A short distance and rising up hill, we arrived at our next destination, Rockburn. It is a fine stone house, but not the original structure that had been destroyed by fire prior to the hostilities. The wounded Mosby was brought into the cottage where he remained until morning. By sunrise, two surgeons arrived, William Dunn, the battalion's doctor, and Talcott Eliason, from Upperville, who had attended Gen. Stuart. They were able to remove the bullet that had traveled upward and lodged in Mosby's right side.

On the MHAA "Mosby Ride" with Walter Kansteiner and the author on point

The Rangers immediately established a protective cordon around their wounded commander. Mosby's men knew that the Yankees would be scouring the countryside once they realized that the wounded officer at Lakeland had been Mosby. The Rangers arranged to transport Mosby southward by a series of stops in friendly homes, and eventually to his folks' place at McIvor Station in Amherst County. Over the course of this journey, Mosby was hidden at Glen Welby, Waveland, Wheatland, and, after a week or so, on to his parents' home when he had regained strength enough for the journey.

While the moving of Mosby secretly transpired, William Chapman and "Dolly" Richards put the Rangers into a series of actions to throw the Yankees off. Any Union camp or picket position was attacked. Federal patrols were harassed or ambushed. If it was blue, it became a target. Conflicting rumors about Mosby's condition helped confuse matters, too. The strategy was successful. If the Yankees ever got close they were always too late!

Of course, we know Mosby recovered and returned to the battalion that by then was a regiment. He survived the War and went on to a long, active civilian career, which is a story for another book!

After Burke finished the Rockburn interpretation, the mounted contingent about-faced and, amid a leisurely paced chatting, returned to the Rector House where refreshments were served and pleasant conversations were observed on the lawn.

Since he has moved back to Mosby's Confederacy, Steve ("Big Yankee Ames") is our only ranger to have helped with subsequent MHAA Mosby Rides; however, we are still proud of our contribution to preserving the heritage.

A youthful John Gott discovered a trunk full of Lakeland relics in the attic of his family's house in Marshall

Side note: When noted historian John Gott was a young lad, he was helping his grandmother and aunt move from their house on Main Street in Marshall. After everything had been loaded up, John was instructed to go back through the house to make sure they had not left anything. It was empty until he got to the attic. Sitting in a corner was a large, dusty trunk. Curious as to why something so obvious had been left, John opened the trunk. Among the items inside he found a window sash with bullet holes in the pane, a blood stained bonnet, and a spent bullet. Wow! When he returned to his family, and told them about the trunk, they told him to never mind!

It seems John's grandmother and aunt were Lakes and Mosby had not spoken kindly of the family afterward (he believed they had sent him off with a servant who would have given him up to the Yankees). Apparently the family would not even allow the name Mosby to be uttered in their house. The Lake women told John that the trunk contained items connected to the wounding of that bad man (Mosby)!

I never asked John how he managed to save the trunk and its contents, but he did. John eventually sold most of the collection to Bob Daly of Middleburg where we first encountered the treasures. After Bob's death and the auction of his collection, I do not know where the artifact collection went, but at least we have the photos.

Bob Daly, Andy Harris, and the author in the Welbourne library in October 2003 - Bob holds a framed presentation of a portion of Sarah Lake's bloody bonnet, the bullet removed from Mosby, a CDV of Sarah Lake, and the waist belt Mosby was wearing at the time of the wounding at Lakeland. The letter from John Gott verifies the authenticity of the items - attached to the belt is a hand-written note by Mosby verifying its authenticity. The author holds the carbine purported to be the weapon used to wound Mosby at Lakeland.

Loudoun Heights

Did Mosby suffer setbacks and occasional defeats? Yes. The painful loss of Ranger lives at Loudoun Heights stands out among all others. Loudoun Heights looks across the Shenandoah River to Harpers Ferry. The Union camp at Loudoun Heights was situated in Loudoun County in a valley between the Short Hills and the Heights, and on the eastern slope of the Heights.

A foot of snow and bitter cold made for a miserable ride for the Rangers during the wee hours of January 10, 1864. They had assembled at Upperville the previous afternoon, and ridden through sub-freezing temperatures as far north as Woodgrove, Ranger Henry Heaton's family home, where the Rangers halted to thaw and recover. Mosby relied on the recon and input of Frank Stringfellow, one of Gen. Stuart's famous scouts. The

Rangers continued their frozen march over the several miles remaining to reach the rendezvous with Stringfellow.

As the attack on the Federal camp began, something went wrong. The sleeping Union camp was surprised, but gunfire on one wing of the attack hit prematurely and all prior planning unraveled. The Yankees managed to rally and effectively counter the Rangers. Although the Rangers came off with prisoners and captures, their gain was unequal to the loss of some of their best men and officers. Ranger accounts tend to place the cause of the disaster at the feet of Stuart's scout, but who can say for certain.[6]

Because the Loudoun Heights Fight is considered to be Mosby's most serious defeat, it garners a lot of interest from Mosby scholars. The various accounts of the fight do not provide an easy interpretation as distances are given in general terms and some landmarks are vaguely referenced, as is the description of the route taken by the Rangers. It probably all made sense to the chroniclers who wrote their firsthand accounts; however, it has been a challenge for modern researchers to determine a more accurate picture of the fight.

Bringing clarity to the Loudoun Heights Fight has been a focus of our studies from the beginning, and is a required site to visit on each trek. Initially we simply pulled over onto the access road at the foot of the hill, snapped photos, and discussed the possibilities. We never reached a satisfactory explanation, but we persevered. "Rule 4: Persistence, and then a little more…!"

Growing braver with each expedition, on the 2003 trek we finally ventured further up the hill toward the house that *The Guidebook* identified as the headquarters of Major Cole, the Union camp commander. As we scurried about, trying to be inconspicuous and respectful of the property owners, a door on the side of the house opened, and a woman stepped out!

Uh-oh! Were we too close?

Not to worry! She greeted us with a warm smile and a welcoming hand. Francesca Edling quietly said, "You must be Mosby scholars. Yes, this house was used by Major Cole as his headquarters. My family and I have lived in this house since 1954, when my parents purchased the farm."

This Loudoun Heights home was used as Maj. Cole's headquarters

For the next hour, Francesca gave us an orientation to the land surrounding the site. She explained the local interpretation of where the Union camp spread out and the fight occurred. Her barn, old but rebuilt since The War, sits on the original stone foundation. Homes and private yards sit over the fields where the Yankee tents had been pitched. Portions of the original Hillsboro-Harpers Ferry Turnpike that wound its way up from the Potomac River are still visible. The existing highway (Rt.671) surface is 15-20 feet below and east of the original turnpike that runs along the front of Francesca's property. Parts of the old stone retaining wall are still doing their job. Loudoun Heights Lane is part of the old turnpike and is the last remaining unpaved section that is still in use. For weeks after Antietam and Gettysburg it saw an endless stream of wagons carrying the dead and wounded homeward past what is now Francesca's front door.

From John Divine and other local historians, Francesca's family learned the history of their home and neighborhood. There had been a blacksmith shop located not far from the camp site on Loudoun Heights Lane that turns off the turnpike and goes past Francesca's barn. John Brown had his horses shod at the blacksmith's the day before his raid on Harper's Ferry. He mentioned to the smithy that he was going to hear fireworks coming from Harper's Ferry the following night. Francesca heard this story from the blacksmith's great-great-granddaughter.

Francesca Edling discusses Loudoun Heights with our ranger, Burke Nebeker

While we chatted with Francesca, a vehicle drove in from the highway and pulled up next to us on Loudoun Heights Lane. A young man stepped out from the driver's door. He was not in uniform, but he could have been a dapper soldier from a war-era tintype. Francesca introduced him as Mark Cullinane, her up-hill neighbor. Mark informed us that his family had owned most of the Heights at one time, dating back to the early 1800s. Mark grew up here and had, over the years, found relics and artifacts to support the local opinion that this was the location of the Federal camp.

Further exploration revealed the old bridge over the creek, Piney Run, where the Yankees had a strong picket posted. On another trek, we explored down the Branch River Road that meets the Harpers Ferry Road at the bridge. Mortally wounded Ranger Lt. Tom Turner reportedly was brought to the Levi Waters' home. Some Mosby experts locate the Levi Waters' house on this road, so we wanted to check it out as this site did not fit our understanding taken from the accounts. The Rangers were beating a hasty retreat south on the Harpers Ferry Road. To turn off and head east on Branch River Road seems to be out of the line of march for the Rangers and too close to the Federal camp. In addition, and on a previous trek, Mark took us to his parents' home on Pine Hill Lane, which turns off Rt.671. From family deeds and maps dating to the early 1800s, we could verify that the Levi Waters house was at the junction with Rt. 671. That was a serendipitous moment, plus Mark's family took us all on a hayride to the top of their property to show us the wartime gun placements that had protected Harpers Ferry.

Further research has revealed that Levi Waters was living in the house on Branch River Road at the time of his death, not at the time of the fight. It makes more sense that the house where Lt. Turner gasped his last breath was the traditional location.

After the frigid disaster at Loudoun Heights, Mosby realized that he could not let his men wallow in sorrow and self-doubt. As painful and sad as it was, the Rangers needed to move forward. It is another example of Mosby's qualities as commander. For the next few weeks, he posted each of his companies to active picket duty, guarding and patrolling the roads leading into the heart of Mosby's Confederacy, keeping the men active.[7]

From this experience, Mosby learned to rely on his own reconnaissance and to consider that maybe daylight actions could be more successful. The Rangers had been beaten but they were not defeated. They continued their mission successfully until the end of The War.

Over many successive treks, we continued to explore the surrounding area. It was important to us to be able to place the Rangers' attack as precisely as available information could provide. We believe now that we have achieved our goal. In 2005, while sitting in Francesca's kitchen trying to slowly savor the best apple pie I have ever eaten, managing to inhale every last crumb, we began talking about getting a historical marker placed. Francesca and her family were supportive of the notion.

During 2006, we worked with the Virginia State Department of Historic Resources, and with Francesca, Tom Evans, and Don Hakenson to organize a campaign to erect an appropriate maker commemorating the fight at Loudoun Heights. On January 10, 2007, the dedication ceremony was held. In cold, but not the sub-freezing weather that Mosby and his Rangers faced, the new historic marker was unveiled. Representing the Historic Mosby's Rangers, Burke Nebeker rendered M.C. duty, and Don Hakenson gave a moving interpretation of the fight. Francesca and her husband, Geoffrey, performed the honors in a colorful service. We were proud to have been the sponsor. Being able to give back to those who have assisted us in our endeavors has become an important aspect of our mission.

Burke Nebeker hosting the marker dedication – January 10, 2007

Don Hakenson and Steve Boudreau compare notes at the marker dedication at Loudoun Heights

Geoffrey and Francesca Edling unveil the Loudoun Heights marker

Don Hakenson interprets the fight at Loudoun Heights; the stonework was donated by Mark Cullinane - 2013

Honoring the Rangers

HMR rangers at Col. Mosby's grave, Warrenton, VA

An important element of our mission, written in our corporate by-laws, is to honor the men who served with the 43rd Battalion Virginia Cavalry, Mosby's Partisan Rangers. Honoring the Rangers occurs in several forms. One is that each of our members has chosen a Ranger to personally represent or portray. I honor Robert Stringfellow Walker. As our members have come and gone over the years, we have witnessed a worthy collection of Rangers in our ranks: James F. "Big Yankee" Ames, Fountain Beattie, A.G. Babcock, Billings Steele, Charley Grogan, James Wiltshire, Harry Hatcher, Sam Chapman, David S. Briscoe, Henry C. "Cab" Maddux, Bushrod Underwood, Joe Nelson, and William "Major" Hibbs, to name some of the more notable Rangers. Some of our women members have also chosen to portray civilians who were prominent in Mosby's Confederacy: Amanda Virginia "Tee" Edmonds, Sallie Walker, Eliza "Miss Beck" Elgin, Sallie Settle and others. When representing a Ranger, our member researches and learns as much as possible about that person so a proper and accurate historical figure can be presented.

Another method for honoring the Rangers has been to be in communication with the descendants of the men who rode with Mosby. Robert Walker's grandson, Frank S. Walker, and I have become good friends. Burke Nebeker has become friends with several members of Fount Beattie's family. Descendants of the Spindle brothers have joined our treks. We have visited many times with George Wiltshire, grandson of Lt. James Wiltshire. George even guided us on one of our annual Mosby Rides. Of course, our friend and colleague, Don Hakenson, is related to several Rangers, and there are others!

During our treks we often seek out and find the final resting places of Rangers. The method for honoring the Ranger evolved from our campfire ritual. Once we confirm a grave marker, preparations are made. Before the honor is presented, a person present will plant a Confederate First National flag at the headstone. Each person present has a small, travelling cup for the purpose. Since you are not allowed to pour your own dose of "Frog Juice," you pour for the person to your left. Once the cups are ready, someone who knows about the Ranger will offer a toast. It is a solemn, private ceremony.

A note about the "Frog Juice:" to accommodate personal tastes and beliefs, it can be any number of beverages. While we desire to honor the person, the beverage should not be too pleasant or we might end up honoring too much! For a number of years now, the alcoholic version of "Frog Juice" has been Jaegermeister. Sometimes we will honor eight or more Rangers in the course of a day's itinerary. On an afternoon in 2013, historian and colleague, Eric Buckland and I presented honors to the fifteen Rangers resting in the Sharon Cemetery in Middleburg. By the end of the afternoon, things began to glaze over a bit. So we have learned to be considerate and judicious when pouring for our neighbor. Honor the Ranger, but think of your head in the morning!

One of my proudest trekking days came in 2008. On Veterans Day, we brought together two Ranger grandsons. Yes, grandsons! Frank Walker (Ranger Cpt. Robert S. Walker) and George Wiltshire (Ranger Lt. James G. Wiltshire) had been our Mosby friends for several years by then. I believe they were aware of each other before this day, but had never actually met. Both Frank and George are wonderful Virginia gentlemen, and have been supportive of our mission. It was my desire to return the favor in some small way.

The author, Frank Walker, Andy Harris, Don Hakenson, Katy and George Wiltshire at Fairview Cemetery

Don Hakenson, Andy Harris, and I drove with George from his farm west of Middleburg to Culpeper and converged on the Fairview Cemetery. Meeting us there were George's daughter, Katy, and Frank and Bernice Walker. Fairview is a fairly large cemetery. After a short bit of scouting, we found the marker for James G. Wiltshire. Making sure that all gathered had a properly filled toasting cup (I always carry an extra set plus the "Frog Juice"), George planted a First National flag at his grandfather's grave. Don presented a stirring toast to Lt. Wiltshire's memory.

Frank Walker and George Wiltshire honor Ranger Lt. James Wiltshire

While in the cemetery, we also did honors for Ranger Robert M. Mackall, a former mayor of Culpeper and one of the last surviving members of the 43rd (d. 1934). In addition, Don cannot visit Fairview Cemetery without honoring another celebrated Confederate soldier, William Downs Farley. "Farley the Scout" was one of Gen. Jeb Stuart's most capable officers, and fell in the fight at Fleetwood Hill on June 9, 1863.

Following the ceremonies at the cemetery, George led us to his boyhood home, the A.P. Hill House in Culpeper. Gen. A.P. Hill lived in this house before and during The War.

George Wiltshire approaching his boyhood home, the A.P. Hill House

The current owner was home and was a gracious guide on a tour of the house. George regaled us with childhood memories while we walked through the gorgeously restored rooms.

Afterward, we all drove to Orange where we had lunch at the Elmwood Café. Frank pointed out the location of a large white house that had served as Gen. A.P. Hill's headquarters during the Confederate defense of the "Rapidan Line" in 1863-1864. Then we trooped over to the Graham Cemetery west of town. Herein lies the Walker family plot. Cpt. Bob Walker rests, surrounded by his wife and all six of his sons, and other family members. Once all were ready with "Frog Juice"-filled cups, Frank planted the First National and offered an inspiring toast to the memory of Captain Bob. Frank and George entertained the gathering with family stories. It was an intimate and memorable ceremony, one that causes me to smile whenever I think of it. We all went our separate ways, taking with us the warm glow generated by the ceremonies on that proud, fun day.

Ranger grandsons, Frank Walker and George Wiltshire at Captain Robert Walker's grave

A puzzling phenomenon

Col. Mosby's grave sits among the graves of his family in Warrenton Cemetery. Nearby is the obelisk memorializing Ranger Richard Montjoy, captain of Company D, whose untimely death was widely mourned. Not far from Mosby and Montjoy is Ranger Joe Nelson's family plot. Mosby's headstone is substantial, not ostentatious, but straight forward like the man. My first visit was in 1985; my second was in 1995. Both times I placed a pebble on top of his headstone. It was something I did to honor the colonel's memory. Every visit afterward, not only pebbles but coins, too, were resting on top of Mosby's headstone. The first few observations of coin-leavings saw only copper pennies. Since then, it has not been unusual to see coinage of all denominations stacked on the headstone. Pebbles are still seen, but on occasion there have been a couple dollars' worth of change. Sometimes only a smattering of coins appears, as if someone comes to "clean" the top of the marker from time to time. The enigma for me: what is the significance of the coin leaving? How did the custom start, and how do the coins disappear? There are 46 Rangers at rest in the Warrenton Cemetery. The only headstone to be decorated with coins is Mosby's. It is an intriguing phenomenon that hopefully one day will be solved!

The puzzlement: Coins and pebbles placed on top of Col. Mosby's headstone – why?

---

[1] Williamson, *Mosby's Rangers*, pp.61-63; Keen-Mewborn, *Regimental*, pp.56-57

[2] Stokes, Claiborne M., *Ayrshire*, Unpublished manuscript, August 2000

[3] Williamson, *Mosby's Rangers*, pp.137-141; Scott, *Partisan*, pp.197-199; Keen-Mewborn, *Regimental*, pp.110-112

[4] Jones, *Ranger Mosby*, pp.255-256; Williamson, *Mosby's Rangers*, pp.342-350; Scott, *Partisan*, pp.446-451; Keen-Mewborn, *Regimental*, pp.244-248

[5] Williamson, *Mosby's Rangers*, pp.328-338; Munson, *Reminiscences*, pp.249-252; Scott, *Partisan*, pp.388-390; Keen-Mewborn, *Regimental*, pp.235-241; Jones, *Ranger Mosby*, pp.245-250

[6] Williamson, *Mosby's Rangers*, pp.124-132; Scott, *Partisan*, pp.179-182; Jones, *Ranger Mosby*, pp.164-170; Keen-Mewborn, *Regimental*, pp.100-103

[7] Keen-Mewborn, *Regimental*, p.103

Chapter Ten: *A Never Ending Journey*

The commonly accepted date for the end of The War Between the States is April 9, 1865. Confederate General Robert E. Lee surrendered to Union General Ulysses S. Grant at Appomattox Courthouse. Most southerners accepted that their effort to gain independence had failed.

Carter Hall

Following Gen. Lee's surrender of the Army of Northern Virginia at Appomattox Courthouse, much confusion existed throughout the South. Until he received word from his commanders, Mosby was not about to surrender his command, not while Confederate forces were still actively fighting for independence. Mosby sent Lt. Channing Smith and a few other Rangers to Richmond seeking direction. Unable to give military advice due to his parole, Gen. Lee merely suggested that the Rangers go home and start to rebuild their state.

While waiting for Lt. Smith to return, Mosby sent a contingent to Winchester to confer with Union Gen. Hancock who commanded the Federal army in the Valley. Eager to obtain Mosby's surrender, Hancock agreed to a meeting to discuss terms. There would be a temporary cease-fire in effect until the meeting at noon on April 18. The Union position would be represented by Gen. George Chapman at Carter Hall, the home of George Burwell in Millwood

On the 18th, Gen. Chapman and his escort arrived at Carter Hall early and waited, and waited…. Was Mosby going to be late? The Federal officers began to feel a little anxious. Would Mosby honor the truce or would he launch an attack with force? Union Col. James H. Kidd optimistically observed that Mosby had given his word, and "Mosby's word was law in that section."

Finally, with the blast of a bugle, a mounted column of gray-clad troopers seemed to erupt from the woods in the east, cantering down from the mountain. At the head of the column was Col. Mosby. With Mosby were his battalion officers. All were superbly mounted and attired in their finest uniforms. Col. Kidd wrote that Mosby "rode proudly," looking like "a highland chief coming to a lowland council." A grand spectacle it was!

A cordial greeting was exchanged between Gen. Chapman and Col. Mosby. Then general introductions among those assembled followed. Soon all were engaged in warm conversations like long-lost friends rather than battlefield opponents.

When the hospitable Mr. Burwell called the group to dinner, the seating arrangement around the dining table placed the antagonists in alternating places: blue, then gray; blue, gray. Table talk was amiable and included discussion of previous engagements and simple shared conversations. Col. Kidd was amused to hear exchanges between Mosby's men and the Union officers, when the Rangers would already be familiar with the Yankee. Blue: "Where did I meet you?" Gray: "There was no introduction. I met you in your camp, though you were not aware of it at the time." Oh…!

After the meal was finished, terms of surrender were presented by Gen. Chapman. Mosby declined the offer, indicating he needed more time to obtain direction from Confederate authorities. Gen. Chapman leniently allowed another 48 hours of temporary truce, and set the next meeting for the Clarke Hotel in Millwood.[1]

Don Hakenson at the former Clarke Hotel, Millwood, VA

The Millwood meeting did not go well on the 20th. Tensions were high on both sides. Trust was low. Rumors that Mosby was to be executed rather than paroled heightened the anxiety. Through a panicked misunderstanding, the Rangers made a precipitous exit, and returned to Salem. Rather than surrender his command, on the 21st Mosby disbanded the 43rd Battalion in Salem. This enabled each Ranger to decide the issue for himself. Mosby rode south, aware that the Federal authorities considered him to be an outlaw. Mosby eventually did obtain a parole, made peace with the Federal government, and went on to an active, productive civilian life. But that's another story for another time.[2]

Because of the colorful imagery created by the episode at Carter Hall, it was another target of interest. Since 1979, Carter Hall has been owned by Project Hope (Health Opportunities for People Everywhere). The original buildings are now operated as The Carter Hall Conference Center. On the 2013 trek, we were able to arrange a visit to Carter Hall.

Trekkers discussing the approach of Mosby and his officers

Our cordial hosts were staffers Victoria and Bert. We were guided on a tour of the major rooms of the main house. The facility is gracefully maintained. The living and dining rooms are appropriately sized for large group functions. It is easy to visualize a hundred Civil War soldiers dining together and in a style befitting their mission. Carter Hall: a surrender negotiations conference then; a modern conference center today.

From the front veranda, we discussed the episode and considered the approach of Mosby and his officers. We decided that it is imperative for us to replicate the Rangers approach. It is on our to-do list for a future trek. What a grand spectacle it will be!

Carter Hall Conference Center staff, Bert and Victoria, reenact Mosby's arrival to the surrender negotiations

There is No End

Approximately three million men served in the military during The War. So far as I know, no one has calculated how many civilians served the war effort; however, it has been suggested that nearly every American household was touched by The War. It is estimated 620,000 soldiers died during the conflict, more than any other war in which the United States has been involved. For a number of reasons, The War is the seminal event in U.S. history, not the least being that a majority of contemporary Americans can connect to an ancestor who fought in The War not so many generations ago. The last Civil War veterans were dying around the time I was born. We were connected.

With so many Americans involved and impacted, it is not surprising to encounter an abundance of personal wartime accounts. These stories surface occasionally in newly discovered letters, dairies, and journals, and as family histories are recovered. It is this wealth of information, continuously jump-started by "new discoveries," that will keep the journey alive. The Mosby lore is only a small segment of interest, but it is the magnet for my never-ending journey.

---

[1] J.H. Kidd, *Personal*, pp.445-449

[2] Monteiro, Aristides, M.D., *War Reminiscences by the Surgeon of Mosby's Command*. Richmond, Virginia: 1890. Reprinted by Butternut Press, Gaithersburg, Maryland, 1983, pp.202-207; Munson, *Reminiscences*, pp.267-268; Williamson, *Mosby's Rangers*, pp.388-392

Bibliography

Adams, Charles S., *Military Operations In Jefferson County (Virginia & West Virginia) 1861-1865.* Shepherdstown, West Virginia: Privately published, 1994, revised 1996.

Alexander, John H., *Mosby's Men.* New York: The Neale Publishing Company, 1907. Reprinted by the Butternut Press, Gaithersburg, MD

Ashdown, Paul and Caudill, Edward, *The Mosby Myth: A Confederate Hero in Life and Legend.* Wilmington, Del.: Scholarly Resources, Inc., 2002.

Baird, Nancy Chappelear, *Journals of Amanda Virginia Edmonds: Lass of the Mosby Confederacy, 1857 - 1867.* Stephens City, Virginia: Commercial Press, 1984.

Baker, Norman L., *Valley of the Crooked Run: The History of a Frontier Road.* Delaplane, Virginia: Summerset Printing, 2002 (First Edition).

Beitzell, Edwin W., *Point Lookout Prison Camp for Confederates.* Leonardtown, Maryland: St. Mary's County Historical Society, 1983.

Bonnell, John C., Jr., *Sabres in the Shenandoah: The 21st New York Cavalry, 1863-1866.* Shippensburg, Pa.: Burd Street Press, 1996.

Brager, Bruce, *Combative to War's Very End: Even U.S. Grant had high praise for the Gray Ghost of the Confederacy.* Military History Magazine, Leesburg, Virginia: Empire Press, October 1986.

Brown, Kathi Ann, Nicklin, Walter, and Toler, John T., eds., *250 Years in Fauquier County: a Virginia Story.* Fairfax, Virginia: GMU Press, 2008.

Brown, Stuart E., and Brown, Ann Barton, *Carter Hall and the Civil War.* Berryville, Virginia: Virginia Book Company, 2003

Brown, Peter A., *Mosby's Fighting Parson: The Life and Times of Sam Chapman.* Westminster, Maryland: Willow Bend Books, 2001.

Brown, R. Shepard, *Stringfellow of the Fourth: The Amazing Career of the most successful Confederate Spy.* New York: Crown Publishers, 1960.

Bryan, Charles F., Jr. and Lankford, Nelson D., eds., *Eye of the Storm: A Civil War Odyssey, Written and Illustrated by Private Robert Knox Sneden.* New York: The Free Press, 2000.

Bryan, J., III, *The Sword Over the Mantel: The Civil War and I.* New York: McGraw-Hill Book Company, 1960.

Buckland, Eric W., *Mosby's Keydet Rangers.* Centreville, Virginia: Privately printed by the author, 2008.

Buckland, Eric W., *Mosby Men.* Centreville, Virginia: That Fateful Night Press, 2011.

Buckland, Eric W., *Mosby Men II.* Centreville, Virginia: That Fateful Night Press, 2011.

Buckland, Eric W., *Mosby Men III.* Centreville, Virginia: That Fateful Night Press, 2012.

Buckland, Eric W., *Mosby Men IV.* Centreville, Virginia: That Fateful Night Press, 2013.

Burks, Ned, and Morris, Mary T., *Through the Shadow: A Boy's Memories of the Civil War in Clarke County by Samuel Scollay Moore, D.D.* Berryville, Virginia: Clarke County Historical Association, 1990.

Castleman, Virginia Carter, *Reminiscences of an Oldest Inhabitant: A Nineteenth Century Chronicle.* Herndon, Virginia: Herndon Historical Society, 1976.

Chappelear, B. Curtis, *Maps and Notes Pertaining to the Upper Section of Fauquier County, Virginia*, Warrenton, Virginia: The Warrenton Antiquarian Society, 1954.

Cooke, John Esten, *Wearing of the Gray: Being Personal Portraits, Scenes and Adventures of the War.* New York: E. B. Treat & Co., 1867, 601 pages. Reprinted by Indiana University Press, Bloomington, Indiana, 1959

Crawford, J. Marshall, *Mosby and His Men.* New York: G. W. Carleton & Co., 1867. Reprinted by Invictus, Decatur, MI, 1998

Crouch, Howard R., *Like a Hurricane: the Men, Mounts, Arms, and Tactics of Colonel John S. Mosby's Command*. Catlett, Virginia: SCS Publications, 2013.

Curtis, I.S., "The Attempted Capture of General Crawford," *Confederate Veteran*, vol. XXIII, 1915

Ellis, Garrison, *Tracking the Gray Ghost: the Mosby Paradox*. Virginia Country Magazine, vol.1. Middleburg, Virginia: the Country Publishers, 1983.

Evans, Thomas J. and Moyer, James M., *Mosby's Confederacy: A Guide to the Roads and Sites of Colonel John Singleton Mosby*. Shippensburg, Pa.: White Mane Publishing Company, 1991.

Evans and Moyer, *Mosby Vignettes, Vol. I - V*. Privately printed. Fairfax, Virginia, 1993-1996

Fairfax County (Va.) Civil War Centennial Commission, *Fairfax County and the War Between the States, 1961*, Reprinted by the Fairfax County Park Authority, 1998.

Fauquier County Bicentennial Committee, *Fauquier County, Virginia: 1759 - 1959*. Warrenton, Virginia: Virginia Publishing, Inc., 1959.

Frobel, Anne S., *The Civil War Diary of Anne S. Frobel*. McLean, Virginia: EPM Publications, 1992.

Goodhart, Briscoe, *Loudoun Rangers: History of the Independent Loudoun Rangers, U. S. Vol. Cav. (Scouts), 1862-65*. Washington, DC: Press of McGill & Wallace, 1896. (Reprinted by Olde Soldier Books, Inc., Gaithersburg, Maryland, ISBN 0-942211-76-6)

John K. Gott, *High in Old Virginia's Piedmont: A History of Marshall (formerly Salem), Fauquier County, Virginia*. Marshall, Virginia: Marshall National Bank & Trust Company, 1987.

Hakenson, Don, *Reminiscences of Frank H. Rahm of Mosby's Command & an Analysis of Ranger John H. Lunceford: Traitor or Coward? Or Unjustly Accused!* Alexandria, Virginia: Privately printed by the author, 2008.

Hakenson, Donald C. and Dudding, Gregg, *Mosby Vignettes, Volumes VI and VII*. Privately printed: Vol. VI, 1st Printing, Feb. 2002, 109 pages; Vol. VII, 1st Printing, Sept. 2003

Hakenson, Don, *This Forgotten Land: A Tour of Civil War Sites and Other Historical Landmarks South of Alexandria, Virginia*. Privately printed, 2002 (ISBN: 0-914927-38-8)

Hakenson, Donald C. and Mauro, Charles V., *A Tour Guide and History of Col. John S. Mosby's Combat Operations in Fairfax County, Virginia*. HMS Productions, 2013

Hunter, Alexander, *The Women of the Debatable Land*. Washington, DC: Corden Publishing Co., 1912. Reprinted by Ulan Press, San Bernardino, California, 2015

Jacobs, Charles T., *Civil War Guide to Montgomery County, Maryland*. Rockville, Maryland: Montgomery County Historical Society, 1996.

Janney, Asa Moore and Janney, Werner, *The Composition Book: Stories from the old days in Lincoln, Virginia*. Privately printed, 1973. Sixth printing 1987.

Jones, Virgil Carrington, *Ranger Mosby*. Chapel Hill: The University of North Carolina Press, 1944.

Jones, Virgil Carrington, *Gray Ghosts and Rebel Raiders*, New York: Henry Holt & Co., 1956.

Keen, Hugh C. and Mewborn, Horace, *43rd Battalion Virginia Cavalry, Mosby's Command: The Virginia Regimental Histories Series*. 1st edition. Lynchburg, Va.: H. E. Howard, Inc., 1993.

Lawrence, Lee, ed., *Dark Days in Our Beloved Country: The Civil War Diary of Catherine Hopkins Broun*. Warrenton, Virginia: Privately published.

The Loudoun County (Va.) Civil War Centennial Commission and the Loudoun County (Va.) Board of Supervisors; *Loudoun County and the Civil War*. Leesburg, Virginia: Potomac Press of Leesburg, 1961

Mackall, Mary L., Meserve, Stevan F., and Sasscer, Anne Mackall, eds., *In the Shadow of the Enemy: the Civil War Journal of Ida Powell Dulany*. Knoxville, Tennessee: The University of Tennessee Press, 2009.

Martin, Michael J., "A Match for Mosby?" America's Civil War Magazine. Leesburg, Virginia: Cowles History Group, vol. 7 no. 3, July 1994.

Mauro, Charles V., *The Civil War in Fairfax County: Civilians and Soldiers.* Charleston, South Carolina: The History Press, 2006.

McLean, R. James, *California Sabers: The 2nd Massachusetts Cavalry in the Civil War.* Bloomington, Indiana: Indiana University Press, 2000.

Melville, Herman, *Battle Pieces and Aspects of the War* 1866. Reprinted as Battle Pieces: Civil War Poems of Herman Melville, Edison, New Jersey: Castle Books, 2000.

Meserve, Stevan F., *The Civil War in Loudoun County, Virginia: A History of Hard Times.* Charleston, South Carolina: The History Press, 2008.

Mewborn, Horace (ed.), *From Mosby's Command: Newspaper Letters & Articles by and about John S. Mosby and His Rangers.* Baltimore: Butternut & Blue, 2005.

Mewborn, Horace, "Operations of Mosby's Rangers: Mosby's Confederacy." *Blue & Gray Magazine*, vol. XVII, issue 4. Columbus, Ohio: April 2000.

Mewborn, Horace, "Operations of Mosby's Rangers: The Shenandoah Valley." *Blue & Gray Magazine*, vol. XVII, issue 6. Columbus, Ohio: August 2000.

Mewborn, Horace, "Operations of Mosby's Rangers: Railroad Raids and the End of the War." *Blue & Gray Magazine*, vol. XIX, issue 1. Columbus, Ohio: October 2001.

Mitchell, Adele H., ed., *The Letters of John S. Mosby.* Printed by the Stuart-Mosby Historical Society, 1986, 319 pages

Monteiro, Aristides, M.D., *War Reminiscences by the Surgeon of Mosby's Command.* Richmond, Virginia: 1890. Reprinted by Butternut Press, Gaithersburg, Maryland, 1983

Mosby, John S., *Mosby's War Reminiscences and Stuart's Cavalry Campaign.* New York: Dodd, Mead and Company, Second Edition, 1898. Reprinted 1958 by Pageant Book Company, New York

Mosby, John S., *The Memoirs of Colonel John S. Mosby.* Boston: Little, Brown and Company, 1917.

Mosby, John S., "With Mosby's Men in '64," *The Illustrated American*, vol. xx no.1, June 27, 1896.

Munson, John W., *Reminiscences of a Mosby Guerrilla.* New York: Moffat, Yard and Company, 1906. Reprinted by Olde Soldier Books, Gaithersburg, Md

Norfleet, Elizabeth Copeland, *Woodberry Forest: A Venture in Faith.* New York: The Georgian Press, 1955.

O'Neill, Robert F., Jr., *The Cavalry Battles of Aldie, Middleburg and Upperville, June 10-27, 1863.* Lynchburg, Virginia: H. E. Howard, Inc., 1993.

O'Neill, Robert F., Jr., *Chasing Jeb Stuart and John Mosby: the Union Cavalry in Northern Virginia from Second Manassas to Gettysburg.* Jefferson, North Carolina: McFarland and Company, Inc., Publishers, 2012.

Parson, Thomas E., *Bear Flag and Bay State in the Civil War: The Californians of the Second Massachusetts Cavalry.* Jefferson, North Carolina and London: McFarland & Company, Inc., Publishers, 2001.

Penfield, Capt. James, *The 1863-1864 Civil War Diary of Captain James Penfield, 5th New York Volunteer Cavalry, Company H.* Ticonderoga, New York: Press of America, 1999.

Phillips, Edward H. and Phillips, Loving H. (ed.), *The Lower Shenandoah Valley in the Civil War: The Impact of War Upon the Civilian Population and Upon Civil Institutions.* Lynchburg, Virginia: H. E. Howard, Inc. 1993 (part of the Virginia Civil War Battles and Leaders Series).

Ramage, James A., *Gray Ghost: The Life of Col. John Singleton Mosby.* Lexington, Kentucky: The University of Kentucky Press, 1999.

Ramey, Emily G. and Gott, John K., eds., *The Years of Anguish: Fauquier County (Va.), 1861 - 65.* Warrenton, Virginia: The Fauquier Democrat, 1965.

Ray, William C., *Mount Gilead: History and Heritage*. Sixth revised edition. Leesburg, Virginia: Privately published, 2014.

Richards, Adolphus E., "Mosby's Partizan Rangers," pp.102-115; *Famous Adventures and Prison Escapes of the Civil War*. New York: The Century Company, 1904.

Rogers, Larry and Rogers, Keith, *Their Horses Climbed Trees: A Chronicle of the California 100 and Battalion in the Civil War, from San Francisco to Appomattox*. Atglen, Pennsylvania: Schiffer Military History, 2001

Scheel, Eugene M., *The Civil War in Fauquier*. Warrenton, Virginia: The Fauquier National Bank, 1985.

Scheel, Eugene M., *Loudoun Discovered: Communities, Corners and Crossroads*. Five volumes. Leesburg, Virginia: The Friends of the Thomas Balch Library, 2002.

Scott, Major John, *Partisan Life with Col. John S. Mosby*. New York: Harper & Brothers, Publishers, Franklin Square, 1867. Reprinted by Olde Soldier Books, Gaithersburg, Md.

Siepel, Kevin H., *Rebel: The Life and Times of John Singleton Mosby*. New York: St. Martin's Press, 1983.

Southern Historical Society Papers, "The Monument to Mosby's Men," Vol. XXVII. Richmond, Virginia: January-December 1899.

Stokes, Claiborne M., *A History of Ayrshire Farm*. Unpublished manuscript, August, 2000.

Tate, J.O., "Southern Heroes: Mosby Rides Again." *Southern Partisan Magazine*, vol. XIV, 4th Quarter. Columbia, South Carolina, 1994.

U.S. Army Ranger Hall of Fame, *http://www.ranger.org/resources/Documents/RHOF%20Documents/RHOF_Master_List.pdf*

Vogtsberger, Margaret Ann, *The Dulanys of Welbourne: A Family in Mosby's Confederacy*. Berryville, Virginia: Rockbridge Publishing Company, 1995.

Von Borcke, Heros, *Memoirs of the Confederate War for Independence, Vols. I & II*. Edinburgh, 1866. Facsimile reprint: Morningside Books, Dayton, Ohio, 1985.

The War of the Rebellion: A Compilation of the Official Records of the Union and Confederate Armies. 70 vols., 4 series. Washington, D.C., 1968.

Welton, J. Michael, ed., *My Heart is So Rebellious: The Caldwell Letters, 1861 - 1865*. Warrenton, Va.: The Fauquier National Bank.

Wert, Jeffry D., *Mosby's Rangers: From the High Tide of the Confederacy to the Last Days at Appomattox, the Story of the Most Famous Command of the Civil War and Its Legendary Leader, John S. Mosby*. New York: Simon & Schuster, 1990s.

Wert, Jeffry D., "Blazer's Mission – Destroy Mosby in One Deadly Encounter." *Civil War Times Illustrated*. Vol. XIX, no. 7. Harrisburg, Pennsylvania, November 1980.

The Western Reserve Historical Society, *The James E. Taylor Sketchbook: With Sheridan Up the Shenandoah Valley in 1864: Leaves from a Special Artist's Sketch Book and Diary*. Dayton, Ohio: Morningside House, Inc., 1989.

Williamson, James J., *Mosby's Rangers: A Record of the Operations of the Forty-Third Battalion, Virginia Cavalry, from its Organization to the Surrender*. New York: Ralph B. Kenyon, Publisher, 1896. Reprinted by Time-Life Books, Collector's Library of the Civil War, 1982.

Williamson, James J., *Mosby's Rangers: A Record of the Operations of the Forty-Third Battalion, Virginia Cavalry, from its Organization to the Surrender*. Second Edition, New York: Sturgis and Walton Company, Publisher, 1909.

Williamson, James J., *Prison Life in the Old Capital and Reminiscences of the Civil War*. West Orange, New Jersey: 1911. Reprint by Kessinger Publishing.

Woodward, Harold R., Jr., *For Home and Honor: the Story of Madison County, Virginia during the War Between the States 1861-1865*. Privately published: Madison, Virginia, 1990.

Index

* indicates member of Mosby's Partisan Rangers

4

8

A

B

C

D

E

F

G

H

J

K

L

M

N

O

P

Q

R

S

T

U

V

W

NOTES